From Mt. San Angelo

From
Mt. San Angelo

Stories, Poems, & Essays

Edited by WILLIAM SMART

MT. SAN ANGELO
SWEET BRIAR, VIRGINIA
VIRGINIA CENTER FOR THE CREATIVE ARTS
LONDON AND TORONTO: ASSOCIATED UNIVERSITY PRESSES

Associated University Presses
440 Forsgate Drive
Cranbury, NJ 08512

Associated University Presses
25 Sicilian Avenue
London WC1A 2QH, England

Associated University Presses
2133 Royal Windsor Drive
Unit 1
Mississauga, Ontario
Canada L5J 1K5

Library of Congress Cataloging in Publication Data
Main entry under title:

From Mt. San Angelo.

1. American literature—20th century. I. Smart,
William. II. Title: Stories, poems, and essays.
PS536.2.S76   1984   810′.8′0054   84-3066
ISBN 0-8453-4508-7

"The Mt. San Angelo Copper Beech," a woodcut by Jacques Hnizdovsky, appears on p. 5.

The illustrations from Blake's *America: A Prophecy* are reproduced with the permission of the Lessing J. Rosenwald Collection of the Library of Congress.

Excerpt from "Long-Legged Fly" by William Butler Yeats: Reprinted with permission of Macmillan Publishing Company and A. P. Watt, Ltd., from the *Poems* by W. B. Yeats, edited by Richard J. Finneran. Copyright 1940 by Georgie Yeats, renewed 1968 by Bertha Georgie Yeats, Michael Butler Yeats, and Anne Yeats.

Excerpt from "Meditations in Time of Civil War" by William Butler Yeats: Reprinted with permission of Macmillan Publishing Company and A. P. Watt, Ltd., from *The Tower* by W. B. Yeats. Copyright 1928 by Macmillan Publishing Co., Inc., renewed 1956 by Georgie Yeats.

Printed in the United States of America

This book is dedicated
to all the artists
who have ever needed
a quiet place to work.

There on that scaffolding reclines
Michael Angelo.
With no more sound than the mice make
His hand moves to and fro.
Like a long-legged fly upon the stream
His mind moves upon silence.

William Butler Yeats
"Long-Legged Fly"

Contents

What I Do in Here Is All That Matters

I

In the early sixties, when I was teaching at Skidmore in Saratoga Springs, New York, there was, out on the edge of town about a mile-and-a-half from the college, a mysterious place called "Yaddo." From the road all you saw were woods, and two large, stone gateposts on each side of the entrance drive. I don't recall if there were actual gates or a sign saying KEEP OUT—PRIVATE PROPERTY, but that was the feeling you got—that this was a very private and exclusive place, sort of like those estates in James Bond movies where secret agents learned the deadly devices of their trade. All I knew about Yaddo was that it was something called an "artists' colony" and that famous writers, artists, and composers came and hid out there from time to time. Occasionally we'd actually see one. Malcolm Cowley gave a talk at the college once, and I heard that *he* was out there, and that all the scruffy-looking younger men and women who came into the hall with him that night were also out there.

Another time a woman named Aileen Ward came to the lounge of the English House and read a chapter from a book she was writing on John Keats, and again there was a little gang of Yaddo people accompanying her. After the reading, there was sherry and cookies, and everyone separated into their own groups: the Yaddo people in one corner, the younger members of the English Department in another, students in another, and the senior members of the department and a couple of Honors students clustered around Miss Ward, talking about "Endymion." At some point I noticed a very unusual-looking man (he had coal-black hair and the chiseled features of an Eskimo or American Indian) standing against a wall by himself, and I decided to go up and introduce myself and find out who he was.

"Galway Kinnell," he replied.

"'*Gal*way'?" I said, perhaps arching my brow slightly. "You must be a poet."

Without smiling he replied, "I am."

To try to redeem myself I said, "It's a great name for a poet. Did you make it up or is it real?"

Alas, Galway Kinnell and I didn't hit it off at that first meeting, and I didn't see him again for several years. Then one evening I went to a party to celebrate the publication of his second book, *Flower Herding on Mount Monadnock,* and when I got a chance to talk to him I apologized for the way I'd acted that first time. By then I think I was beginning to realize that Auden and Frost and Eliot weren't the only living poets in the world, that there might even be one or two I'd never heard of. Considering the fact that I was almost thirty years old and the Creative Writing instructor at Skidmore, this was a rather late awakening. On the other hand, it might still not have occurred if, about a year before, I hadn't met another writer from Yaddo, and this time got to know him fairly well during the month he was there.

I met Marvin Cohen at a reception for Hortense Calisher, who had just published a new novel. The reception was held at a coffeehouse in Saratoga called Café Lena where Yaddo people liked to go to hear folk music and where, the previous summer, I had acted in a play. I had learned by now that whenever you met someone from Yaddo, the first question to ask was simply, "What do you do?" and the Yaddo person would answer, "I paint" or "I write" or "I write music," and you took it from there. So:

"What do you do?"

"What?"

"What do you *do?*"

"Just a minute." He twisted something in his ear and I saw he was wearing a hearing-aid, even though he couldn't have been over thirty. "Say it again."

"I said, what do you do?"

"I write."

"What sort of writing?"

"Fantasies about my imaginary life. What do *you* do?"

"I teach at Skidmore."

"Oh, I thought you were from Yaddo. I just got here this afternoon."

"Where from?"

"The City."

He was wearing a black coat several sizes too big for him and the knot of his tie was half-twisted under his collar. His shirt was a green-and-orange flannel outdoorsman's shirt, but his face was pale and pasty, as if he hadn't been outdoors in years.

"Where in the city?"

"Avenue C. You know it?"

I shook my head and said, "Only through Galway Kinnell's 'The Avenue Bearing the Initial of Christ into the New World.'"

"What's that?"

"A poem."

"I don't read poetry."

A writer who doesn't read poetry? I thought.

He looked straight at me and said, "I bet *you* write poetry."

I shrugged. "A little."

"I could tell."

"How?" I asked.

"You just look like someone who writes poetry." He grinned. "No offense!"

The next time I saw Marvin Cohen I was sitting in my office grading papers, and from down the hall I heard a voice asking my chairman, "Is there a guy named Bill Smart here?" I heard Joe give directions back to my office, and a moment later Marvin appeared in the door.

"I happened to be going by and saw the sign English House and figured I'd find you here." He looked at the papers on my desk and said, "Writing?"

"Grading papers," I said.

"You want to go get a Coke?"

It was spring, very warm in fact, but Marvin had on a long overcoat and an old hat, and the hearing-aid wire went from his ear down under the collar of his coat. I noticed girls glancing at him as we walked along the street. He had a strange loping walk, and his shoes slapped the pavement like clown shoes. After we had passed a couple of dozen girls, he said, "How can you stand it!"

"You get used to it," I said.

Marvin shook his head in disbelief and continued to stare at every girl we passed. When I greeted one I recognized from a class, Marvin said, "What's her name? Maybe I could call her up and get a date. You could fix me up. Tell her you have this terrific friend—say I'm a poet! How about it?"

That evening I told my wife about Marvin Cohen coming by the office and speculated on what my chairman probably thought. She suggested that perhaps I ought to say something in an off-hand way tomorrow about Marvin being from Yaddo and not anyone I knew. "You know how Joe is." I did indeed.

A few days later I paid my first visit to Yaddo, arriving precisely at the appointed hour and finding Marvin sitting on a stone wall next to a porte-cochère, like a toad on the palace steps. The house behind him looked big enough to have fifty rooms. Before I even got out of the car he said, "Did you bring something?" I nodded, turned off the engine, picked up the envelope lying on the seat beside me, and got out.

"You want to see the 'Italian Gardens'?" Marvin asked, and led me around the outside of the house and down a long lawn. At the bottom we walked around pools full of lily-pads and statues of nymphs and fawns. "Nineteenth-century decadence," Marvin said; then, "Who are some of the writers you like?"

It was so abrupt, I had to think a moment before replying.

". . .Hemingway . . .Faulkner . . .Fitzgerald . . ."

"F-f-f-*Fitz*gerald," Marvin shouted, stuttering for the first time. "Christ!" and explained for two minutes why Fitzgerald was such a bad writer.

When he was finished, I asked, "Who do *you* like?" looking for a chance to get even.

"Cervantes!" he said, and that ended that.

Coming back up the hill he pointed out the tower in which Truman Capote had written *Other Voices, Other Rooms* and sniffed to indicate what he thought of the history of the place.

"Are there any famous writers here now?" I asked.

"Philip Roth," he said, "another one of your Fitzgerald types." Then he glanced at me and said, "Instead of asking if people are *famous,* why don't you ask if they're any good?"

All this was so upsetting I was sorry I'd come and I'd be damned if I'd let him read my stuff. We walked up the lawn in silence. Ahead of us the house sat huge and impervious, all gray stone and windows that reflected silvery blackness.

"Want to see the inside?" Marvin asked as we reached some marble steps.

"Sure," I said, "but I can't stay."

"It'll be quick. We're not supposed to bring people in from outside. It's like *The Magic Mountain* here."

The interior was just what I expected—high, baronial ceilings, wooden beams, carved-wood chairs so big two could sit side-by-side as uncomfortably as one, a couple of nineteenth-century, Russian-looking sleighs, an enormous stained-glass window depicting some historical scene, and old sofas and armchairs covered in frayed velvet and damask.

"They say Edgar Allan Poe wrote 'The Raven' here."

"I wouldn't be surprised," I said.

"Come on, I'll show you my room," he said, starting up the stairs, "but don't talk. They're very strict about that."

As we turned at the landing, I whispered, "I feel like I'm being

14

snuck into a dorm," and Marvin sniggered. Going along the hall-way, I heard a typewriter being typed in the distance and won-dered if it could be Philip Roth.

When we got to his room, Marvin took a key out of his pocket and unlocked the door. But when he opened it, I was surprised to see another door right behind it. It was like opening a door onto a boarded-up wall, like a cartoon without a caption. Marvin opened the second door, then closed them both behind us. "This took a while to get used to," he said. "I kept closing the wrong door first."

The room was huge and full of sunlight. There was a narrow bed and a spindle-legged writing table with a straight-back chair and an old overstuffed chair with a floor-lamp standing beside it. Through the windows I could see the gardens at the foot of the lawn. Marvin's coat and tie were hanging over the doorknob of what must have been the closet. On top of the dresser I could see pill bottles and a box of saltines and two candy bars. Sitting on the floor beside the dresser was a cheap little canvas bag with a rip in the side and a piece of rope for one of the handles.

"What's it like, being here?" I asked.

"Too quiet. I miss hearing people being shot at night."

"God, what I wouldn't give for a room like this." I sighed, looking at his desk. "You should try writing on a card-table in the bedroom."

"I have."

"With a wife and three kids?"

"No, just my girlfriend sometimes."

"That's a little different," I said.

"He nodded, then stepped over to the desk and picked up a large manila envelope. "Here," he said. "Tell me what you think."

I glanced down at the envelope. On the front was written

The Self-Devoted Friend
by
Marvin Cohen

When I looked up, Marvin was looking at the envelope I was holding in my hand, the one I'd gotten out of the car with.

"Listen," I said, "I've decided I don't want you to read it after all. I don't think you'd like it."

"Don't be stupid," he said. "You probably won't like my stuff either."

It was so unlike my own precious sensitivity, my Holy Devo-tion to an idea of art so high I could hardly finish a paragraph, that instead of withholding I simply handed it over and said, "Look, I've got to go," and started for the door.

"I'll see you out."

Again, as we went down the hall, we could hear a typewriter ratta-tat-tatting softly in the distance.

Back outside Marvin said, "Look, you can't call me here, so I'll call you sometime next week. Your number's in the phone book, isn't it? There aren't any other Smarts?"

"No, I'm the only one."

"Okay, I'll give you a call."

Driving out, down through the pines and past a little pond, I saw two women walking along the road. When they smiled, I smiled back, wondering if they were writers or painters or what. You couldn't tell anything about an artist just by looking. Most of them were very ordinary and unimpressive, hardly noticeable.

The next time I saw Marvin, a week or so later, he told me the piece in the *Kenyon Review* was clever in a nasty sort of way but everything else was too sentimental and romantic and why didn't I just write the way I talked. I said I couldn't, I took writing too seriously. He shrugged and asked what I thought of *The Self-Devoted Friend.*

"It's strange," I said. "Surrealistic. I *like* it, but I think there's a limited audience for that sort of thing."

"You're right!" Marvin said, and burst out laughing. "I may be the only one who likes it."

The last time I saw Marvin was near the end of his stay, one night when I got him to come to our house to babysit while my wife and I went to a party. My wife was a little nervous about leaving Marvin with the kids, but I told her he'd be perfectly fine, in fact they'd probably love him. And of course they did; when I picked him up at Yaddo he had a grocery bag full of Cokes and potato chips and candy-bars, and I suspect he even brought along the manuscript of *The Self-Devoted Friend* to read to them at bedtime. My wife, naturally, prepared a long list of instructions on each of their bedtimes, what snacks they could have, the number where we could be reached, and of course the numbers of the Rescue Squad, Police, and Fire Department. I'm sure she was very nervous all evening. But when we got back, they were all asleep in their beds and all the lights were off but a single lamp next to the chair in which Marvin was reading. He didn't hear us come in. (I had told him not to turn off his hearing-aid, but I assume he had: it was probably the only way he could read.) Anyway, everything was fine, I actually got out my wallet and paid Marvin the standard babysitter's fee, and as I drove him back out to Yaddo he recounted all the things they'd done. He said he'd expected hourly phone calls from the Rescue Squad, Police, and Fire Department, checking up, but everything had gone fine. And he had indeed read part of *The Self-Devoted Friend* to Paul (who was six then) and he thought Paul had liked it. "He's smarter than you, Smart," and we laughed.

"Marvin, I *like* it," I said. "I think it's terrific. All I said was it's too strange for *most* people."

"Well, I couldn't write the sort of stuff 'most people' like if my life depended on it."

In the silence that followed, all I thought about was Marvin's wonderful self-confidence and my own total lack of it, and how much I envied him. How much righter *he* was, and what a coward *I* was.

Then Marvin interrupted my thoughts by saying, "I really envy you . . . having a wife and kids. . .lots of friends. . .living the way you do. You should see my place, all the cockroaches, my mattress on the floor. . . ."

"But you have time to write," I said.

"Yeah, well. . . ."

I didn't want to hear anything that might disillusion me, so I changed the subject. Because I was turning into the gates at Yaddo, I said, "How's it been, being here?"

"Okay, it turns out." My car lights lit up an opossum crossing the road, head down, hairless nose and long tail, like a huge rat. "The time and silence don't mean as much to me as most people—I've got plenty of that back in New York—but I've enjoyed the dinners." I smiled. Marvin went on: "I like the company at dinner-time, and of course the food's a lot better than I usually eat."

"It'd be the opposite with me," I said. "What I need is the time and quiet."

"You ought to apply," Marvin said.

"I probably couldn't get in."

I hoped he would say "Sure you could," but all he said was, "You ought to at least try."

I pulled up behind the mansion. All the lights were out, it was totally dark. I thought about the twenty or thirty writers and painters and composers asleep inside.

"I hope they left the door unlocked," Marvin said. He went over and tried it and came back to the car. "Listen," he said, "let's get together sometime if you're ever in New York. I'll show you Avenue C."

"I'll try," I said, "but I never get into the city. You know how it is."

"Yeah, well, if you ever do."

"Right. And let me know next time you're here."

"Sure."

We shook hands and said, "See ya," and I went around the circle under the tall pines, my lights flashing across their trunks, and back down the road and out onto the highway home.

I never saw Marvin Cohen again. The next year I left Skidmore, I was in England a couple of years, and ever since then I've been down in Virginia. We never wrote to each other. But I've kept up with his career in an accidental sort of way by noticing occasionally when he published a new book. New Directions published *The Self-Devoted Friend* a few years after he was at Yaddo. Then there were more books, which I never read but loved for their crazy titles: *The Monday Rhetoric of the Love Club & Other Parables; Baseball the Beautiful; Fables at Life's Expense; Others, Including Morstive Sternbump: A Novel; The Inconvenience of Living; Aesthetics in Life & Art: Existence in Function & Essence & Whatever Else Is Important, Too.* Then, strangely enough, my son Paul, who's twenty-seven now, ran into Marvin at a party in Greenwich Village, and when he told him his name Marvin asked if he was related to a guy named Bill Smart who used to live up in Saratoga Springs? And when Paul said I was his father, Marvin said, "I babysat you! It's amazing! The only time in my life I ever babysat, and you survived!" and told Paul all the details of that evening and I'm sure asked him if he recalled *The Self-Devoted Friend.*

II

Ever since I was eighteen I have been trying to find time and a place to write. When I was in college the dorms were noisy and there was always a roommate to contend with. I couldn't work in the library because you could neither type nor smoke there. I searched through all the college buildings and found an abandoned squash court in the basement of the assembly hall, but the dean wouldn't let me have it. I tried for a while to work in classrooms at night, carrying over a typewriter and all my papers, but classrooms were depressing with their blackboards and chalk-dust in the gutters that held the erasers and all the empty chairs and three or four times a night a janitor or security-man or fellow student sticking his head in the door and asking what I was doing there. If I could have rented a room off-campus, I would have done so, but I didn't have enough money even for the college bills, let alone a sanctuary. My senior year I was finally able to get a room without a roommate and everyone despised me because I stayed in it and was short with anyone who interrupted me by barging in or even knocking on the door.

After college I got married and went to graduate school to avoid the draft and tried to write at night on the kitchen table while my wife sat in our tiny living room, reading. To get to the bathroom she had to cross the kitchen, and for the first couple of months I'd look up and smile whenever she entered. After mid-night I became very conscious of the people in the downstairs apartment and would close up the typewriter and shuffle to-gether all the pages on which I had started stories, put them in a corner, and go to bed. Undressing in the dark, I could tell by her breathing that my wife was not asleep. . . nor waiting up for me either.

When she got pregnant, I quit graduate school and went to work for a publisher, traveling around the Pacific Northwest promoting college textbooks, because I thought I'd be able to write at night in hotel rooms. But by the time I got to a hotel and had had dinner and finished writing my daily report, it would be after nine and I was too exhausted to do anything. So I started getting up at 4:30 in the morning and making a glass of instant coffee with hot water from the bathroom faucet and trying to write on glass-topped dressers with notices about room-service and local beauty parlors stuck under the glass, but it was just too depressing.

So at the end of a year I quit again and we moved with our baby to a little one-room cabin my wife's grandfather had built down in the Missouri Ozarks, a little cabin with a cistern and an outhouse and a woodstove. But by the time we had the place habitable and I had made a little shack for myself out in the woods, winter was upon us. First thing every morning I'd go out to my shack and light the kerosene heater to warm the place up while I went back and had breakfast; but the days just got colder and colder and the shack never warmed up. I would sit in front of my typewriter with the heater between my legs and gloves on my hands, cap pulled down over my ears and arms stiff in a red Mackinaw, and try to write.

In less than a year we gave up on the cabin and moved back

east, and my wife, as supportive as possible under the circumstances, went to work and let me stay home. Every morning she'd leave at a quarter to nine, dropping our son off at a house where he was kept five mornings a week. I set my typewriter up on a card-table in our bedroom, and as soon as they were out the door I'd start to work, because I only had three hours: at noon they'd be back and I'd have to have lunch ready, then Paul would be put down for his nap and she'd go back to work. Logically, I felt that three hours every morning, five days a week, ought to be enough: my former teacher, John Malcolm Brinnin, had told me of a friend of his who had a job and still managed to write a novel every year simply by getting up early in the morning and writing a page a day. Yes, I knew about Trollope, who could turn it on and off like a faucet. But I was neither Trollope nor Brinnin's friend; I felt more like Proust or Flaubert, who, when asked how his writing had gone, said he had spent the morning putting in a comma, and the afternoon taking it out again. Downstairs I'd hear our landlady running her vacuum cleaner; out the window I'd see her half-witted husband working in his vegetable garden. When the phone rang and she turned off the vacuum cleaner, I could hear every word she said. All morning every day she was either vacuuming or talking on the phone.

The next year I returned to graduate school to finish my degree, and my wife got pregnant again. The next year I went to Skidmore. Now we had two children, a three-year-old and a baby, and I was back supporting us again. The first year at Skidmore, it was all I could do to keep up with my classes. I taught three sections of freshman composition, with twenty students in each, and they all had to write a theme a week—sixty papers to grade every week, from September to May. And I was also teaching a section of the "Mainstreams of English Literature" course and having to stay up till two or three every night reading *Beowulf* and *King Lear* and *Paradise Lost* and *Pilgrim's Progress* and *Vanity Fair* and *Great Expectations.* There was no time even to think about writing.

The next year it eased up slightly—at least I was teaching *Beowulf* etc. for the second time—and I talked our landlord into letting me convert a section of the attic above our kitchen into a little "study." The heat came up through an open register, and along with it all the screams and yells of a woman and two kids trying to get through the fifteen waking hours of every day. But no, that wasn't the problem; the real problem was just how few hours each week I got in that room. We lived several miles out in the country, and I couldn't run back and forth to my "study" between classes. I remember the *sounds* from weekends and the summer, for those were the only times I ever got up there. Then we had our third child.

One night at a party I recited my Litany of Complaints to the only person I thought could understand, a painter on the faculty who also had three young children. "How do you manage," I asked. (No question mark, because it wasn't a question.)

"I have a studio," he replied.

"What do you mean, you have a studio?"

"I mean I have a studio. . .away from home. . .and I go to it every day."

"What does it cost?"

"Nothing."

I was drunk on the mere thought of it. "Christ!" I said.

"Would you like to see it?"

The next day I went there, to a little house right in the middle of campus, near the library, that I'd never noticed before, just assuming someone lived there because there were curtains at the windows. I knocked at the door and my friend came and opened it and let me in. Inside, he led me through another door and into a large room full of the trappings of a painter: a couple of easels with canvases on them, large tables covered with brushes and tubes of paint, finished paintings hanging on the walls—all permeated with the wonderful smell of oil and turpentine and linseed oil.

My friend wanted me to see his work; I, in my Machiavellian way, wanted to find out if there were any more empty rooms in the house and, if so, would he let me use one. I would do anything to have such a room: only use it when he wasn't there, be absolutely still, never disturb him, polish his shoes if he left them outside the door.

"It won't bother *me*," he said. "There are a bunch of empty rooms upstairs. I'd appreciate it, though, if you wouldn't take one directly above me."

I was so happy and excited—it was like getting your first bike or first car or first anything you've ever waited a long time for— that all I wanted to do was run upstairs immediately and see it (ride it, drive it), and my friend (my *friend*) smiled to see how much his generosity meant to me, and we went right away. There were two empty rooms upstairs that weren't above him, and I took the smaller one because it was farther away. It had formerly been a child's bedroom: the wallpaper was covered with rock-ing-horses and teddy-bears and tin-drums; red and blue and yel-low.

"It's perfect!" I said. "How soon can I move in?"

"Whenever you want."

I went home and told my wife and she was as happy as I was; it's no fun living with someone who's miserable all the time. The next day my friend had a key made and sent it to me through inter-campus mail. That evening I drove back in with all my gear piled on the back seat of the car: a little table, a straight-back chair, my portable typewriter, a couple of cardboard boxes full of stuff I was working on, a ream of blank paper, a little electric pot to heat water in, a spoon and cup, an ashtray, a wastebasket. I moved them one by one from the car into the house when no one could see; it was like I was setting up a rendezvous for illicit trysts. Because the house sat right in the middle of campus (a sidewalk that went to the library passed right in front of it) I knew I had to be very secretive. I didn't want anyone to know I was there, *especially my best friend,* and that's because he, too, was a writer, trying desparately to write at home in a bedroom, in a house with a wife and two children, and I knew if he saw what *I* now had, he would put irresistible pressure on me to let him share the bounty by taking the other empty room. But that would be impossible. Bert and I were totally different kinds of writers: he worked fast, typed like a newspaper reporter, while I worked slowly, putting down words carefully (too carefully) and throwing away pages and starting over. I knew I wouldn't be able to do a thing if, from across the hall, I could hear *his* type-writer going a mile a minute, or if, in a long moment of silence from his room, he could hear another silence coming from mine, and out of curiosity sat listening for an hour and only heard a couple of pecks at the keys. No, it was impossible: to let Bert know I had the room would have been the same as giving it up.

It took half-an-hour to unload the car because anytime I saw anyone approaching or coming from the library, I stayed in the house, waiting till the person was out of sight before going to get my next load. When I finally had everything in and arranged the way I would begin using it the next day, I sat in the stillness for perhaps twenty minutes staring at the rocking-chairs and tin-drums and teddy-bears on the wall behind my typewriter, then leaned forward and did something I'd never done before: I wrote something directly on the wallpaper. WHAT I DO IN HERE IS

ALL THAT MATTERS. Satisfied, I got up, snuck out the front door, and went home.

So it wasn't *quite* true, a year later, when I said to Marvin Cohen that I had no place to work except on a card-table in the bedroom, but it wasn't as far removed as it would appear. It was true that I did have a room now, but it was still far from the kind of conditions a writer actually needs. I still had to teach five days a week and, even though I was able to improve my actual teaching schedule slightly by getting my courses bunched together end-to-end, I still had no more than a couple of hours at a time for writing, and whatever time I could deprive my family of on the weekends. Though my wife was as supportive as she could be of my need to write, still she got resentful when I took off every Saturday morning to go to my room, leaving her alone still another day in a house out in the country with three little kids. And knowing that my selfishness made *her* miserable created so much guilt that even when I was in my studio it was difficult concentrating 100% of my mind on my writing. If it was a beautiful day and she had wanted us to go on a picnic and I had said, "I'm sorry, but I can't," her resentment would haunt me all day and I'd dread going home to the bitterness I knew awaited me. I thought often of the opening lines of Ransom's poem, "Prelude to an Evening":

> Do not enforce the tired wolf
> Dragging his infected wound homeward
> To sit tonight with the warm children
> Naming the pretty kings of France.

Sometimes I'd try to rationally explain the special needs of artists, but she'd get angry and say, "Don't think you're so special just because you want to be a writer. Other people are just as important as artists, and *they* don't get everything they want." I said it wasn't *special* treatment I wanted, just the same chance that people in other occupations had. Doctors and lawyers didn't have to do other jobs in order to support themselves and only get to practice medicine or law in their spare time.

"Doctors and lawyers get *paid* for what they do," she said. "Finish something and get it published and then you'll be able to quit teaching and write all the time."

But I knew that was a pipedream. For the story in the *Kenyon Review*—which was not a totally insignificant publication—I'd been paid fifty dollars. For a piece I'd written on Robert Frost

23

for *The Reporter* I'd been paid seventy-five. I knew that even when a poet got a poem in *The New Yorker* he might get only $100, and that was a lot. For poems in most little magazines all poets usually got were two copies of the magazine. When Bert had an essay published in *The Hudson Review,* an essay that had taken him half a year to write, all he was paid was something like $150 and a year's subscription. While it was true that occasionally a serious writer wrote a book that became a bestseller and made a lot of money—Salinger, Updike, Bellow—the chances were infinitesimally small. Might as well try to win the Irish Sweepstakes!

Once, when I wrote John Brinnin about it, he wrote back a long, solicitous letter that came down to just one thing: in order to write or paint or do anything in the arts, you had to be "ruthless": abandon one's responsibilities to everything but one's art. Unless you had money, there was no other way. Well, I didn't have money, and I didn't have the guts to be *ruthless;* so I would have to stay home, earn a living, try to be at least half a husband and father, and just do my best to be a writer on the weekends, in the summers, and during the few hours I could snatch whenever I could.

III

Simultaneous with all those complaints about never having enough time and an isolated place in which to work went another thought: that perhaps I was a dilettante, and I merely dabbled at writing regardless of how seriously I pretended to do it. After all, there were plenty of artists who had to work under similar conditions—indeed, far worse: utter poverty, poor health, physical handicaps—who nevertheless managed to do something. I thought of D. H. Lawrence who seemed to have been able to write anywhere, under the very worst circumstances. I had read a description once of Lawrence sitting in bed writing while three other people were in the same room, talking; he would look up occasionally from the novel he was writing to enter the conversation, as casually as if he were writing postcards. I remembered a scene from *David Copperfield* in which David sat at night writing contentedly while his darling "child-wife," Dora, sat beside him, holding his pens or playing with her little dog Jig. Why did I think I needed a cork-lined room, all so precious and perfect, when much better writers had not? For myself then, no excuses: the problem lay not in the less-than-ideal circumstances of my life, but simply in a void at that core of the self out of which good work must inevitably come.

Discount *me* then, still I knew that the Lawrences, Trollopes, and Copperfields were anomalies. I thought of Yeats in his tower, Thoor Ballylee:

> A winding stair, a chamber arched with stone,
> A grey stone fireplace with an open hearth,
> A candle and written page.
> *Il Penseroso*'s Platonist toiled on
> In some like chamber, shadowing forth
> How the daemonic rage
> Imagined everything.
> Benighted travellers
> From markets and from fairs
> Have seen his midnight candle glimmering.

I thought of Hemingway's description in *A Moveable Feast* of "the hotel where Verlaine died, where I had a room on the top floor where I worked," a room in which he could take as long as he wanted:

> . . .sometimes when I was starting a new story and I could not get it going, I would sit in front of the fire and squeeze the peel of the little oranges into the edge of the flame and watch the sputter of blue that they made. I would stand and look out over the roofs of Paris and think, "Do not worry. You have always written before and you will write now. All you have to do is write one true sentence. Write the truest sentence that you know." So finally I would write one true sentence, and then go on from there.

I thought of Faulkner writing *As I Lay Dying* on the bottom of a wheelbarrow during the long nights in the boiler-room at the University of Mississippi and all those other rooms of one's own in which a writer might sit for hours on end staring into a fire with neither guilt nor fear of interruption. I knew then that the problem for artists was seldom laziness, but not having the time to work as slowly as they would like.

Analogies came to mind: that quiet rooms were as necessary to artists as operating rooms were to surgeons, and that just as surgeons needed bright light and all sorts of refined equipment and many assistants, so artists needed quiet and isolation. But therein lay the problem: surgeons *had* operating rooms and all the conditions essential to the practice of their profession, whereas artists did not. And the reason they didn't was because they had to be famous before they could possibly earn enough money to provide themselves with the proper conditions for practicing their professions.

So that's what Yaddo and the other places like it were for artists: temporary facilities essential to the practice of their professions. No wonder then that Yaddo and the MacDowell Colony had so many distinguished alumni—Thornton Wilder and Willa Cather and Robert Lowell and William Carlos Williams and Aaron Copland and Milton Avery and Eudora Welty and Flannery O'Connor and Saul Bellow and Katherine Anne Porter and Leonard Bernstein (the list could go on and on!): it was because the sanctuaries they provided had in a significant way contributed to the quality of work those once-unknown writers and painters and composers had been able to accomplish at them. No wonder Thornton Wilder said of MacDowell: "How I needed it, needed to hear myself think and to get out of all this tumult with which I was both deeply engaged and not unhappy, but in which there was no chance, really, to explore oneself." And Frances FitzGerald had said, "The MacDowell Colony is a beautiful desert island. It offers silence and time for the most unadulterated form of concentration." And Philip Roth had called Yaddo "the best friend a writer ever had." These artists' colonies, in other words, were no different than Yeats's Thoor Ballylee or Hemingway's "room on the top floor" or Faulkner's boiler-room. They simply provided those sheer essential conditions necessary for the deep concentration of creativity.

The Virginia Center for the Creative Arts is such a place, and this book represents the work of some of the writers who have worked here at Mt. San Angelo over the past few years. It is the first of a series of annual anthologies we will publish to acquaint readers with some of the best writers of our time. All the stories, poems, and essays in this collection are being published here for the first time—a rare sort of book these days. Thirty years ago, book-length anthologies of "new writing" were one of the most exciting formats in publishing, and anyone who recalls such series as *New Directions, New World Writing, discovery, The Berkley Book of Modern Writing,* and the *New American Review* will remember the wonderful discoveries one always made in their pages: things like William Styron's "Long March" (in *discovery* in 1952), and Ralph Ellison's "A Coupla Scalped Indians" and Ionesco's "The Bald Soprano" (in *New World Writing #9* in 1956), and the first publication of Philip Larkin and Derek Walcott in America (in *New World Writing # 10,* also in 1956), and William Gass's "In the Heart of the Heart of the Country" and Philip Roth's "The Jewish Blues" (in *New American Review* in 1967). That is quite a precedent to try to live up to, but I think there are stories and poems and essays in this book that are just as outstanding and will take similar places in contemporary American literature.

In addition to an annual anthology, from time to time we will also publish individual collections of poetry or fiction by the most promising young or neglected mature writers who have come to the Virginia Center, for one of the great opportunities a place like this affords is the chance to discover writers (as well as visual artists and composers).

Without the generous help of a number of people, this book could not have become a reality and first among them are the authors who contributed work they might have published elsewhere. Second, I want to thank Jack Wheatcroft for bringing Thomas Yoseloff down to Mt. San Angelo, and Tom for having the vision and courage to enter into a unique publishing venture—the first ever—with an "artists' colony." And finally, I want to thank my wife, Juliana, and our daughters, Sarah and Jessie, for letting me have so much *time and solitude.*

William Smart

JOEL AGEE

I Bow to Chin Shengt'an

Three hundred and fifty-odd years ago, a Chinese scholar named Chin Shengt'an was shut up in a Buddhist temple for ten days together with a friend on account of rainy weather. To pass the time, the two men recounted all the happy moments they could think of. Later Chin Shengt'an wrote thirty-three of them down and interspersed them among his now famous commentaries on the play *Western Chamber,* ending each one with: "Ah, is this not happiness?"

Here is one of Chin Shengt'an's happy moments:

Having nothing to do after a meal I go to the shops and take a fancy to some small thing. After bargaining for a while we still haggle about a small difference, and still the shop-boy refuses to sell it. Then I take out a little thing from my sleeve which is worth about the same as the difference and throw it to the boy. The boy suddenly smiles and bows courteously saying, "Oh, you are too generous!" Ah, is this not happiness?

For a long time I imagined that there was something Chinese in my character, simply because I love works like Chin's "Happy Moments" so much. But now that I've started adding a few of my own moments to his I notice with interest how different we are. Where a Chinese artist selects a blossom to paint, the Westerner picks a bouquet. Even a flowering plum branch by van Gogh resembles a plum branch by Chih Pai-Shih only by virtue of their common subject. Chin's happy moments are in fact everyman's; mine are mine only. His are as plain as uncarved blocks of wood; mine are chiseled and shaped as nearly in my own image as I could make them. Yet the nature of beauty is communicable from culture to culture and from language to language, and so is the nature of happiness. I once saw an Oriental man bowing before Raphael's *Madonna.* I bow to Chin Shengt'an.

At the peak of the countercultural explosion of the last decade I meet a small band of melancholy German hippies who invite me to join them on a trip to the mountains to take some LSD with them there. Since the hippies seem to be nice, and the mountains happen to be the Swiss Alps, and the acid is a brand called "Orange Sunshine" that is esteemed for its purity, I decide to go along, and leave my wife and our three-year-old daughter at the campsite where we have been staying. The acid trip consists of four thousand six hundred and seventy three years of soul-rending torment, during which I wander in and out of an Alpine lake in a circle of perpetual misery, drowning again and again, sloshing my way through marshland back into new lives, only to pass the same grinning tangle of barbed wire that heralds the next inevitable drowning. Eventually I collapse and watch dozens of very large insects stabbing my legs and sucking their furry black bodies full of my blood, and I come to the conclusion that I am in hell and that because hell is eternal I'll not only be here forever but have always been here, always, always. Suddenly one of the hippies appears. His face is radiant with compassion; he calls my name. Holding me by the hand, he leads me to a wood-block house with a porch where some ten or twelve Swiss people are singing an ancient song in four-part harmony, and tears of gratitude pour from my eyes. It is time to go home. In the car, my hirsute companions reveal themselves, by the kindness in their eyes and their beatific smiles, to be angels. Back at the campsite, I step out of the car and see my little daughter running up to me, laughing with glee. Before I can kiss her she is gazing into my eyes and exclaiming: "Happy! You're happy!" and I realize with a pang of self-reproach how selfishly happy I've been and how much she needs me to be happy. "Where were you?" she asks. I point to the snowy peaks in the distance. "You're happy!" she says again, and this time her delight is so great she breaks into a dance, whirling her arms and kicking up her feet. "Gina! Where did you learn to dance like that?" She throws her hand back and points to the mountains. Ah, is this not happiness?

Every few years I remove myself at one blow from the sources of all my cares and ambitions by living in complete solitude without clocks or newspapers, books, or TV, somewhere on the fringes of wild nature, for several days at least, with the purpose of living to no purpose other than my heart's content. It never takes long before I begin to receive the divine fruit of perfect self-indulgence, a delight so maniacally glad at not having to give account to anyone that all I can do is grin and whoop and dance around the room laughing—ah, is this not happiness?

I get out of bed on a sudden buoyant impulse and, without any conscious purpose, sit down on the couch in the living room, feeling neither bored nor expectant, neither sleepy nor quite awake, comfortably poised in that fertile zone intermediate between waking and sleeping where we would all be geniuses if we could only dwell in it for a while. Fortunately I don't know I am there. I vaguely think of playing the guitar, but my body has settled into such pleasant immobility that it would take an effort to leave the couch; and then the thought of my limited skill, the predictable chords and runs I would play and the stumbling (and equally predictable) variations I would attempt, decide the issue. My eyes close, and I find myself playing imaginary music—at my usual level, but with a singing resonance unachievable on my guitar. Pretty soon, though, I'm playing the blues awfully well— a languidly thumping bass beat, sharp plangent chords abruptly smothered with a palm, wild lonely phrases twanged out in C, in F, in G7, strings pulled off pitch to just the right ache of expression, and then the resolving chords, a different feeling with each reprise, laconic, sad, angry, lewd, a song without words and without need of words. And then it occurs to me that I have never heard a guitar played better in all my life. I think to myself: why not add a bass? And lo, there is a bass. The guitar, relieved of its rhythmical duties, lets loose a gorgeous series of melodic flourishes—jazz, I suppose, but there is a prayerful, ragalike lilt to it; and sure enough, a tabla is added. And then I think: "let's have a piano," and there is a piano, and it mingles strains of Chopin with the raga-blues of the other instruments. The effect is sublime and unlike any music I have ever heard. In the back of my mind I think: "if you could only record this or write it down, you would astonish the world." But since that is impossible and, in any case, unnecessary, I give myself over completely to listening. Ah, is this not happiness?

I am in Minneapolis attending an Indian powwow in order to write about it for *Life* magazine. The photographer assigned to take the pictures tells me he plans to proceed along the lines of a motto he attributes to the American Marines: "Go in, get the job done, and leave." After three days, his indelicacy and arrogance have angered the Indians and cast a shadow over the trust given me in the beginning. The feeling of being an unwanted stranger among joyfully dancing and congregating people produces an unbearable headache, and the relentless boom-boom-boom of the big drums is starting to feel like torture. A young man with a first-aid kit passes by and I ask him for an aspirin; but when he hands me the little tin box, I find myself unable to open it. "Hand it over," he says. "It took a white man to build this thing, it takes an Indian to open it." I'm unable to smile at the joke, and all I'm able to think to myself, stupidly, is: this is numbness. I take three aspirin tablets. After a while the headache disappears, leaving the numbness. The dance floor is full of men in brilliant costumes, and all of them are wearing feathers in their hair. Suddenly the director of the powwow sits down next to me and watches the dancers for a while without talking. "I hear you tried to talk to that photographer," he says. "I hear you tried to make him more sensitive to us." I nod. "That's good," he says, "that's good." We watch the dancers together. "This is the crow dance," he says then. "You see, they're moving like big birds, pecking and looking around for enemies. And you'll notice the feathers in their hair: here . . . here . . . here . . . here . . . and here . . ." and as he explains, his fingers thread through my hair and lightly touch my scalp. Ah, is this not happiness?

At a time in my life when all prospects, material and spiritual, professional and romantic, are gloomy, when I am still hurting from the recent collapse of an absorbing love affair, friendless and seemingly incapable of making friends, preoccupied by alternating thoughts of suicide and of escaping alive into the astral realm with the help of an occult manual, I learn about a trip to Cuba available to "North American youth," all expenses paid by the Cuban government. I sign up just in time; a week later I am in Havana sipping cuba libres made with ersatz Coke and enjoying an astonishing popularity with my fellow travelers, all of whom consider me "politically correct," "sincerely militant," "hip and groovy," or "a hell of a nice guy," depending on their ideological bent. What's more, Cuban girls consider me exotic. (We still speak of young women as girls in the present tense of 1964.) A haze of perfumes, glances, smiles and lingering touches begins to cloud my political vision. Inspecting the proud militia, I notice how breasts and buttocks improve on the uniform's baggy design. A young worker demonstrating advanced techniques of cigar manufacture massages her product with tenderness. The spokeswoman for the industrial planning commission has lips that kiss the air as she denounces the U.S.

31

embargo. Suddenly I'm introduced to a black girl in a black evening dress who produces a flutter in my heart and an ache in my groin. She has absurdly long lashes, glitter on her cheeks, a studied hauteur in the tilt of her chin, and she does not find me exotic: she snubs me. Two hours later I see her divesting herself of ostrich feathers in a nightclub. The men go wild and shout her name: "Désirée! Désirée!" I return to the North American youth at the hotel, sidestep a caucus of militant blacks and another caucus of militant women, and go to bed, avid for sleep and oblivion, never suspecting, no, not even dreaming, that this glistening siren, this Désirée, will eventually lure me to an institution that was not included in our official itinerary, a remnant of decadence called a *posada,* a tryster's haven where the ceilings are covered with mirror-glass and the walls faintly resonate with moans and cries and the rhythmical jangling of bedsprings; or that we will walk the streets hand in hand feeling like gods in our languid sufficiency unto each other; or that she will see me off at the airport and wave until she vanishes among the receding palm trees by the edge of the runway. Half asleep in the humming airplane on the way home I can feel the caress of her hands and the strong embrace of her thighs. Ah, is this not happiness?

Waking up from confused dreams one morning I see before my closed eyes a heart rising like a sun from a murky substance into a region that is clear and spacious. Opening my eyes, I see right in front of me several men and women sitting around a table that is covered with a red and white checkered tablecloth. Even though I have never seen them before, and even though they are no more than an inch and a half tall, I am certain that they are my closest relatives. They greet me warmly, my heart responds of its own accord, and they vanish. Ah, is this not happiness?

My wife, who is also my dearest and most understanding friend, has little feeling for classical music, which to me is almost as precious as love itself. How often have I invited her to a concert or asked her to sit down next to me and listen to a record, and noticed her struggling against sleep or restlessness after a short while! One Sunday morning I put on a recording of Beethoven's *Emperor* Concerto while she's making breakfast in the kitchen. Just after the second movement begins with that lofty and tender song that somehow, incomprehensibly, makes a single gesture of hope and heartsickness, generosity and resignation, my wife comes into the room with an expression on her face as if she's about to remember something important. We look at each other, listening, and both of us begin to weep. Ah, is this not happiness?

SALLIE BINGHAM

Captain Bud

It began as the kind of rumor that cooks, coming out to work, whispered to each other at the bus stop. Somebody, some white woman in the suburbs, had been kidnapped. Nobody knew her name, although they knew the rest of the details. She had been taken from her house, from her chaise longue in fact, where she had been resting in the middle of a hot day. She had been bundled into a car trunk, still wearing her negligee, and the trunk had been closed and the car had been driven away. Her husband had found one of her white satin mules in the drive.

A day later, everybody knew her name because it was in the papers. It was Mrs. Ronald Doll, and she lived in a brick house not far from ours.

Then it seemed that nothing more would happen. She had been gone three days, and then it was five. The FBI was brought in as soon as it seemed that the kidnapper had carried her across the state line, but the FBI could find no clues.

There was speculation, after a while, that she had wanted to go or at least had not put up much of a fight. She was a pretty young woman without any children to keep her busy, the kind who spent afternoons at the country club letting the tennis pro rearrange her grip. So it was thought—or at least, our cook thought—that she could have gotten herself home, after a week, if she had really wanted to.

I was eight years old that fall and enrolled in third grade but there was so much sickness going around I spent most of my time at home. I was a scrawny child, the kind who would have worn her brother's undershirts, if I had had a brother. I was willful, too. The kind of child who can walk into a living room and set every grownup's teeth on edge. I spent most of the time in the kitchen, wearing my bathrobe, which smelled permanently of pine vapor rub.

Milly, our cook, tried to tone down the talk when I was around but after a while, Tom Roberts and Lea would get started full swing. Nothing was said that I couldn't have repeated to my parents. It was the way it was said that signified: Lea would put her hand to her mouth, or Tom Roberts would kick her foot under the table. Then Milly would be severe with them, "You two quit your fooling and get out of my kitchen," she would say.

Tom Roberts said openly that he was suspicious of Mr. Doll who did not seem to be doing much to retrieve his wife. Tom's suspicions were justified when we heard that Mr. Doll had known where Mrs. Doll was all week. The kidnapper had left a note with directions and a demand for money, but because the amount was very large, Mr. Doll ignored the whole thing. Perhaps he believed, along with Milly, that Mrs. Doll would make her way back, with or without shoes, when the time came. Then the FBI smelled out the ransom note, and after that poor Mr. Doll had no peace.

A week later, we saw his picture in the paper, holding his wife in his arms. She had on a man's clothes, not good ones, but she still had nothing on her feet. According to the newspaper, the FBI had laid a clever trap and caught the culprit and his victim as they were leaving a gas station.

Lea read the whole piece out loud. It told how Mrs. Doll had kept the culprit busy in the car with mathematical games. "She went to Miss Pierson's the same as you, Louisa," Milly said, "and look where it got her. If she hadn't of known those games, he would have done something awful to her."

"It looks like he must have done something to her—all that time," Tom Roberts said.

Lea giggled and Milly gave her a look. "I guess he knew better than to stick his neck out," Milly said. "Even that kind of low-down colored boy knows something."

Tom Roberts said, "It wasn't his neck I was thinking about."

Milly pulled the metal roaster out of the oven. "Get out of my kitchen, now. I've got to start they supper."

"I'm going to watch for Daddy," I said, knowing when I had worn out my welcome.

It was one of my baby habits to stand in the front hall in the late afternoon and watch for my father. When I was three or four, I had believed my waiting would make him come, but I had long outgrown that.

That evening, my mother came downstairs in her rose-colored teagown to meet him. She didn't see me, standing beside the curtain—I already had the fatal ability to blend in—and so I overheard the conversation.

"John, I'm scared to death," my mother began.

"Why, what is it?"

"That terrible business with poor Ann Doll. They aren't sure that man they caught is the one that did it."

"They'll find out, before long."

"Yes, but in the meantime, what if he's on the loose?"

My father chuckled. "Afraid he'll come and get you?"

"It's not me, it's Louisa."

"I don't think he fancies little girls."

"That kind of . . . animal—" my mother said, and stopped. "Why, he could just walk right in that front door!"

"Tom and Lea and Milly wouldn't let him."

"They'd probably just go all to pieces," my mother said. "And you know with my commitments, I can't watch her night and day."

My father said, "I can't imagine anyone wanting that little scrap of humanity."

"Hush, John!" My mother sounded scandalized. Then she laughed. Arm in arm, they turned away and started up the stairs.

I did not see them again until they had eaten their supper and were ready to go out. They came down to the kitchen to kiss me goodbye. Mother had on her pale blue silk dress which Daddy had brought her from New York and the necklace I later learned he had given her the day I was born. She kissed me, smelling of a French perfume I thought was called Knee De Gay. "Now, don't listen to those dreadful programs," she said as Daddy brushed my forehead with his lips.

As soon as they were gone, Tom Roberts set the big brown radio with the cloth face in the middle of the kitchen table. He climbed up on a chair to plug the cord into the socket next to the lightbulb. The cord swung like something alive; I watched it all during "The Green Hornet." Lea was ironing a fleet of my mother's nightgowns and Tom was supposed to be doing the flat silver; at least he kept the water running although Milly told him it would not take the place of elbow grease. The drone at the end of the program announced my bedtime. Even Tom was not bold enough to suggest that I stay up for "Inner Sanctum."

Lea took me up to bed. She jerked off my shirt, ran a washcloth over my face and pushed a comb through my hair. Then I put on my pink flannel pajamas and she tucked me into bed; I wriggled to loosen the top sheet. Lea never kissed me. When I kissed her, she laughed and looked away. "Now go to sleep. Don't let me hear you up."

"Lea?"

"What?"

"Is that man that kidnapped Mrs. Doll still around here some-place?"

"As far as I know, they've got that devil locked up in the county jail."

"How do they know he's the right one?"

"They don't yet. But you still don't have a thing to worry about."

"What if he's out there, under the trees . . ."

"If he is, he isn't coming anywhere near this house. Tom Roberts says your Daddy's going to hire us a night watchman. He's going to get us a captain from the police."

Uprooting the tight sheet, I set up. "A captain?"

"That's what he said. He'll be marching around this place with a gun in his belt—" She made the ritual gesture of loosening a gun in a holster—"and as soon as he hears a sound, he's going to fire: Bang! Bang!"

I heard Milly's chair scrape back in the kitchen. Lea looked startled. "Get to sleep, now. No more foolishness. That captain will be here in the morning."

Next morning after breakfast I heard a car come up the drive. I ran downstairs. There were two policemen waiting at the door. My father had already left for work but my mother was up and dressed to receive them.

One of the policemen was tall and thin and scraggly and the other one was fat. I hoped for the thin one.

They talked about various things which did not seem to have anything to do with the situation, and I admired their blue uniforms, their broad shining belts and their holsters. I had never seen a holster up close before and I had not realized how loose and ready the pistol appeared to be. It could be snatched out without a hitch.

After a while the fat one went back to the police car and drove off.

Mother began to show the thin one around. She started with the room next to the kitchen which was supposed to be the servants' dining room but which was never used because our people preferred to sit in the kitchen. She explained to our policeman that he could use that room for himself; there was a radio for him to listen to the news, and she would have a good reading lamp moved in. My mother believed that everybody read. Next she took him into the kitchen and introduced him to Milly and I learned his name: Captain Bud. Milly bobbed her head and did not look up from the carrots she was scraping. Tom

Roberts was going through the linen drawers in the pantry when Mother introduced him. He looked out the window and smiled. Lea was upstairs, making beds, but by lunchtime she knew everything about the Captain. He was forty-three, not doing well on the police force, and never married.

My mother explained to the Captain that we were having an alarm system installed for when he was off duty, and that he should supervise the job. Then she went upstairs and I was left to show the Captain the outside.

He was swinging his hands, in the front hall, as though he had seen plenty of mirrors and gold chairs and chandeliers in his time. "I cover the wedding receptions," he told me. "Acres and acres of this kind of thing."

I took him outside. We went around through the west porch and down to the sunken garden and up again by the kitchen stairs. He stopped to lift up a clay pot. "Who takes care of the plants?" he asked, and I explained that Jacob was supposed to but was shiftless and allowed things to run wild.

Further along, there were four leggy begonia plants which Jacob had been told to put into bigger pots for the terrace. Captain Bud tapped out the old root balls and found four right-sized pots and popped the root balls in. Then he told me to get him some water. I ran into the house and brought him back a big silver pitcherful. He laughed and said he had meant the hose but water was water. He soaked the four pots and set them on the wall where they would get the right amount of light, and then he was ready to continue the tour.

We went to the vegetable garden and Captain But got down on his knees to look at the tomatoes, burst open on the ground. "Why didn't anybody bother to pick them?"

"We did for a while but Daddy said they gave him upset stomach."

He stood up and brushed off his hands. "Not meaning any disrespect, but rich people don't know how to live, as a rule. It's like those weddings. They have frozen capon flown in from New York. One of my old roosters would have more flavor if you boiled him up with onions."

"Have you got a farm?"

He laughed. "I've got a two-bit frame house and a half acre of poor land out at Woodside. And my chickens."

"Could we go see them?"

He looked at me. "You're plenty old enough to be in school. What's wrong?"

"I've got a cold."

"I see your nose is running. Here." He rummaged in his pocket and handed me a tissue.

I thanked him and wiped my nose. He made me keep the tissue. "You don't have to be afraid, it's not a catching cold," I said.

"You're a thin little thing. Don't you eat?"

"Oh, I eat plenty." I had already formed an opinion of the kind of girl he would like and I knew it was not a weakling with no appetite. "I eat the cornbread Milly makes, with lots of butter, and I eat collard greens. Mother says they're greasy."

"Nigger food," he remarked.

"Mother doesn't like me to use that word."

"Now, don't mistake me—I've seen some fine people working in these big houses, bringing up the children and taking care of everything and never once laying a hand on money or jewelry even when it's lying around asking to be taken."

"The kidnapper is colored," I confided. "Did you hear about it on the radio?"

"Read it in the newspaper. Don't think about it, Little Bit. There are bad apples in every race."

Then we went around to the front porch and I saw the alarm-system truck had pulled up. Captain Bud went over to the head man, who said he wanted to see the woman of the house. Captain Bud explained that he was the new watchman, and that it was his responsibility to oversee the installation. Then he said, "I'll see you later, Little Bit," and I knew enough to make myself scarce.

In no time at all, I learned the Captain's daily routine. As soon as I came home from school, I would run around to the sunken garden and find him strolling down the gravel path. He made the entire tour of the house twenty times, stopping three times for coffee and the bathroom.

After a while, it seemed to me he was not making quite so many tours. I would find him on the back porch when I came home from school. He had found a box of tools in the furnace room and he was making a windmill. The thin blades of the windmill were joined to a shaft which connected, in turn, to the figure of a sharp-jawed wooden man; his arm moved jerkily when the blades were turned. Captain Bud whittled a tiny saw and a stack of logs no bigger than matches. The saw was attached to the wooden man's hands and could be made to move back and forth across the stack of wood. Then he painted the whole thing, giving his man a pair of bright yellow trousers and eyes which came out too blue.

I went along to put the windmill up in the vegetable garden. It was a warm fall day, but frost the night before had felled the tomato vines. Captain Bud drove the stake for the windmill down into the ground and nailed his man on top. Right away, the blades began to turn, and the little man sawed in a frenzy. I clapped my hands. "We're going to dig you your own vegetable patch, next spring," the Captain told me, looking over the layout of the garden. "We'll have you some tomatoes, and a row of lettuce." Then we went inside to listen to the five o'clock news.

The kidnapper's trial went on all fall because of the lack of circumstantial witnesses. Mrs. Doll was "in confinement"; later, I found out she was having a baby, which mystified me. So there was really no one to speak against the kidnapper except for a boy who had seen him in a gasoline station, and he had nothing but good to say. Captain Bud and I grew used to the high droning voice of the prosecuting attorney and the peevish squeals of the culprit's lawyer. Finally one day the kidnapper himself took the stand and talked just like Tom Roberts.

After that, Captain Bud began to walk a new route around the house. "That's to throw them off," he explained. Some days, he seemed distracted and hardly noticed me. I thought he was suspicious of Tom Roberts, and I explained that Tom never left the house and did not know how to drive a car, let alone play mathematical games. It turned out that was not what the Captain meant. He said we were generally surrounded by evil and he was trying to outwit it.

On the days when he didn't notice me, I followed him anyway, imagining that I was stepping in his invisible footprints. After a while, he would always look back at me and smile. Then I would run up beside him and tell him some tale from my own day at school. When I had finished, he would offer me a scrap from his own life. He told me his mother was old and sick and depended on him; he also said he had a no-good brother who was a drunk. He said the check my father gave him every Friday went just about nowhere, and he was going to have to give up his little place at Woodside and sell his chickens. I nearly cried when he said that. Then he fished behind the box bush in the sunken garden and pulled out a paper bag. "Cold weather gets into my bones," he explained, although it was a warm day. He tipped the sack to his mouth.

After that, we stopped by the box bush on every round. By

five o'clock, he was looking much too red in the face, and I wanted him to go home without listening to the news. But I couldn't persuade him. There had been a break in the case that day and he wanted to hear the kidnapper's wife, who had been found somewhere in South America. She was supposed to speak against the kidnapper, but although Captain Bud leaned into the radio and turned the volume up high, what she said didn't seem to amount to much. He was a poor provider, she said, which was why she had gone to South America, but that was because he always had his head in the clouds.

"That's those games," the Captain said, shaking his head, and then he finally went out and got into his car and drove away.

After that, we spent more time in the sunken garden. It was turning cold, and I would pinch my arms and dance to keep warm. Finally five o'clock would come, and then the news, and then the Captain would drive away. One afternoon, a few minutes after he'd driven off, I heard a terrible crash down at the gate.

I ran down with Tom Roberts and Lea behind me; Milly stayed on the porch. The Captain's car was nudged up against the front gate, and there was broken glass everywhere. The Captain himself was sitting in the middle of the road. His legs were spread wide apart and his hands were resting on his knees.

"What's done happened now?" Tom Roberts asked, peering at the Captain from a safe distance.

Lea asked, "You hurt, Mr. Bud?"

I ran to him and knelt down to look in his face. He was smiling. "Hello, Little Bit," he said.

I started to feel his shoulders and arms. I thought I would be able to feel the end of a broken bone if he had hurt himself. I was afraid he might be sitting in a pool of blood, but I did not dare to tell him to get up in case something inside was broken.

Tom Roberts said, "Better call the police."

Captain Bud closed his eyes and passed one hand over them. "I am the police," he said.

Tom backed off then. Captain Bud went to his car and looked it over. A liquid of some kind was draining down onto the road. "I'll just walk back up to the house and call the wrecker," he said, and he took my hand and started back up the hill. Lea and Tom Roberts followed some distance behind.

"Mother gets home at five-thirty," I told him. "She'll have a fit!" He didn't even answer.

In the house, he went directly to the telephone and said something short to the person on the other end. Then he washed his face and hands in the kitchen sink and dried himself on a dish-towel. "That'll have to be washed, now," Milly said. Captain Bud turned on his heel and marched out. I ran after him. As we started back down the hill, Lea shouted at me to come back.

At the gate, Captain Bud sat down in the ivy and smoked a cigarette. I kept asking him what he was going to do if my mother came home first. "There isn't anything for me to do, Little Bit," he said.

Then the wrecker drove up. Captain Bud and the driver appeared to be friends; they waved at each other cheerfully. "Broke down again, Bud?" the driver asked. I was horrified to think that this had apparently happened before.

They hooked the car up to the wrecker and I waved to the Captain as he climbed into the cab. I saw him offer his friend a cigarette. Then they drove off.

My mother turned into the gates a few minutes later. She asked me what I was doing, standing in the middle of the road, and I told her I was hunting wildflowers.

For a while after that, everything went smoothly. Captain Bud was nearly always where I expected him to be when I came home from school, and he paid fewer visits to the box bush in the sunken garden. As we walked around the house, I told him a few choice items from my day at school. Sometimes he would laugh. Other times he would seem bored and then I would improve on my tale, exaggerating a little to make it more interesting. One day not long before Christmas, he asked. "How come you never have any friends home to play?"

"They like to play with dolls."

"I saw that big collection of yours."

"They're not to play with. They're just to collect." I did not add that none of the girls in my class would have been interested in keeping me company on Captain Bud's rounds.

He grumbled a lot as Christmas approached, saying his mother was getting worse. She needed constant care, and he would put her in a home if he had the money. On Christmas Eve, she fell and broke her hip, and Captain Bud spent his day off getting her arranged. He said she would be in the hospital for a long stretch and the doctor did not expect her to walk again.

I went to my room and sat down by my new dollhouse. The thin-legged doll family was still gathered around the Christmas tree, bending stiffly over the tiny silver and gold packages my mother had made. Captain Bud came in the door and looked darkly at the scene. "I wish I could park mama in one of these empty rooms, where I could keep an eye on her," he said, and then he stumped off, without stopping to look at any of my presents.

That afternoon, about four o'clock, I heard the alarm begin to shriek. It was a new voice in the house. I ran out into the hall and collided with Captain Bud, careening toward the stairs. I thought he was going down to the basement to throw the switch, but instead I heard a shot, and glass splintered in the front hall.

By then Lea was standing behind me on the landing, holding onto my jumper strap. I broke loose and ran down the stairs.

Captain Bud was standing in the middle of the hall with his pistol in his hand. "It's just a little mistake," he told me. The big window was broken behind the marble bust of my grandfather. The bust itself had lost an ear.

I hunted around among the broken glass for the ear. It was heavy and cold, and there was no way to stick it back on. "They're never going to let you stay, now," I said, beginning to cry.

Captain Bud smiled. "The way it was, Little Bit, I saw that head against the light, I thought he was coming through the window."

"And your mother's in the hospital. How are you going to pay for that if you get fired?"

"I don't know," he said, and then he got into his car and drove away.

I washed my face and combed my hair and waited for my mother to come home. As soon as she opened the front door, I ran to her and buried my face in her fox fur. I said somebody had tried to break into the house and the Captain had fired at him and hit the bust by mistake.

My mother started to tremble before I had finished, and then she tottered out to the kitchen to ask for corroboration.

Lea and Tom held back while Milly spoke. "Yes'm," she said, "we did hear that alarm go off about four o'clock. Captain came running down the steps, drew his pistol out and shot. Man got away, but that don't matter. He won't come fooling around this house again."

"Yes, Lord," Tom said. That was going too far, and I saw Milly give him a look.

My mother staggered toward the stairs, begging someone to bring her up some tea.

Later, when I asked Milly why she had said that, she just glared at me.

"I like him, too," I said hastily.

"They's worse," Milly said.

Captain Bud had the whole of New Year's weekend off as a reward for his services. When he came back to work, he looked pale and his hands were trembling when he turned on the lights in the front hall. "Dark earlier and earlier," he said. I started to explain that actually it was beginning to go the other way, but he shook his head as though he was shaking my words out of his ears.

At five o'clock, the verdict on the kidnapper was read over the radio: guilty. There had just been a kidnapping up north and a baby had been killed, an important one, so the punishment had been jacked up: death in the electric chair. "Poor bastard," the Captain said.

"But he did it," I said, searching his face.

"Who knows?" the Captain said. "Maybe he did, and maybe he didn't. In this country, they always find somebody."

I went out to the hall to wait for my father. I felt disturbed, all the way through. It had never occurred to me before that an innocent man could be punished for something he didn't do.

I heard my father's car on the drive and at the same time, Captain Bud came down the hall from the kitchen. On the other side of the glass front door, my father appeared in a circle of light. Captain Bud snatched his pistol out of the holster and aimed.

I screamed. My father walked into the house. "What is the meaning of this?" he asked when he saw the Captain's pistol.

"We heard somebody coming, we didn't know who it was," I said.

The Captain slowly put his pistol away. "My nerves are all to pieces," he said.

"This is the end, the limit," my father said.

I ran to him and threw my arms around his waist. "His mother is sick, she broke her hip, his brother is no good—"

My father undid my hands. "Your superiors will hear of this," he told Captain Bud.

Later I helped Captain Bud get his things together. I shuffled his magazines and his bottles and his chewing gum and cigarettes into a shopping bag while he stood to one side and watched. After a while, he said to me, softly, "I singed his tailfathers, didn't I?" He didn't wait for me to answer. "Yes, I singed his tailfeathers good," he said.

My mother was waiting in the front hall to tell him goodbye. She shook his hand and made a little speech about bad luck. She said she'd do her best to keep this little incident off his record. Captain Bud smiled all the time she was talking; I never had seen him smile so much. By the end, his smile had become a grin. Then he walked to the front door and opened it and walked out.

I ran after him. My mother pulled me back into the house. "What is this?" she asked, turning me toward the light.

"He was going to help me make a garden in the spring."

"I never knew you wanted a garden. I'll order some seed catalogues."

"He was going to take me to see his chickens."

"Unsuitable," my mother said, after a moment's thought.

"His mother just broke her hip!" I wailed, but she interrupted me.

"Go up and wash your face. I want you calmed down in time for dinner. Your father's in a state; I can't have two of you on my hands. Tell Milly you can eat with us if you calm down in time."

I calmed down in time. Dinner with my parents was a rare treat. We did not talk about the Captain, and my father was unusually irritable, but we had artichokes; the leaves, neatly arranged, made a green pattern on the white plates.

MARGUERITE GUZMAN BOUVARD

Tea Ceremony

Through the doorway, the pared earth,
fishbone trees and shadows
scattered like ornamental rocks,
a garden serene as the Ryoan-ji in Kyoto,
and the sky an unplowed field.

It tells me that the days I herd
like an animal trainer, urging
each hour onto its chair,
cannot be driven,

that I must follow the hours
moving across the lawn
like stately beasts.

It tells me that a simple room,
a table for writing, a cot, a few chairs
leaves space for the ochres
and purple of the heart.

In this room, I draw up a straight-
backed chair for my grandmother.
I sit by the bedside
of my aunt dying in Rimini.

We don't need to speak, our thoughts
the fragrances of green tea.

DAVID BRADLEY

Growing Old

I

Many things are said to be passed on. Sleepiness can be passed on, and yawning can be passed on. Time can be passed on also. . . .

Miyamoto Musashi
A Book of Five Rings

risk: The possibility of loss. The term is commonly used to describe the possibility of loss from some particular hazard, as fire risk, war risk, credit risk, etc. It also describes the possibility of loss by an investor who, in popular speech, is often referred to as a *risk bearer.*

insurance: Protection against risk. To secure such protection private contracts are made according to which, for a consideration of a premium paid by one party, called the insured, another agrees to indemnify the insured should he suffer losses specified in the contract. . . .

Sloan and Zurcher
Dictionary of Economic Terms

Once, when I was fairly young—nine or ten I think; certainly not more than eleven—my mother went away overnight. My father fixed me dinner and made sure I washed behind my ears and put me to bed on my mother's side of the double bed that my parents shared. Sometime in the middle of the night I was shocked from sleep by a crash of breaking glass and the thud of something meaty hitting the floor. And then I heard my father call my name.

I found him on the bathroom floor, amid the shattered remains of a water glass, supporting himself with his knees and one hand, groping, with the other, for something to hold on to. His glasses had slipped and hung from one ear. He looked up at me, unable, in his myopia, to really see me. There was fear in his naked eyes. His breath came in rasps. "Help me, David," he said.

I could not help him—he weighed more than two hundred pounds. In the end I could only walk beside him as he crawled back into the bedroom, and try to steady him as he struggled up onto the bed. He would not let me call anyone. He said he was all right. He told me to return to the bed myself, to go back to sleep.

I did not go to sleep. I lay there and listened to his breathing. And I wondered what I would do if he were to stop.

I had no doubt about what it would mean. My father had the idea that a breadwinner was a sort of king, entitled to all duty, honor, respect and obedience, and so, whenever he found my demonstration of these virtues wanting, he would seek to motivate me by impressing upon me that his hard work was all that stood between me and destitution. When he was pleased with me he would reinforce my sense of security by taking me down to his basement study to show me where the insurance and other papers were, "just in case anything should happen" to him. The insurance, he said, would keep my mother and me going for six months. He never said what would happen then. My imagination filled the vacuum with images from Charles Dickens.

And so I lay there listening, timing my father's breathing to the millisecond, tensing in terror if the sound of his inhalation came even a moment late, hatching wild schemes: if he failed to breathe again I would get the vacuum cleaner and use the blower end to force air into his lungs like they did on "Ben Casey"; I would pull the wires from a lamp and shock him back to life à la "Dr. Kildare." I do not know when I went back to sleep. Or how.

My father never mentioned that night. It is possible that he forgot it. I never did. Through all my years of childhood listening to my father breathe was a constant preoccupation. When he would nap in the afternoon I would sometimes stand at the door of the bedroom, listening. If I was too far away to hear, I would watch his chest rise and fall. At every hesitation I would tremble, fearful not for him, but for me. For I had accepted the definition of my father that he himself promoted; he was my security. And I was afraid not that he would die, but that he would die before I was old enough to take care of myself.

I did not simply stand in fear; I moved in it. My father was, I knew, in his fifties, which seemed to me ancient. Death was an immediate inevitability. And so I saw myself in a race with the Reaper, trying to grow up before my father grew old, trying to reach my day of independence before he reached his date of death. I began to do odd jobs at an earlier age than most children, even in those times. I tramped through the snows of winter trying to sell flower seeds to farmers. My dog was not to me a pet but a factory that regularly produced puppies which could be sold for profit. I secretly took to skipping lunch at school. I opened a bank account about which my parents knew nothing— or so I thought—and fed it with every penny I could. When I grew old enough to have a real job, summer and part-time, I worked industriously and desperately, hanging around after my shift, trying to grab fifteen minutes worth of overtime worth thirty-seven and a half cents. I reacted to my first seasonal layoff with the depression one would expect of a breadwinner with a family of six to support. I went to work no matter what—one morning I was so sick and dizzy I fell out on the grill, but I lasted until the middle of my shift. Then they took me to the hospital and performed an emergency appendectomy. I went back to work in less than two weeks.

Going to college was, for me, an escape from a decade of terror. I had a scholarship, and with that money and what I could earn I was independent. The financial aid people established a figure for what they called a "parents' contribution" to my up-keep. I did not ask my father for money. I did not even tell him about it.

I know exactly what the effect of that escape was: my father disappeared. He and I had somehow agreed that his meaning to me was simple security. That was his purpose, the source of his power. And when that was gone, he was gone. Oh, I loved him. Thought of him. Was bound to him by respect and ritual. Bought him Old Spice aftershave each Christmas. But as a factor in my decision making, a source of comfort or terror, punishment or reward, my father disappeared from my life. I think he knew that, and I think it bothered him; once my mother murmured something about my father wishing there was something he could do for me. There wasn't. We had made sure of that.

II

The true artist will let his wife starve, his children go barefoot, his mother drudge for his living at seventy, sooner than work at anything but his art.

G. B. Shaw
Man and Superman

On a pleasantly warm evening in late July 1979 my father reappeared in my life. I was nearing twenty-nine then, living in a rented walk-up in New York's East Village and commuting, during the academic year, to teach at a university in Philadelphia. And I was working on my second novel.

As I saw it then, my professional existence depended on that novel. My first book, published four years earlier, had been a "literary success"; the reviews had been impressive, the sales had not. That was the beginning of what I had once thought were apocryphal publishing nightmares. Now I knew they were not apocryphal. But I believed that this new book would get me beyond them—would get me some attention, more work, and maybe even a little clout, all of which I felt I needed in order to write the way I wanted to.

I needed money too, but a new book would take care of that, albeit indirectly. In two more years the university would be deciding whether to give me tenure or fire me. With a second book published I had a chance to keep a job that paid me adequately and still left me time to write.

It all came down to timing. If I could finish the book by February or March of 1980 it could be published before the tenure decision, but in order to make that deadline I would have to work almost nonstop through the summer of '79.

I did. Until that pleasantly warm evening in late July when my mother called to tell me that my father, complaining of pain and palsy in his legs, had been taken to the hospital. She did not say that she would like me to come home. But at midnight I got on a Greyhound and I rode for six hours, which is a long time to be alone with yourself and your thoughts—especially if you are finding it hard to like either.

My thoughts were of my father, of course. I had quickly evaluated the known factors—his age (seventy-three), his physical condition (he was a diabetic with chronic high blood pressure who carried fifty pounds of excess fat), his personal habits (a high-saturated fat, high-sodium diet, an aversion to regular exercise, a fondness for snacks that verged on the neurotic), the implications of his recent medical history (a broken leg, indicating a brittleness of bone, the loss of sight in one eye, due probably to decreased circulation and therefore indicating a loss of cardio-vascular efficiency)—and concluded that, no matter what the current problem might be, my father could very well be dying.

But while my thoughts were of my father they were not exactly *for* him. They were for me. Because I was afraid.

I was afraid, to begin with, of going home. Oh, I had gone home before, and I understood the tension inherent in being an adult returning to a place in which I had always been a child, and in which I was going to, in a sense, have to act like a child. Usually, at the end of the bus ride I would find a father to pick me up and provide me with room and board, and a mother who would cook and wash my clothes and, if I did not do it within ten minutes of arising, make my bed. I would be taken care of. I would also, to some extent, be bossed around. Not directly or offensively. But my normal routine and habits would be interrupted. I would rise and go to bed earlier. I would eat more regularly—dinner at six o'clock instead of when I got hungry. I would wear clothes around the house, go to church on Sunday, not drink, swear, or have sex. And I would be asked, especially by my father, in subtle and indirect ways, if I was sure I knew what I was doing with my life.

Lately I had come to terms with the tension, and had grown adept at avoiding any conflict. I was more secure in my independence, and so could enjoy giving a little up for a while, able to accept gifts that, when younger, I would have refused. Lately home had become a haven.

But at the end of this bus ride I was not going to be taken care of. I was going to have to take care—of business, of people, of my own emotions. I was going to have to be precise; calm, collected—concerned but more than slightly dispassionate; it wasn't going to do any good for me to start crying in a corner. This time I was going to be an adult returning to a place where I had always been a child but in which I was going to have to act like an adult. I was afraid I could not pull it off.

I was afraid too that there would be a problem of money. My

father, a minister, had never earned more than seven or eight thousand dollars a year; I could not imagine that he had much money put aside. And I didn't earn much; my job was good for me because it allowed me time to write, but it covered my expenses only because I had kept them minimal. My independence was dependent on a lack of dependents. But if my father died I might very well have to help support my mother, and I was worried what I would do; I could easily find a job that paid better—but it would be one that would leave me little or no time to write. I wondered if I would do that. I was afraid I would not.

And I was afraid that there was something horribly wrong with me. For it had not escaped my notice that I was not reacting to the possibility of my father's death with emotions born of pure love. I was acting properly so far, but I was thinking selfishly. I was, in fact, more than a little annoyed at my father—annoyed that he had taken such lousy care of himself, annoyed that he should interfere in my life at such a crucial time. And I was somewhat testily wondering not just what was wrong with him, but how long the disruption would last. I told myself that I did not really feel that way, that I was unconsciously repressing more tender emotions in order to maintain the necessary calm.

But I did not entirely believe it. Because I recognized that one of the reasons I was on that bus was to minimize my father's ability to interfere with my future. For while I had no illusion that anything I could do would really make a difference, I knew that, if I were not there and anything bad did happen I would forever feel somehow at fault. My bus ticket was my proof that I had done what I could—my receipt for guilt insurance.

III

Albany: Where have you hid yourself?
How have you known the miseries of your father?
Edgar: By nursing them, my lord.

William Shakespeare
King Lear

. . . and his big manly voice,
Turning again towards childish treble, pipes
And whistles in his sound. Last scene of all
That ends this strange eventful history

52

Is second childishness and mere oblivion
Sans teeth, sans eyes, sans taste, sans everything.

William Shakespeare
As You Like It

After four weeks of tests performed in three different hospitals the doctors decided that my father had a fairly rare disease that had about ten names, the least unpronounceable of which was Guillain-Barré Syndrome. They didn't know what caused it but they could predict what it would do: paralyze my father. The weakness in his legs would spread upwards throughout his voluntary and semi-voluntary muscles, probably becoming so extensive that he would need assistance from a respirator in order to breathe, possibly becoming so complete that he would be unable to blink his eyes. If the disease became extreme the functions ordinarily governed by his sympathetic nervous system—heartbeat, blood pressure—might become erratic. All of this would be treated with life-supporting machines and drugs—for the disease itself there was no known cure, not even a widely accepted treatment. That was the bad news. The good news was that the disease would go away.

Nobody knew what caused that either, but it almost always happened. After only a few weeks, two or three months at most, the lost functions would return, and the paralysis would begin to descend as it had ascended. The patient would almost always be fully rehabilitated in less than two years; the disease killed less than one patient in ten or twenty, disabled, in any significant way, less than one in five. It was a fairly benign disease as neurological diseases go; the doctors, almost affectionately, called it GBS.

I was obscenely pleased with the diagnosis. To my father it was a sentence to weeks in chains in a dark dungeon, but I could not see that; to me it meant that my appearance as the concerned son was going to be a cameo role, that my father's interference in my life was going to be both brief and mild.

But on a quiet evening late in August my father's case of GBS became extreme. His breathing grew labored and uneven, his heartbeat sporadic and inefficient, and his blood pressure went through the floor. He was moved to an Intensive Care Unit. I was called in and dressed in a yellow gown and white surgical mask, which were supposed to keep me from killing my father

53

with the microbes I carried in my body and on my clothes, and sent in to see him.

My father lay on a shockingly white bed, spread out like a component stereo, most of his vital functions in the control of a machine. A nurse came and stood beside me, and quietly explained what everything did. I was no stranger to technology or medical terminology, but I understood only ten percent of what she said. At least I was better off than my father, who was a stranger to technology and medical terminology, who had been born into the era of the Stanley Steamer, who refused to travel by plane, who had taken a year to conquer his distrust of a calculator I had bought him. The machines would be terrifying him. And so I leaned over to try to explain it to him as best I could. But I saw his lips moving weakly behind the oxygen mask. He was saying: "Take me home."

It should have made me cry; instead it made me furious. I did not know why, but I wanted to grab him and shake him, to take him on a guided tour of his own body: See this, old man? This bottle is your stomach, and this tank is your lungs, this compressor is your diaphram, this pump is your pancreas. You still have a heart, but this thing here is what makes it beat. And this is a picture of the beat. This number here is a count of beats in the last minute, and this one is the number of them that haven't done you or anybody else a damned bit of good. You can watch these numbers and see how well you're doing. You're not doing too well. So tell me, how the hell am I supposed to take you home? Maybe we could swing a private nurse and an ambulance, but what about the tow truck and mechanic? "Take me home," my father was saying.

I said, "I can't," and went away.

IV

Grow old along with me!
The best is yet to be,
The last of life, for which the first was made.

Robert Browning
"Rabbi Ben Ezra"

The land of faery
Where nobody gets old and godly and grave

54

Where nobody gets old and crafty and wise
Where nobody gets old and bitter of tongue.

William Butler Yeats
"The Land of Heart's Desire"

My father lay in the Intensive Care Unit for over a month. I did not see much of him; the academic year had begun and so I was dividing my time between New York, Philadelphia, and the hospital, which was in Pittsburgh. Even when I was there, the ICU visiting hours limited the time I could spend with him to a total of one hour a day. The rest of the time I spent sitting in the special waiting room, along with my mother and the others who had loved ones working out their destinies in Intensive Care.

The doctors had discovered that the event that had put my father in the ICU was a myocardial infarction—a heart attack. The cause was unclear; it could have been brought on by GBS, or it could have been a result of his struggle against the disease. The effect, however, was perfectly clear: my father's heart was seriously damaged. This put him in a paradoxical situation. In order to recover fully from GBS he would need to do hard work in physical therapy. The damage to his heart might make that impossible, or dangerous. And so he might be faced with the choice of being a cripple for the rest of his life, or of killing himself trying not to be.

He might end up helpless either way. I could not imagine what impact that would have on him. He had always been proud and jealous of his independence; he was the kind of man who would ask directions of a stranger and then take a shortcut of his own. He was never comfortable with something unless he did it himself. Now he might not be able to do anything himself. That might drive him, quite literally, insane.

Which he might be already, made that way by his current helplessness and by the frustrations of being unable to communicate (a tracheotomy had eliminated his ability to talk, and his hands were too weak to make meaningful signs) and of having to squint at the world through one horribly myopic eye (the nurses tried to keep his glasses on, but that was both difficult and dangerous). I feared that he might survive in some half-senile state, his weakened body and feebled mind constantly taking him on unpredictable voyages into irrationality or second childhood.

But I also feared that his mind would be unaffected. For despite his pride in his own independence, he was terribly fond of being obeyed, agreed with, and waited on. He was authoritarian as a matter of philosophy, dogmatic as a matter of occupation, and impatient as a matter of course. As an alert invalid he might easily become a tyrant.

I realized that I had never dealt with those things before. As a child I had chafed under them helplessly, and I had, in adulthood, found a rather ordinary compromise: I stayed out of sight. When I spoke to or visited my father, I concealed my thoughts and feelings and behavior—not entirely, but enough to keep the peace.

But the success of that practical compromise had prevented me from considering the philosophical question: what *did* I owe my father? Did I owe him obedience or even its semblance? Did I owe him a part of my future? Where was the line that separated an overly demanding parent from an ungrateful child? I had never before wrestled with that question. I wrestled with it now, and found it hard going, not only because it was the worst possible time, but because I had ever before me what seemed a shining example of filial duty: the life of my father himself.

Two years before I was born my father left the community in New Jersey where he had been pastoring for fourteen years and returned to the town in western Pennsylvania where he had been raised and where his mother, then eighty years old, still resided. For the next dozen years my father "looked after" my grandmother, providing for her what has come to be thought of as an ideal environment for aging persons. My grandmother had her dinner and breakfast and slept at our house, enjoying contact with younger people, balanced meals, supervision for her medical problems—she developed diabetes and cataracts—but she also went to her own home every day, where she could have privacy and independence in the home that had been hers for nearly half a century.

It had always seemed to me that my father had done a wonderful thing for my grandmother. And so I began to think that perhaps there was some way in which I could do the same thing. It seemed possible. I would have to make a longer commute, by car, but it would not kill me. And I discovered that my father did have some money that, properly reinvested and added to his social security and my albeit meager pay, would allow him and my mother and me to live comfortably. Or would have, if he had not been sick, and if I had not been me.

Because when I looked into the matter in earnest I discovered that what can only with great charity be called a system of medi-cal assistance in this country is based on a bizarre illogic: we are more concerned with preserving the life of a person of any age, fetus to nonagenarian, than we are with providing for the needs of the life so preserved. My father's medical bills would be taken care of for a few more months . . . so long as he stayed in an institution. After that he could continue to receive care, but only in an institution and only if everything he had worked to build, the things by which he so often defined himself—house, sav-ings—were gone. Leaving nothing to take care of my mother but social security and me.

I wasn't going to be much help. My ability to earn money was limited. I would not get so much as a tax break from the IRS. If I did not complete the book I would probably be fired. And I too would lose everything I had been working for.

I realized that the example set by my father was illusory, inappropriate, and dated. My father had not made much of a sacrifice to take care of his mother. He was forty-three when he moved, had been married for over a decade, and his career had developed to a point where he could live where he chose—much of his work involved travel anyway. And he did travel, some-times for more than half the year. He could do that because it was really his wife who looked after his mother, who prepared the balanced meals, washed the sheets, cleaned the room, ad-ministered the daily injections of insulin. My father paid the bills, and got on with his work. When my grandmother died it was my mother who was at her bedside; my father was playing host to a meeting of the church youth group. It was not as cold as it sounds—my grandmother was in a coma. But my father had, at the end, made a choice about where to be, and the hard implications of that choice had been somewhat softened by the fact that he had my mother standing in for him.

I was fourteen years younger than my father had been, was not married or equipped with a permanent or portable lover, and my career was at the point where I could not be anywhere I wanted to be. I needed New York and the contacts it afforded, access to the kinds of research facilities available only in urban areas. If I tried to follow my father's example I was going to become a male version of the old maid daughter whose entire role in life is to take care of the folks. That was impossible for me. For I had been trained from youth to believe that a man works, and that he sacrifices other concerns to do his work, that if he does not he is not much of a man. When I was four it had been necessary for my mother to undergo surgery. After the operation was successfully completed, my father left me on a short business trip, leaving her in the hospital and taking me with him. I enjoyed the trip and, a few weeks later, begged to accompany him again. He asked who was going to take care of my mother. I suggested that we put her back in the hospital. That had become something of a family joke—"ain't he a chip off the old block?" It was no longer funny. Because the kind of thinking that would have made it possible for me to accept the complete sacrifice of work to care for my father was totally foreign to me.

My understanding of all of that did not relieve my guilt about the feelings that were the result of it. For even if my father's sacrifice had been less than I had once thought, someone else's had not been: my mother's.

When my mother acquired the responsibility of my grandmother she was in her mid-thirties and childless, living sixteen miles from New York. It was possible that, left to herself, she might have found other outlets for her talents and energy. Even had she had a child, in that environment she could have done a dozen different things: gone to school, started a business, engaged in research. I knew she could have because she had done all those things in the limited term available to her while I was still fairly young . . . but only after my grandmother was dead. Given the social mores of those years of her prime—that late 'Forties and 'Fifties—my mother's sacrifice was so laudable and expected as to seem almost no sacrifice. In the present day it seemed tragic. Even *wrong*. Even though I loved my mother I realized that I could never choose as a mate a woman like her, who would be satisfied with that kind of life. Which meant, of course, that I was never going to do for her what my father had been able to do for his mother.

That hurt me. Because my father's reappearance had made my mother reappear as well, and it seemed to me she was far more deserving of concern than my father. She was calm, resigned, almost serene, waiting while her mate of nearly fifty years fought for life, to see what the rest of her life was going to be like. It was probably not going to be anything good. She had not only nursed my father's mother, she had nursed her own. Now she might have to be a nurse again and it was not going to be an easy kind of nursing—it was going to sap her strength and probably leave her destitute. I wondered what, in time, that might do to her love for my father. I knew damned well what it had done to mine; I had thought the Thought.

The Thought was unconscious. But when I look back now I see that in the later stages of my father's illness I was acting on it: checking with his lawyer to make sure his affairs were in order; moving papers from his safe deposit box; figuring out how to arrange his finances. I called it Being Prepared for the Worst. What it was was preparing. For I changed nothing in my life, and made no arrangements to.

And so when my mother called to tell me the doctors had said my father was dying, I said I'd take the first plane out, and went back to sleep. And when I sat and listened to the doctors tell me in their precise jargon that my father's veins had turned to sewers because his kidneys had gone on vacation, but his lungs were on wildcat strike and his heart was taking frequent coffee breaks and that his body just wasn't working very much and that, should it decide to quit altogether, they were not going to make any "heroic efforts" to get it back on the job and were in fact considering a gradual layoff of the automation that gave an illusion of operation, I did not protest or even question too strongly. I took it in good humor. I even made a weak joke. Because I had already thought the Thought: wouldn't it be better for everybody, him, my mother, and of course, myself if he just died?

It was not evil to think the Thought. It was natural, I believe, and rational. But I sometimes wonder if somehow my father did not hear me think it. If he did not know, more consciously than I did, that his only son was contemplating his final dissolution as a kind of final solution. I wonder if the Thought was not more dangerous than the germs those masks and the yellow gowns were supposed to protect him from. I wonder if, apart from GBS, multiple myocardial infarctions, pneumonia, septicemia, pulmonary edema, and convulsions, it was not the Thought that killed him.

V

"How's mom these days?"
"Okay," Tony said.
"Tell her I was asking for her."
"Asking for her isn't anything," Tony said.

Raymond Chandler
I'll Be Waiting

Time travels in divers paces with divers persons.

William Shakespeare
As You Like It

59

My father has been dead for three years now. A lot has happened in that time. My mother survived the trauma and loneliness and has found new ways to use the talents and abilities that
for so long supported others; she has become an accomplished
public speaker, a manager of property, an expert in local history,
the part-owner of a business. She has a life of her own, and she
could easily disappear from mine. Except that I won't let her.

For in those three years I have done a lot of thinking about the
way I handled my father's dying. I have faced two hard facts. I
handled it about as well as I could, given the circumstances. And
I did not handle it very well at all.

There are many reasons for each of those facts, but there is
one reason for both of them; I had let my parents disappear
around some corner in my life, and I had brought them back only
when I wanted to; when it was convenient. I had made them into
abstract symbols—"parent-things," easily loved, easily dealt
with. In the name of avoiding friction or disapproval or hurt
feelings or jarred sensibilities, I had put them out of sight, and I
had put me out of their sight, and I had drifted blissfully in the
illusion that it would go on that way forever, or that, when it
could not, it would not be a problem. When it became a problem,
I found myself dealing with everything at once—with emotions
and practicalities, ancient wounds and fears. I was shocked not
only by my father's death, but by his very reappearance in my
life in a new and different role. I found myself without any idea
of how I should behave or what I should do that was based on a
real sense of who I am and the world I live in and on who he was,
really. The morals of the situation were outmoded. I had developed no ethics. I was therefore doomed to act both immorally
and unethically.

And so I have taken steps to keep my mother from disappearing. I have asked her to accept the realities of my life; to understand that, while I am not married I am not, precisely, a virgin,
that I do suffer from a hangover now and again, that my language
is not always suitable for the ears of babes. I have asked her to
come and hear me speak when I am appearing nearby, to meet a
few of my friends and business associates, to become aware of
the pressures of my business, while at the same time facing some
of the realities of that business herself—she is a partner in a
bookstore.

And I have asked myself to become conversant with the
realities of her life. To do a bit of research on the aging process,
to become a bit of a gerontologist as she once became a
pediologist, to become as sensitive to the portrayal and treat-

ment of older people in the media as I once was to the portrayals of the young. To deal head up with the practicalities of her existence; to be aware of the social services in her area, the laws that apply to her finances, and to set some money of my own aside in preparation for the time when she might need it.

I have also made myself face the realities; to recognize that someday I am going to have to face the implications of my mother's mortality. I know there are certain things I am not going to do in order to take care of my mother; I will not marry, or go and live nearby, or, except in direst circumstances, pursue a more lucrative occupation.

But there are other things I could do, if I were properly prepared. And so, cold as it sounds, I run scenarios in my mind, imagining the worst, trying to expand the limits of my love, my sense of duty, my sense of honor, against the day when they will be tested. That day is coming, unfortunately; my mother is dying.

My mother has no illness. She appears to be in excellent health. She is dying only in the sense that everybody is, in the same sense that I am. Only my mother is doing it faster. For each passing day probably represents a greater percentage of the time she has remaining to her than it does of that remaining to me. It is possible, of course, that I could predecease her—airplanes crash, even relatively young men have heart attacks, and there are mortal dangers aplenty on my city's streets. But, barring improbability or misfortune, my mother will die before I do. Which means that each passing moment has greater significance for her than it does for me. This is a source of some anxiety, because I do not know exactly how fast my mother is dying. If I did, I would act differently. If I knew that this day, this month, this year would be her last, her time scale would mean more than mine. As it is, I do not know. My mother could live another twenty years, or even thirty. And so my evaluations of importance are only approximations.

But still they are different than they used to be; I used to live in one time frame, and now I live in two. Now I realize that my postponement could be my mother's cancellation, and I ask myself, when I consider a change in my life, how important is it that I do this? What are the values, not only in my terms, but in hers?

At the same time, I have realized that my mother has had a life, and that I must have one too. Despite love and concern and calculation I cannot live in the shadow of a deathbed or an invalid's chair that may be two decades away. Still, I know that my mother may one day need me, a thought that almost made me hate my father. It does not make me hate my mother. In fact, it almost makes me happy.

For I have realized that all the emphasis our society places on growing up has concealed a cycle working in our lives. We do not simply grow up and away from our parents, circumstances bring us back to them again. And I would like to think that, if we take the time to prepare, and if we do not expect too much of ourselves, that need not be so terrible.

MARTHA CLARK

Woman Picking Flowers

It saddens me to watch her
picking flowers in the evening,
bending always in the same direction.

First she's young and the cows are curious;
then she's old and the flowers are dandelions
and she's picked them once today.

All around her are birds that she cannot describe,
a road through the woods, her feet in the grass,
all around her the hum and ripple of insects.

It saddens me to watch her, so lost
in what she does, the cows facing west,
the orange sun, now sitting the way a mother might.

MARTHA COLLINS

White Tree with Branches

The tree in the library courtyard has blossomed with snow.
Not little clumps, or bunches, or lines
on the branches, but big white clusters that make
you think as you think when blossoms appear on the trees
before the leaves, as in plum—
                              or with the leaves,
as in pear, as in the story in which the bride's bouquet
is a bent black branch, laden with green and white—

or the photograph of twenty nuns in their white
lace dresses, white lace veils, their hair long
and curled for the last time, their hands clasped
around white candles wound with flowers—

We take things in through the corners of our eyes.
We forget before we know, letting things sink.
The white fields we dream may be the random sides
of the road—
                rolling fields with grass, fields
with cows, clouds like smoke, hills with trees
perhaps in the valleys, fields that come together
like thighs at the place that seems like the end
of the road, clouds like blossoms, blossoms like fields—

The old road home, that leads to this new white place.

Gray

Honest A.
More honest a:
a day's where I begin.

Gray sky. Gray sea.
The dulled horizon underlined.
Burled sand, beached stone. Some bones.

My hands, numb and white, curled.
You gathered stones and shells.

A few gulls. Slight white waves.
The terns could not be seen.

Those early days how brown you seemed.
Hair, eye, brow, beard, skin
still tan in winter.

After your call the cold rain came.
I closed the window part way.
Like rain I was beginning again.

I stared. Stared.

Canescent leaves in evening light
outside the shingled house.
The dried marsh where you
supposed a tiger.

That night I dreamed a last line.
Morning? you wrote. *Morning?*

Elusive figures chalked
on the pale slate of late sleep.
A dog barked. The morning train hooed by.
Light rain rained on the low roof.

Gray is your color. Grey.
He was so grey, he stunned rain.

Later days we shunned touch.
The chairs did not help
or the lit fire.

Gray and bare the hill itself at last.
Gray grays gray.

The back half of the cut worm writhes.
The head does not complain.

The least least tern sleeps more than I.

I see you less than ever now.

We hurt in the same place.

JAMES MADISON DAVIS

Lady of Spain

When people ask me what I do, I tell them I "play organ." Then I watch. If the corners of their mouths rise, if they smirk in the slightest way, I immediately remove them from my list of potential friends. I will not be the friend of barbarians, and crude thoughts are the essence of the Visigoth. Given society as it is now, I am left with few friends. There is Leopold, my landlord— he is eighty years old and rather erratic; Twyla, the palm-reader who lives across the hall; and Mark, a photographer who often gets me jobs at weddings. If I were to tell people I "sell organ," I could easily be without any friends. Barbarity is infectious, and during the current plague, one must make allowances.

To equate *the* organ with that *other* organ shows the cast of the contemporary mind. No further proof is needed. They're sexually obsessed. They look for a chance to fondle whatever they can get their hands on. As Twyla says, it's merely another proof of the final days of decadence. We have no immunity that the Greeks and Babylonians did not have, and this maniacal devotion to sexual interests is more than conspicuous in the eyes of shoppers strolling in the mall where I am forced to play.

I have endured this job for a mere week. Though I am obviously the best organist of the three salesmen, I have been retained through the Christmas season only. It isn't, after all, playing skills that matter, but sales alone (as Mr. Conchis continually points out), and I haven't sold very many, so far. I was quite confident of a transaction yesterday. After I convinced her that one of those wheezing, plastic horrors for one hundred and twenty-nine dollars was no bargain, I was certain she would go for a better model. Instead, she left. She was obviously only in here because she was looking for a thrill. Yes, even with a child in tow, she was on the prowl for a liaison in the dim alcoves where the instruments are ensconced. She didn't say so. She didn't have to. It was manifest in the tremble of her hairy upper lip. She wanted to have sex with me. And we had barely introduced ourselves! That's the kind of "civilization" we live in. That's the modern world for you.

So today Mr. Conchis assigned me to sit atop this flimsy platform with tinny ornaments on the side, fingering tunes for tasteless libertines as they shuttle in and out of stores with squalling brats and packages that would challenge Atlas himself. At the moment I am playing "Raindrops Keep Falling on My Head." One of the conga switches is thrown, so there are fake drums and an obnoxious rhythm boom-chickety-booming out of the machine. It's like a nightmare featuring Xavier Cugat and Little Ricky. My nausea is immeasurable.

Mr. Conchis has ordered me to play from in one of two books: *Tunes for All Time* or *Merrie Melodies of Christmas.* Neither has an organ work worthy of the pulpy paper they are printed on, but huge, distracting numbers are arranged over the staffs so that blithering idiots can thump out inferior songs without learning anything about music. Of course, anyone who would play these "tunes for all time" is already severely musically deficient. It goes without saying. Why else have seventeen buttons providing accompaniments that make wind-up monkeys sound like the London Philharmonic? Never mind the niceties of harmony. Nor the thunder of pipes on a major chord. No! Never mind the immortal Schumann, the titanic Couperin! Thumpa-thumpa, instead. Boom-chickety-boom. We can play our two thousand-dollar instrument with one hand and leave the other free for fondling.

Oh dear. Mrs. Suburbia looketh on. Her face is the color of school paste; her hair the texture of Brillo. Even the blue bag she holds against her belly cannot conceal her rotundity. She smiles. Her teeth are too white to be *de natura*. I smile back. Who knows but what the porcine dear might have an appreciable sum to spend on her mentally moribund spouse. One look at her tells you his clockwork has been unwound for years. How else could he have fulfilled his marital duties? It's such a shame ugly people have sex. It's what gives it a bad name. She still smiles. I'd like to roll the organ on top of her for what she's thinking. You can just forget it, dear. Go home to your husband. He has a stronger stomach than I.

She holds her hands up to her mouth and calls out, "Do you know 'Lady of Spain'" My God, do I? that's one of the "tunes of all time!"

I nod and finish up "Raindrops" with a flourish of my own

devising—imagine using all ten fingers on both keyboards!—and while Mrs. Suburbia applauds I go right into "Lady of Spain." I have a delicious little entrée of my own devising, but Mr. Conchis gives me an icy glance, so I switch on a background rhythm. I doubt Mrs. Suburbia would notice whether I did it with the "March," "Tango," or "Waltz." She sways along with the tune. She no doubt feels sexy, the severest delusion I could impose on her. *O Dieu, prends pitié!* I hear her whiny voice. She's singing along. Maria Callas may rise from her grave.

There are also voices to my left. Am I condemned to a hell where Mitch Miller is Satan? It's three degenerates with marijuana-inspired tee-shirts. They spread their arms like the Osmonds emoting.

> "Lady of Spain I adore you
> Take down your pants, I'll explore you
> Open your snatch up for business
> And Lady of Spain I'll love you!"

"Get the hell out of here!" Conchis yells. The punks run away (probably to ravish some nubile twelve-year-olds behind the junior high), but six or seven people are applauding. What other proof do you need that the Tartars are inside the walls? Even if the song does merit worse. I finish "Lady of Spain." Mrs. Suburbia leaves a quarter on the platform and bustles off. I leave it there. You can't buy me at any price, honey. I'm no lounge lizard.

"Mr. Conchis?" I call out. "Mr. Conchis?"

"What is it, Colin?" He is barely polite, but he steps up on the platform while I go on to play "You Light Up My Life" very slowly, like the dirge it deserves to be.

"Mr. Conchis, do you think it would be possible for me to play some sacred music?"

"Sacred music?" He squints.

"Christmas music. I had in mind that part of Schubert's Christmas Eve Mass—"

Conchis puts his hands on my shoulder. "Colin, Colin, Colin," he mutters. "You're not here to perform. I've told you a thousand times."

"They'd really sit up and take notice," I say. "They ignore this Muzak."

"People don't want music, Colin. They want tunes. Look, we're trying to introduce a little music into people's lives. The joy of making music. In turn, that gives me the joy of making money. Now imagine, there's this husband wandering around in this mall right now. He don't know what the hell to give his wife. He looks up. There's you playing the organ, and it sounds beautiful, you know what I mean? One of these songs takes him back to when he was dating his wife at the drive-in, in a 1957 Buick.

"But shit, no. He knows his wife is too damned stupid to play an instrument. She ain't had agile fingers since he got rid of the Buick. But hey! Looky there! All that beautiful music is coming out of one finger. One finger! The organ's doing it all. Hell, that's what he'll give her—the Gift of Music. Now, sure, she needs it like a hole in the head, but it'll look nice in the living room, and maybe he'll get a helluva good time on Christmas night."

"That's all people think about these days."

"Well, hell, the poor prick's trying to save his marriage, regain his youth. We're doing a social service, Colin, but it only works if you play with one finger. He gets a little happiness; I get a little profit. When he finds out his wife is too dumb to follow the numbers and he's sick of having the television interrupted by songs nobody'd recognize, he sells the thing back to me—at a reduced price—and I have it back on the floor, as a Pre-owned, in time enough to make another profit on it by Valentine's Day. Christmas, Valentine's, Mother's Day. It's like a natural cycle, Colin. You don't want to mess up the flow of nature by showing off, do you?"

"No, sir."

"Good." He pats me on the shoulder. I cringe. "See? I've trusted you with all the secrets of my business. I like you, Colin. Play some Christmas stuff. Get everybody in the buying spirit."

"Yes, sir," I say. Sure, he likes me. Isn't Conchis a Greek name? The Greeks had their little posterior interests, didn't they? It's so obvious what he wants.

And there's no doubt about it, because as soon as he leaves he heads straight past the shoe store and toward the deli on the north causeway of the mall. This is where he buys his coffee, and I have a theory the beverage supresses the sexual desire in people who do not have the moral strength to otherwise control themselves. That's a rather obvious explanation of why Americans drink millions of gallons of the bilgewater dispensed at soda fountains and vending machines. The British, you will note, drink tea. The South Americans, with their burgeoning population, drink coffee. Need I say more?

And there she is, in the window. *Ange pur! Ange radieux!* Of course! It is Thursday. Time to rearrange those gnomish shoes. Such a person of beauty among ugliness! Such a pure fleck of gold among the licentious dross swirling past! Her long hair can only be described as flaxen; her eyes as cool aquamarines. How horrible for a pristine being like her—for Beatrice, for Laura, for Yseult—to be thrust into the mud-trodden ways of commerce! She was there last Thursday and I knew instantly she was a kindred spirit, but she finished her demeaning task of dressing the window and was gone before I went to lunch. We have no mutual friend. How shall we be introduced? How can I introduce myself without seeming forward? I smile. She doesn't seem to notice me. I watch her as if transfixed, the dull booping of "Good King Wenceslas" droning out. I'd just as well be playing a tuba. She is standing on a stepladder, pinning green bunting near the ceiling. Oh to marry that wisp of a girl! To take her in my arms and protect her from the crudities and deformities of this contemporary morass. Oh, my *celeste* Aïda!

She is my Muse. Inspiration fills me. I look back for Conchis and do not see him. I will show her what an organ is for. I wind up "Wenceslas" quickly, and turn about three-quarters sideways to her. I turn off the preposterous instant rhythm buttons and increase the volume. I loosen my shoulders and bring down my fingers onto those sharp first notes of Bach's *Toccata and Fugue*. The very ceiling vibrates, shoppers are stopped in their tracks, and miracle of miracles! she looks out at me. I do not miss a beat, nor shift my eyes from hers, and move up the scale into the quicker parts. Oh, I am rolling! E. Power Biggs, envy me! The magic of this moment! The smile on her sweet lips! She lets the bunting drop. She covers her mouth with her hand and climbs down. She calls a matronly woman and points out at me. She presses her wrinkled lips as if trying to hold in her emotions, then heads for the back of the store, undoubtedly to weep at the splendor of a fine love being offered through the medium of music.

Yes, this is what the years of practice were for! I don't even think what I am playing. My fingers dance across the keyboard as if my hands were possessed by Euterpe herself. I finish the final thunderous chord and drop my head. I was so enraptured, I was not even aware of my surroundings—except for her, my angel. I pull my handkerchief and pat the perspiration on my upper lip, and then hear it. Applause! The shoppers are standing all around me. They clap loudly. Like Saint David among the Celts, I have carried a sacred message into the wilderness and moved the heathens. Music, real music, the immortal Bach—how could they not forget their unnatural obsessions?

Some call up congratulations to me, but I ignore the vulgar

herd. Where is my angel? She is out of the window. There, on the other side of a shoe rack. The older woman is handing her a pen and paper. She writes. Do I dare hope it is to me? How can I? Does she have the courage to delicately offer a meeting? Tea, perhaps, at a suitable place? Perhaps she is part of a salon of dignified poets and *aficionados* of the fine arts: kindred spirits with fine sensibilities. Where do they hide among the crude multitudes?

She hands the note to the older woman. An elderly go-between! What further proof do I need of her sensitivity to decorum? The older woman shakes her head. She folds the paper and calls over a gum-cracking sales girl. Surely, then, the missive is not for me.

"Hey, mister, can you play 'Star Wars'?" asks a peculiar child.

"Go away!" I say. The gum-cracker is on her way. The note *is* for me. Perhaps a request to play her particular masterpiece. *"La vie en rose,"* I'll wager. Yes, that would appeal to the romantic I see in her eyes. She is back in the window, watching, arms crossed, a faint blush. Ah, it is the East and Juliet is the sun!

"This is for you," says the nasal clerk.

"I know," I say. "Thank you." I look back at the window and hold up the note. I've got it, my angel. I hold it between two fingers and bring it up to my nose like a fine cognac to see if any of the scent of her white hands has transferred to the paper. Unfortunately, it is tainted by the smell of shoe leather and, undoubtedly, Miss Gum-chew of 1982. There are possible faint traces of the matron, also. Never removing my eyes from hers, I unfold the note:

Bub, the inner seam of your pants is split.

What? I don't understand. I look down at my trousers. *I am displayed!* My nether parts would be clearly visible to her when she stood upon her ladder. I am stunned, devastated as if a dagger had just pierced my heart. I cover the opening with both hands and inadvertently meet her eyes.

She is smiling. There is a new light in her eyes. She winks and blows me a kiss. I am shattered. Turning my legs under the keyboard, I close the access to my privies, climb down and flee, knees clasped together, screaming like a banshee over my humiliation.

As I climb into my automobile, I vow I shall never return again. Mike, the photographer, has told me of an opening in a skating rink. It might as well be a brothel for all the solicitations which transpire on the ice. I would kill myself were it not so obvious that I am needed to counterbalance the arrant philistinism about us. I take these dreary jobs only to keep body and soul together. Where is the soul without the body? Ah! If only there were some way to dispense with the latter!

CORNELIUS EADY

The Good Look

It is like my Father,
his legs turning to rubber
taking what he believes to be
his last look at our house.
I imagine my Mother, his
crazy wife
standing at the front door,
believing it all an elaborate stunt,
or peeking through
the living room blinds
making as small a target
as possible.

He breathes.
The street reels under his feet,
and now he is a dancer,
luck weezing out his mouth,
propped up by cousins
leading him to the open maw
of the car door

Which is, at the moment
the line that marks
the borders of the world as he knows it,
a line that, once crossed
is forever denied.

My Father
stops at that portal,
and, though totally mistaken
takes a hard look at the house.

Everything the word *goodbye* was ever
meant to imply
is in this look,
a look that, when shown to me later,
second-hand, as
part of a story with a
happy ending

nevertheless
raises the ante.

Victims of the Latest Dance Craze

The streamers choking the main arteries
of downtown,
the brass band led by a child
from the home for the handicapped
The old men
showing their hair (what's left of it)
the buttons of their shirts
popping in time
to the salsa flooding out
of their portable headphones

And mothers letting their babies
be held by strangers
and the bus drivers
taping over their fare boxes
and willing to give directions.

Is there any reason to mention
all the drinks are on the house?
Thick, adolescent boys
dismantle their BB guns.

Here is the world (what's left of it)
in brilliant motion,
the oil slick at the curb
danced into a thousand
splintered steps,
the bag ladies toss off their

garments
to reveal wings.

"This dance you do," drawls the cop,
"what do you call it?"
We call it scalding the air.
We call it dying with your
shoes on.

And across the street
the bodies of tramps
stumble
in a sober language.

And across the street
shy young girls step behind
their nameless boyfriends,
twirling their skirts.

And under an archway
a delivery boy discovers
his body has learned to speak,
and what does this street look like
if not a runway,
a polished wood floor?

From the air
biting insects
drawn by the sweat
alight when possible
on the blurr
of torsos.
It is the ride
of their tiny lives.

The wind that burns their wings,
the spinning, oblivious flesh,
mountains stuffed with panic,
an ocean
that can't make up its mind.
They drop away
with the scorched taste
of vertigo.

And under a swinging light bulb
some children
invent a game
with the shadow the bulb makes
and the beat of their hearts.
They call it dust in the mouth.
They call it horse with no rider.
They call it school with empty books.

While in the next room
their mother throws her dress to chance.
It bumps to the floor
like a muted foot on a bass drum
and when she takes her lover
what are they thinking of
if not a ballroom filled with mirrors,
a world where no one has the right
to stumble
on anyone's foot?

In a parking lot
an old man says this:
"I am a ghost dance.
I remember the way my hair felt
damp with sweat and wind.

When the wind kisses the leaves, I am dancing.
When the subway hits the third rail, I am dancing.
When the barrel goes over Niagara Falls, I am dancing.
Music sounds my bones like metal.

O, jazz has come from heaven," he says,
and at the z he jumps, arcing his back like a heron's neck
and stands suddenly revealed
as a balance demon,
a home for
stetson hats.

We have all caught the itch:
The neon artist
wiring up his legs,
the tourist couple
recording the twist on their

instamatic camera,
and in a factory
a janitor asks his broom
for a waltz,
and he grasps it like a woman
he'd have to live another
life to meet,
and he spins around the dust bin
and machines,
and he thinks: *Is everybody happy?*
And he spins out the side door,
avoiding the cracks on the sidewalk,
grinning as if he'd just received
the deepest kiss in the world.

LYNN EMANUEL

Inventing the Picture of Father in Las Vegas

If I could see nothing but the smoke
from the tip of his cigar, I would know everything
about the years before the war.
If his face were halved by shadow I would know
this was a street where an EATS sign trembled
and a Greek served coffee black as a dog's eye.
If I could see nothing but his wrist I would know
about the slot machine and I could reconstruct
the weak chin and ruin of his youth, the summer
my father was a gypsy with oiled hair sleeping
in a Murphy bed and practicing clairvoyance.
I could fill his black Packard with showgirls
and keep him forever among the difficult buttons
of the bodice, among the rustlings of their names.

Miss Christina. Miss Lorrain.
I could put his money in my pocket
and wearing memory's black fedora
with the condoms hidden in the hatband
the damp cigar between my teeth,
I could become the young man who always got sentimental
about London especially in Las Vegas with its single
      bridge—
so ridiculously tender—leaning across the river
to watch the starlight's soft explosions.
If I could trace the two veins that crossed
his temple, I would know what drove him
to this godforsaken place, I would keep him forever
remote from war—like the come-hither tip of his lit cigar
or the harvest moon, that gold planet, remote and pure
      American.

SUSAN FAWCETT

Casualties

I peer at you, still unblemished on the road,
blue-gray feathers unbelievably delicate.
Your eye remains half open and I wonder
whether you watch me scooping you up,
cradling your head like a baby's.
You are still warm, half a green worm
caught in the tip of your bill.

Of all the hurt birds I tended in childhood
did any live? Were any healed
by boxes lined with rags,
eyedroppers of fluid, nights my flashlight
searched the grass for worms?
The tiny crosshatched fronds on your breast
lift and fall. Once again I cannot know
the hidden damage, cannot cross
the threshold of your strangeness.

When my grandmother lay in a metal crib
writhing for drink, her liver rotted to nothing,
I stood weeping by the bed
and reached for her hand.
Her black eye singed me once, scornful,
amused, before she turned away
and left me aching for the lie
that love can save us.

In Mr. David's Salon for Long Hair

the dryers softly moan, the blown strands
leap and fall in lush blooms.
The women plait each other's hair, soothing the air

with lullaby voices. Mr. David glides among them,
drawing this one's auburn fall across his cheek.
He will not allow the violence

of metal clips, does not believe in cutting.
Above him float huge photographs of women
safe in clouds of hair. One grips a mast, hair

throbbing in the wind, and seems to sail away.
Another watches from her cloak of waves.
If danger flickers, she will disappear

down the dark corridors of her hair.
Mr. David pauses and is young again—
holding his mother's silver-handled comb,

bending to the chestnut curls so long
they tangle at her feet,
gently combing, moving up, past her waist

where gray begins to streak the brown,
moving up from gray to silver
to the crown, pure white.

He has no photographs from Bergen-Belsen
to stop the swift unrolling, her naked head
tips forward, her body strangely small.

ROLAND FLINT

A Letter Home

Mother I'm sure you remember
When I almost hanged myself in the kitchen?
I was 14 and had just inherited
Milking the cows from Allen
Whose time doing chores must have ended
When he graduated from high-school.
I wasn't mad about doing them.

Anyway, that night I came in from milking,
After feeding hogs, calves, chickens,
And hung myself. Of course you remember.
In the kitchen by the sink
We had that towel—I haven't seen one since—
A single cotton loop,
Four feet long, a foot wide,
Hanging from a wooden spool or dowel
Affixed to the wall.
The lower loop must have been
Not quite sink-high: I hung from that.

You came from your radio program
To find me, still wearing my mackinaw,
Chore-cap and buckle overshoes.
My feet were behind me, on the scatter rug,
I was face down and slung forward.
The towel was under my chin,
My hands just off the floor.
Dead still.

You said as soon as you got me free
I started to breathe and get my color.

Thank God I came in when I did thank God,
You cried and cried, rocking
My head and shoulders to you,
Sitting on the floor. It may have been
The last time you held me so.

When I could talk I told you
That I remembered slipping on the rug and falling,
That I must have hit my head on something
And, throat-first, fallen into that loop.

Mother, this month I'm going to be 49,
I've never told you the truth about that night,
And I want to tell you now.
I don't think I meant to die,
But I did hang myself—not quite by accident:
I came in, set the milk pail down, and,
Perfectly idly, deliberate and purposeless,
I put the towel under my chin,
Stretched out, keeping my overshoes on the rug,
Lowered my body, then my hands,
And swung there, as I'd done before—often.
Dreaming, I suppose, but about what?
I don't know any more, maybe I never knew.
The last thing I remember was
A kind of tingling all over
And a sound—like time. Maybe
I was trying to dream about hanging myself,
How it would be, or acting out a movie fantasy
Of my execution by the lynch-mob—
Maybe it was something like that—
But it's possible I was thinking of nothing.

What a nightmare I was to you—
I might have died many times,
From carelessness or experimenting:
I almost drowned when I was 7.
It was just luck I didn't fall 25 feet
To the cement floor of the potato warehouse.
I was side-swiped twice by cars, hit by a truck.
All from recklessness, all my fault.
When I was 15, I dove
From a tree and knocked myself out

On a rock in the river's bottom.
I played on the tops of moving freight cars.
Dove into snow-banks from the roof of a store.
Three times, once driving,
I was in cars or trucks that rolled over.
And once, with a bellyful of beer
I tried to chugalug a (stolen) fifth of
Seagram's whiskey. All this before I was 19.
And before I became as I have now become
Very careful and willing to live,
As you are doing, for a long time.

I have been brooding on all those we know
Who have been killed in a few seconds' surprise.
And about altering this one incident for you—
If not quite removing it
From that list you must have made by now
Of the merciless tricks freak accidents can pull.
We don't have to name our dead, do we?

I'm sorry I lied. I must have thought
I'd catch hell. I know it gave you nightmares.
And I've had mine: when Elizabeth was 2
She was standing on the car seat beside me,
I was driving, we were taking a big curve,
And the passenger door swung open.
She did not quite fall,
But I've dreamed it over, waking and sleeping,
Ever since—and she's almost 19 now.

I'm also sorry I waited
Thirty-five years to tell you.
I hope it makes a difference to you,
It does to me: it reminds me to say
Thank God you came in when you did,
Mother, for the life you gave,
What it's been, what it will be.

for Orva Hastings Flint, 1905–1983

84

Jim

I gave my lunch apple to a horse
Yesterday and remembered the horse,
Who was your "friend David,"
Eating the only copy of one poem
In Minnesota. So last night
I re-read your final book again,
Moving among the Ohio, French
And especially Italian people and animals
Of your last journey.

Some of the resolved gentleness here
Makes me cry, your welcoming
Of the blue spider not so much as
This late acceptance of the self.

I was often moved when you wrote
Of your preferring lions in His name
"Small wonder Jesus wept at a human city."

But I am more moved now when you
Make me believe the turtle's face
To be a man of God, with its
"Religious face," meaning unswervably
Perfect to itself, I guess, to you,
Perfect to me in your language.

Holding the book, I read,
Watching your father and the fat Ohioans
Tremble in my hands.

I close it at last, and
Looking at the jacket-back
I bid the picture and your name good-night,

Then in the dark I try
To sleep right through the
Stone beasts ghosts and angels
Of my stubborn grief who bear
Ohio after Fano.

ANNE HOBSON FREEMAN

The Fence

She's almost a landmark on Lafayette Street—the fragile old lady shouldering into the mile that separates St. Luke's Church from her apartment. She always wears a hat. In summer it's black straw. In winter it's black felt, or, on Sundays, mink to celebrate the upswing in her fortunes when the water rights, attached to her grandfather's ruined iron works, were sold.

This summer evening she is walking back from her apartment to the church, for a congregational meeting. She is custodian of the Church; the vestry created the job in the Depression to keep her and her mother and her sisters from starving.

Now she will not give it up.

Her name, Lulee Cary Lightfoot Andrews, is printed on the program for the Sunday morning service; and her face—with its white hair and coal black eyebrows—on the minds of several thousand tourists to whom she has explained the history of St. Luke's.

Generally, she trumpets the names and dates from her lips, intermittently at first, so that each one seems a single entity, like the first raindrop. Then almost imperceptibly, there is a quickening of tempo; names and dates, dates and names begin to follow faster, rising to a magnificent crescendo—after which, with a jerk of the head that is almost casual, she indicates the pew where Lee worshipped.

Tonight the congregation of St. Luke's has been called together to vote on a proposed addition to the church building. The architect's model sits waiting for inspection in the transept, showing the original church with the new wing that will be wedged into the hill beside it, an ingenious device combining a Sunday school on the street level with a commercial garage underneath.

And that part is perfectly all right with Lulee. She has never been, like so many of her friends, categorically opposed to progress. In fact, she was intending to support the vestry's plan completely, until this afternoon, when she saw that the vestry had gone too far.

The chimes had just finished tolling three o'clock when two young men from the architect's office arrived with the model. Lulee held the door open for them, and the young men shuffled in, with tiny drops of perspiration trailing down their temples, as they bore the future St. Luke's into the present one, the first man backing blindly through the doorway, the second now and then whispering a warning as the miniature steeple careened toward the doorsill.

Finally, they set the model down on the card table Lulee had set up in the transept, and she signed a receipt for it, forcing the pencil to glide in generous loops until it had completed the familiar signature, "Lulee C. L. Andrews, Custodian."

After the young men left, she sat down on the front pew to study the model. She sensed that there was something wrong with it. Not in the strident whiteness of the tiny buildings. She discounted that, knowing that soon enough the soot from the city would soften it to gray. Not in the artificial trees, stuck down like lollipops at even intervals in the plaster frosting to assure the donor of the site, Margaret Taylor Hughes, that the condition of her gift had not been forgotten: "that any building on the site be recessed from the sidewalk twenty-five feet and no less than four magnolia trees and two willow oaks be planted before it."

No, there was something wrong with the original church.

Lulee strained forward in the pew, her back bending till her eyes were level with the tiny steps leading to the tiny portico. Tiny, naked steps, she thought, and then she realized what was wrong.

The iron fence was gone.

Her back snapped straight and she sat there motionless, except for the rapid rise and fall of her chest and the trembling of the twisted fingers in her lap.

She knew it was deliberate. During the first seconds of the shock she dismissed the soothing voice that said, "Maybe they just forgot to put it on the model. That don't mean they plan to tear it down." Because she knew the young minister, Mr. Swift, and those smooth-talking business men on the vestry well enough to know that the fact that the fence was never mentioned in her presence was evidence that this was a surreptitious act.

The architect had included the fence along the side of the

88

church in his model. Why, then, not in the front of the steps? They knew she would object to tampering with the original church. When they brought up a proposal to poke holes in the ceiling for indirect lighting, she had made the junior warden leave the vestry room and walk into the church with her and *look* at what they were about to ruin—plasterwork that architects from all over the country came to see. She stopped them then; so this time they had worked behind her back. "And you deserve it," she could hear her sister saying, as if she were alive today, "If you're gonna play with fire, and write up its minutes, and take up for its doings, then when you get burnt yourself, you deserve it."

In Lulee's tidy mind—where thoughts were generally stored like folded linen on designated shelves—protests, accusations and arguments were exploding now, as if a crate of firecrackers had been accidentally ignited. So she sat very still, until the last explosion. Then out of the debris she began to sort the facts that were important.

It was wrong to tear the fence down; she must not let them do it. The muscles in her body responded to this fact as they would have responded to a physical fact—a door to be opened, a suit-case to be lifted.

That fence was a work of art, designed by the original architect to go with the Greek Revival church. She was always pointing out to people how its delicate acanthus leaves matched the ones in plaster on the ceiling inside.

The fence was useful, too. For more than a century it had been protecting St. Luke's from downtown traffic. You could see it in the Matthew Brady photographs; and all those people back then—President Davis and General Lee—must have passed through its gates a hundred times at least. Which was another reason that the fence should be preserved. As a memorial to great men. Lord knows, there had been precious few passing through it since.

But Lulee knew that it would be risky to use this argument. She'd noticed more and more that young people do not like to be reminded of the past. Particularly Richmond's past and this church's part in it.

As she sat there on the front pew, absolutely still, with these thoughts churning in her mind, Lulee wondered how she was ever going to put them into words. Because she had decided she would have to speak tonight.

And it is what she's going to say, choosing the words that she

89

will use, that is absorbing her attention now, as she walks back to the church from her apartment, with a slapdash supper lying undigested in her stomach.

Her lips are moving silently as she strings words into ropes that she will try to fling across the generations. She is so occupied with words that she does not even look up when she reaches the church and the iron fence she will be fighting for tonight. Her hand reaches out mechanically and swings the gate back on its hinges.

"Hey, Aunt Lulee!" It's her nephew Cary calling from the far side of the portico. She climbs the steps diagonally to say hello to him, though she knows she has his vote already. You can always count on Cary to vote against change. Any change. Tonight he will be voting not just against the idea of tearing down the fence but against the whole notion of putting up a wing. On the very first count, the vestry had numbered Cary Andrews among its unpersuadable opponents.

She can also count of the votes of the members of the Historic Richmond League and the Association for the Preservation of Antiquities. But in this day and age those votes are not enough. She has heard the vestry analyze the membership; it is a mathematical fact that the activists, the unconditional supporters of Mr. Swift and the senior warden, Conway Taylor, have a comfortable margin. To save the fence tonight, she'll have to win some votes from them.

Mr. Swift starts off the meeting with a prayer, asking the Lord for the wisdom to see the special needs of a downtown church, the courage to undertake a bold plan for its survival, and the patience to withhold small personal objections to the architect's model in the interest of a greater good, the future of God's work in this parish.

Afterwards, he sits down in the choir stalls, while Conway Taylor, chairman of the board of the Commonwealth Bank and senior warden of the church, takes over the meeting.

Lulee watches Conway's polished black shoes mount the marble steps to the chancel, then pause and turn to face the congregation. His miracle-fabric suit shows no sign of the heat that has fallen on the city like a sour wash rag; his forehead has no sheen of perspiration on it, as if the heat, too, is aware of his unspoken economic power and does not want to tangle with him.

He begins by explaining the plan to finance the new building with a thirty-year mortgage defrayed by the income from the garage.

Lulee is sitting with her nephew in the Andrews pew, five rows from the front, on the gospel side. She is waiting for a pause from Conway Taylor, a chance to interrupt him and speak out to the crowd. And she can feel her heart pounding in her rib cage—the boom, boom, booms traveling along her veins up to her neck and then into her eardrums, where, reproduced again, they threaten to drown out the sound of Conway Taylor's words.

When she finally does hear the call, it is not, as she expects, a call for comment, but a quick, perfunctory nod in the direction of the by-laws: "If there are no objections to the design, as presented in this model, we will go on to consider . . ."

The boom, boom, booms in her ears are so loud now that she has to shout above them. Her mouth falls open, her lungs inhale and she says, *"Wait!"*

Right away the pounding stops, and she realizes she has spoken too loud.

"What is it, Miss Lulee?" Conway Taylor asks in a voice so subdued it seems to reprimand her for shouting in the church.

Now everyone is looking at her. She can feel the rows and rows of faces behind her burning into her back; see the four rows of them in front twisting on their necks. And for a second she seems to have no muscles in her legs. As she stares in horror at her lifeless knees, they respond without warning, thrusting her small body up against the pew in front, so that she has to grab hold of it to keep from falling over it.

She takes a deep breath, then, and forces out the statement that is lodged in her larynx, expels it with a sudden gust of air, as she has seen her great-nephew expel a dried pea from a hollow tube.

"About the fence," she says, pronouncing the "about" somewhere between "a boat" and "a boot," as Virginians generally do. "I don't think you ought to tear down the fence."

"We don't plan to tear down the fence, Miss Lulee," Conway Taylor says. "Only that portion of the fence that is in front of the steps. The architect believes, and the vestry agrees, that it makes the church seem inaccessible."

"Oh, *please* don't tear it down!" She hears her voice pleading; she won't win votes by pleading. So she reaches back into the closet of her mind, where she has stored so many strings of words and seizes the first one she comes upon.

"That fence is an attraction for the tourists. Just last week a man from Michigan came in here to see St. Luke's and he said, 'Where'd you get that fence?' And I said it had been here since the church was built in 1845. And he said, 'Hang on to that fence. You don't see many churches with a fence like that one.'"

As she mouths the words, she looks around at the faces that are turned toward her. Open, empty faces, but at least open faces—not locked up for the day behind a handsome mask like Mr. Swift's or Conway Taylor's.

"That's exactly what he said," she continues, releasing one hand from the walnut rail and half-turning toward the rows of faces behind her. "It's part of the original church and we ought to hang on to it, don't you know? No tellin' what it would cost us, if we set about to buy it.

"And we need that fence there for protection. A church that's in the middle of the city needs something to discourage drunks from sleeping on the steps. The gates aren't ever locked. Anyone who wants to come into the church, because it is a church, can always do that. But the fence is out there to discourage the others."

What are all those faces thinking? That she's curious and quaint? She doesn't mind that when she's taking people on the tour. But it's not what she needs now.

Yet what else can she say? That they mustn't violate the magic circle? If she starts that kind of talk, they'll think she's crazy. Unless they, too, have stood across the street on a winter afternoon and seen the pale gray spire merge into the sky, while the little fence below it bristles like a porcupine, its iron needles fending off invaders—convoys of trucks, battalions of shoppers. Lord, if she starts to talk like that, they'll think she's lost her mind.

Lulee takes a deep breath and flings out one last string of words.

"That fence is historic. It's a part of Richmond's past. You can see it there in all the old engravings, because it's been here from the start, don't you know? And it was here during the War, when General Lee and all those people came in here to church."

By accident, she's done it—mentioned the name that means so much to her and nothing to these young people except some vague, unwanted link to the days of slavery. And by doing so, she's forfeited their votes.

Lulee's knees collapse, and she sits down.

Sure enough, an arm shoots up across the aisle. It belongs to the young surgeon with the Vandyke beard; the youngest member of the vestry.

"Surely you don't mean to say that we have to keep that fence just because General Lee may have touched it. If you want to know the truth, I'm getting just a wee bit tired of the General and his crowd. It never ceases to amaze me how much time and energy, to say nothing of money, is wasted in this town on building and preserving monuments to losers."

Margaret Taylor Hughes, Conway Taylor's sister, and the donor of the building site murmurs, "That's not fair," while Sarah Winston Smith, founder of the Historic Richmond Guild, leaps to her feet and thunders in a hoarse contralto, "I suggest you read some history, young man. And examine your definition of a loser. Or you may discover that you are one yourself."

A murmur of amusement ripples through the pews. Nearly everybody there has, at one time or another, been a victim of Sarah Winston Smith's tart tongue.

The young doctor is blushing, as he prepares to answer.

But before he has a chance, Conway Taylor intervenes. "We cannot take the time tonight to go into each individual's objections to details in the plan . . ." The words flow from his lips, as smoothly as syrup from a silver pitcher: ". . . the Women's Auxiliary believes we need another oven in the kitchen. The Sunday school superintendent prefers green blackboards. Of course, your vestry wants to hear all of these suggestions at the appropriate time. If you will submit them to me in writing, at the end of this meeting, I will see that they are given full consideration. But now, if we want to get home before midnight, I suggest that someone make a motion that we consider only the primary question: Shall we authorize the contractor to begin construction of the new wing? Or shall we abandon this plan for expansion?"

"I so move," says a voice from the back of the church.

"Second."

"It has been moved and seconded . . ." Just like that, slowly and smoothly and without interruption, the attention of the congregation is drawn away from the fence as Lulee has seen a wave sucked from the shore by the outgoing tide.

"It has been moved and seconded that we confine this evening's discussion to the primary question . . ."

Suddenly, across the aisle and two rows up, Lulee sees a slender arm with thick, gold bracelets on it, waving. It is Margaret Taylor Hughes's arm. Conway Taylor sees it, too, and says, "Yes, Margaret?"

"I want to go on record," Mrs. Hughes stands up and turns to face the center aisle. She is a handsome woman in her early sixties with her gray hair drawn back from her temples in a loose French knot. The vestry assumed that Mrs. Hughes's vote would be controlled by her brother, Conway Taylor. Yet here she is standing up and saying in a voice that is shaking with emotion,

"I want to go on record in support of Miss Lulee. I see no reason to tear down any part of that fence. In fact, if I had known that this new wing would lead to arbitrary changes in the church itself, I would not have given you the land for it."

She turns then and faces her brother, Conway Taylor, squarely. "I wish to have it put into the record, Conway, that I'm ashamed to have my name connected with such meaningless destruction."

As Margaret Taylor Hughes sits down, a hush falls over the entire congregation, and they savor the predicament of Conway Taylor, the way a moviegoer savors the silence right before the draw, when the Best Shot in the West has met his equal.

But if they are hoping to see Conway Taylor shoot it out with his sister, they vastly underestimate him. One of the skills responsible for his success in business is a remarkable tact which can convert a small defeat into a larger victory. He has learned never to linger over a defeat, but simply to plow it under, until it is indistinguishable from the substance of success.

Without even changing the tone of his voice, he says, "The fence or lack of fence is a minor matter, really. Since there seems to be strong feeling for it, I shall instruct the architect to leave the fence intact. Now, if I may return to the motion on the floor. . . ."

So it's over. Just like that. Lulee's words have reached somebody after all. For one split second, across a generation, two minds have connected. A sister has stood up to her brother.

And the fence has been saved.

After the new wing is voted in, by a majority more generous than the vestry anticipated, the meeting is adjourned.

Lulee catches a ride home to her apartment with her nephew, Cary. But she does not hear what he is saying to her in the car. Her mind is still too full of echoes from her sudden victory; her heart, too busy pounding a noisy song of triumph in her ears.

Later, though, as she reaches out to switch off the lamp beside her bed, the noises stop. And in the sudden silence, she realizes that not a word she spoke tonight got through to that young surgeon or his friends. And in the long run, they—not Margaret Taylor or her brother Conway—will be making the decisions for St. Luke's.

Under the lamp beside her bed, a photograph of her father, posing shyly in his regimental uniform, stares at her with dark, almost accusing eyes.

"All right, Papa, what would *you* have said to them? You can't imagine how much things have changed."

94

Now she is remembering another summer evening, more than eighty years ago. A crowd of relatives and friends have gathered on the porch of their house at 4 West Lafayette Street; and they are rocking in their chairs and swapping war stories. Her father rises quietly and walks into the house.

She, who is still a little girl then, runs after him and stops him in the hall. "Why do you *do* that, Papa? Can't you see it hurts their feelings? Why won't you stay with them and talk about the War?"

"Four years were enough for me," he says. "Lulee, let me tell you this much. It was the worst mistake we ever made."

"Forgive us our mistakes." That's what Papa would have said to that young doctor and his friends.

And it's what Christ would have said, too. *Does* say—in one of those newfangled translations of the Prayer Book that she has never liked because they rob the language of its richness: "Forgive us our mistakes, as we forgive those who make mistakes against us."

New words for an oldtime cure for shame. And maybe even youth.

Lulee switches off the light and lets her head fall into the feather pillow.

Less than a minute later, she's asleep.

JAN HAAGENSEN

Captain Farley's Fireflies

Rosser rebuked for drinking by his bride
saw saplings at the end of the field
reared backward like Forrest's killed horse
or Longstreet shot in the neck and shoulder,
and thought by his men to be an angel.

Six men from the whole right wing
saw white through the trees.
Women in the cool dawn
throw themselves in front of horses
and Stuart's winded officers.

Men see two trees
stand in the light like brother and sister
singing hymns to Jackson
as he lay near death from shock.

Captain Farley lost a leg
and pressed it to his bosom
as one would a child
or an Angel of the Lord.

Early's every married officer
got himself killed
or captured by a brilliant moon
furnishing the light of day
to the black troops of Smith's corps

who greet President Lincoln
like the Angel of the Lord.
Staff officers ride through white woods
and stand in half-circles by dawn
at the baptism of Jackson's daughter

before they make camp in fields
as if they'd flee with their brides
from the fireflies found in the hand
of a sleeping officer.

Fireflies in the starlight
take a deep breath
like the lieutenant who's a father
at the baptism of a daughter.

Forrest believed he'd die
at Fort Donelson,
shot through the foaming heart
so he could choke like a man
slapped on the back by a brother.

Tree follows tree through the field
like a blindfolded horse,
a beauty of twenty years,
following a man out of a fire,

while the dogwoods show the whites of their eyes
to the men who loved Jackson
more than he loved the angels.
Cold fireflies fill the heavens
as if they rode blindfolded
at the right hand of Forrest.

Captain White saved the life of Beauty
Stuart's shot horse in a burning field.
Governor Yates,
"he of the ever trembling heart,"

lost his staff and then himself
in the woods with a beauty's daughter
to whom he gave the rank of Major,
as if she fought with Stuart.

Wind holds back the firefly
captured at dark
like a beauty in the arms of Beauty,
or an Angel of the Lord
pressed to the bosom of Captain Farley.

EDWIN HONIG

Making the Rounds in the Hugged House of Mind

(in memory of Karl Weimar)

*The Phi Beta Kappa Poem, Brown University,
March, 1982*

1

Nights drop through the body
like water
through a faulty tap

with the same light-being
of the sky lifting
the worn-out corners of the day

the same smile fading
from the doctor's face
the prognosis still the same

and the mind
like a snake's mouth
widening to devour it

while the body
rumbles through its day
like any other

as when turning
out of bed
with two feet planted

it stands and walks off

sure of doing everything
unendingly.

Whose tenant are you?
What lease do you hold
and when do you move out?

2

Bleakness in the eye
the sky goes rigid
the sea reviles its images.

A flow creases down the mountain
slowing stones
into the swollen lake.

A hand wipes off
the sweat of forests
as they tilt and bend
one tree on another.

In your white face
the eyes web over
the mouth a crack in dough.

Thought crumbles in your ears.

You can't remember
what your grandma said
when she held you
against the dark.

Down on your knees again
you wait for words to rise
and separate the darkness.

3

Total change
is life-as-is betrayed.

So she will not reply at once
if you should broach it

and you will walk your fury off
around the lake
if she says no.

Once spoken
the sense begins
to dive and wrestle
like a rutting kangaroo
until it's openly embraced.

Get going!
Don't waste another moment!
Give it all you've got!

Hearing the hard inane commands
makes you stumble
and that night
the first dream of its kind
begins to nibble
at your groveling heart.

4

Yes, let me hear you blame me
just as you wish—
whenever, whatever.

What you can't see is I'm free,
free not just of you
but of myself as well.

Blaming me brings back
the old throb—
not the heartache
or muscle in the neck
but memories of a cage
cleansed of me
like sucked-out bone.

Yes, go ahead and blame me,
and when you're through
spare me a moment to ask you
to bend with me slowly

so I can enter
your boiling heart.

5

The flimsy mountain stream
waltzes through the meadow.

Stones taken by surprise
rattle grudgingly behind.

It will not be denied.
It plays and dances
with its own flow in mind.

It cannot be contained.
It rushes down the mountainside
and flies into a spray so fine
it can only settle in a mist

Where a huge sea beings to roar
against the rocks it hates
but always must abide.

6

The death of the bison
emptied the plain.

Now winds break us apart.

We hindered the lives
of so many
there is nothing
standing between us.

Even the shade trees
bunched against us
have died in the dark.

And we are alone
far and wide

as though the eye
saw nothing but itself.

O winds of miracle
and madness
raise up one bush
and a patch
of buffalo grass.

7

Is time a dream of empty slaughter,
Gog and Magog in the flames?

And should we dream it quickly
so as it fills us daily
we may feel it seep away?

Hot
we would grow colder.

Cold
we would inflame.

Who is it supports us
sleeping closer to our faces
than the rain?

Should we waken Abel
to let live in the world again?

8

Men live in your hollow chest
who do nothing but surmise,
estimate and surmise
what must seem to be believed,
what must be said of it
and never disallowed
neither raised nor lowered
without a final nod
from one of them.

Of course they sleep—

sometimes all day and night—
one by one or all together
while the world slips by
without them.

And yet for them
the whole world lives nowhere
but in their eyes.

You believe this
as you believe yourself
though once they leave
you may think otherwise.

DAVID HUDDLE

Spider

for Kelley Powers

Have I dreamed you on my ceiling
like this, where with the fly swatter
I could transmogrify your ass
into, as they say smithereens?

Crawl behind those cross-country skis
or somewhere out of sight. Spider, pass
by. Let me be the big creature
who finds your death unappealing.

Fall

for Ron Goble

In my back yard stand apple trees,
two, a Rome and a McIntosh,
neither one pruned or sprayed for years.
They bear a scabby fruit that drops

to the grass and stays till it rots.
If I pick one up to throw, jeers
from far-off crows mock my toss,
my bold wind-up under the leaves.

PETER KLAPPERT

Stages of a Journey Inland

from a notebook, 1978

Tuesday, May 16

even packed to the gunwales and riding down
    low over the wheels, boxes
        and suitcases of books, yellow

pads, blank paper, journals girdled
    together in fat
        rubber bands and CPB

flapping, O'Connor even scattered across
    the rear ledge the
        tattattat typer

bundled in a dog-eared blanket and shirts
    swaying like strap-hangers at
        the windows Balzac even

drugged and sloe-eyed sitting up
    hyper on the front seat stunned
        numb-jumpy sleepless radio

intermittent stale hooch burped
    through a gesso of toothpaste on the
        roof rack the kayak a

long beak over the windshield a gunsight lines
    v-ed to the bumpers
        bump sail snapping dodges

heavily into the ropes and we all
      yaw in the downhill swells—

    The drive was a long reach inland.

*

Flat land, scattered farms west of Richmond,
then the roller-coastering foothills.
Blue haze of mountains at a distance.

The town
        (bank, P.O., State Store,
U-Wash-It, two dozen dusty shop fronts
and a small plaza with a supermarket)
              has been taking a long nap.

*

Mount San Angelo rises above
and well back from the road, a black roof
and white chimneys seen from a highway,
a glimpse of capitols
if the trees are stirring.
           Rough fields
fall away on three sides. Downhill, bottom right,
a group of Holsteins gathers at some trees.

You cross the northbound lane, go down
a dip and across the fat pipes of a cattle guard,
wind past the cows
and a tin-roofed, sledge-footed saltlick up on stilts,
shift down to second by a stand of trees and come
around the top of the *S* and up the rise
over a rattly cattle guard into the lot.

*

Wednesday, May 17

Cracked macadam, gravel, ruts,
bluestone, dandelions, tufts of grass.
The drive circles the grounds—the mansion
and Bill Smart's house a hundred yards back—
then runs straight out between fenced pastures
to a rambling manor-farm barn.
                              Many wings,
many levels of brown roof, gable and hip.
Blue-grey cinderblock. Three silos
east of center, a cottage far east in the foreground.
The west wing, formerly pigs (?), has been made into studios.

*

"I'm so sorry," I said, running up to Jean,
who was painting outside the pasture fence.
"Balzac just chased your composition away."

Thursday, May 18

In the slope below the drive below the boxwood maze
behind the mansion, an old cracked pool
or the foundation of a vanished house.
Downhill from there, west along Route 29, a small lake,
pond colored. I don't think anyone goes there.

Flip-flops and towels. The mailslots are empty,
the tall dim hallway by the telephone is hushed.
Jean Z, Sheba, Balzac and I
gather in late afternoon to drive to the lake
at the college for a swim.

What one wants is fewer prepositions.

Friday, May 19

They are heifers and yearling steers.

A few of the Holsteins somehow
get across the cattle guard in the evening.

Three overweight secretaries from OMB
on their way to *A Delicate Balance* in spike heels,
leaning together and steadying one another
hobbled to a heating grate.

Monday, May 22

Heifers and yearling steers.
Overweight secretaries.
Not even a pc from K.E.

                              *

A derelict, half-hidden boathouse
and a long flat grass-grown dam. Cowpads
and a steep trail down to apple-cedar shade.
A rangey hawthorn and bridge
to nowhere, blocaded and blocked
by a highway ten feet up.
                         Under the bridge
the water moves thinly across the cement run-off
and drops twelve feet through sunlight.
The stream twists like a crab-apple bough.

On the lake side, smartweed and vetch,
one small cedar, scruffy shrubs, a low
barbed wire fence. An aluminum boat,
dented and camouflage peeling and two seats broken,
nuzzles the dam. A rusty coffee can, a board,
oarlocks but no oars. A jump-rope painter.

Tuesday, May 23

I grab myself
by the collar and seat of the pants. I lift myself up
and put myself down in the chair.
I point to the typewriter. I make a fist.

I turn up the air conditioner and bring myself
a cup of coffee. A cigarette? I empty the ashtray
and take the old newspapers
down to the studio kitchen and run the tap until
the cold water runs *cold* and
grab myself hard by the hair and shove
my head under tightening and
twisting my face around hard to the spigot
but I won't
give it up half-wit I yell *Half-Wit!*

Thursday, May 25

The mailslots empty before they fill,
only Carl indifferent to the fat envelopes
addressed in his own hand, often two or three of them
waiting until late afternoon.
                              I was wrong
about the lake: Carl clears the pantry sink,
stacks the d/w, then he's off in the rowboat.
We get bouquets of wildflowers at dinner,
we get local news about beavers.
We also get scolded: please scrape your plates
and put silverware in the soapy bucket. Don't
leave ashes and dirty cups on the table
after Carl has set up for breakfast. Thank you.

Friday, May 26

Not expecting a call
but I stay edgy at dinner.
If the telephone rings it's all I can do
to keep from throwing my fork over my shoulder
It wasn't for me. It never is.

                              *

I *hear* that *lone*-some *whis*-tle *moan*
a-*cross* a *coun*-try *mile*

109

10:30
and east of the mansion
a train comes down the shallow valley
and passes behind the barn.

*

11:00   Five people at the diningroom table
drinking coffee and making conversation
rapping their nails and waiting for the phone
or for the phone to ring for them. I gave up.

Saturday, May 27

I could make a tape loop but I'm
actually typing notes out of Partridge
where I quit two years ago in France: *poisonous child.*

Tuesday, May 30

                    I've read ahead into the *F*s in the appendix,
I've read all my notes, all the discarded scraps lines stanzas
cantos everything cover-to-cover in the CPB all the relevant
chapters in Shirer Paxton Bloch Zeldin de Gramont. I've pinched
teased tickled poked twisted and wrung-out every page
but those eight legal pages of drafts for three or perhaps
four unpromising poems. I'm wore out, living before I was born.

Sero medicina.

Friday, June 2

Saltlick: a dollhouse up on stilts, a disreputable cradle.

Halfway up the hill, above the saltlick,
that little stand of trees: ailanthus,
"The Tree of Heaven," "Paradise Tree."

110

Fuzzy yellow pom-poms like sumac (the guide says)
and nasty smelling. Better at a distance.

If writing about this place, how avoid
that implication? The Paradise Tree is everywhere
around here.
                    Then there's The Crab Apple of Knowledge,
The Poison Ivy of Eden.

Saturday, June 3

A prisoner of paradise.

*

Called and got the furious Papa, given
another number. Music, hubbub,
the closing of a door. The two of us
alone in an unfamiliar bedroom.

Kris bright, cheerful, glad I called,
no plans for coming down to visit.
Had not received second letter
(how is that?), unclear about first.

We talked 45 minutes, but
the tension so swiftly gone
into a line connecting night to night
came back to my neck and my back
just walking back to the
blacked-out silhouette of the barn.

Monday, June 5

                    Downhill from the mansion,
west under dogwood and tulip poplars,
before you come to the boathouse
and the causeway dam,
there's a thinning in the brambles

and the beginning of a path.
                  Two feet in
two rust-stiff strands of wire
seamed in the bark of a locust,
but the fence is slack enough to ease
between and not get barbed.
                 The path dips
to a miniature meadow, a marsh
of jewelweed bright where sunlight
flares through the canopy.
Midway the jewelweed parts
and a fine clear line
—no more than a doodle, really—
marks a boundary.
Simon and Balzac race ahead
and miss the deer signs in the sotted ground.

               I remember jewelweed
in Connecticut. By August those faintly
bluish leaves will rise
on watery stems waist high
and spread, dotted with gold
corn-candy-colored flowers. The light in there
will be pure chlorophyll
but the heavy air, sucked of oxygen
and seething with gnats, will reek decay.

Tuesday, June 6

Blesseder to send than to receive
—I'm on my way, Great God! priority mail.

I have to almost physically *put*
myself in this chair, at this table,
but here installed I'm here unstalled for hours.
Eight pages of drafts for two or three
or perhaps four unpromising poems, suddenly
gobbling up everything in sight—lines, stanzas, cantos, CPB
and Eric Partridge. O'Connor running amok at the mouth.
Sero Medicina: the disease has grown strong by long delay.
Per ardua ad astra: through hard knocks we shall see stars.

Sunday, June 11

We move between the mansion and the barn
across great sweeps of ankle-deep lawn.

Thursday, June 22

Fiction writer needs $$$. Friend of
so-and-so and so-and-so and so-and-so.
Journalism to order. Write Box VCCA.

Everyone furious or supportive:
an exposé (of what?) of us in the *Globe*.
What would Miss Manners say?

We are a tentative community
perched on a frontier. We are
a cantakerous family. We're a bunch
of consumptives at a spa. We're what's left
of the old money, and this is our hotel.

Friday, June 30

There's no place much to go at that lake.
Beyond the jewelweed meadow, the ground
rises through sapling dogwood and beech, stunted
cedars, sumac and riff-raff vegetation,
until the path darkens again among leaves
and pine needles, a smudge under tall trees
jagged along a lake, climbing through laurels
and small, sun-starved blueberries, falling back
into clusters of ground pine, briar, smilax,
suddenly dropping behind roots at a gravelly washout.
The path ends at a second stream, where the lake
arcs in to a swamp and a thick misery of branches
gropes up out of muck.
                    Fifty feet in across the stream
two box-like rocks are completely upholstered in moss.

*

113

So many stinging things—hawthorn, honey
and black locust, osage orange, raspberry,
blackberry, sweet briar, multiflora roses
and hybrids gone feral. Holly, thistle,
cocklebur, wood nettle, smilax (bullbrier,
sweetbrier, catbrier), husks of old horse chestnuts.
And the holly-like barberry, the nightmare plant,
spreading its horned fronds in multiple threats.

Sunday, July 2

Two hours formulating a question for the *I-Ching*.

*

                                              Paddling with a board
ripped from the old pumphouse. Hard, and hard
on the fingers cramped around the pen.
Easier to tack, to point up into
the prevailing west, even in this old boat.
Easier to let the breeze carry me—

                    Not I, not I, but the wind
             that blows through me.

What kind of light did I expect?
                            Easier to zigzag
on the diagonal westward. Water lights
pattern the lake bottom. Water-striders,
long fronds of hornwort combed by a school of minnows.
Red-wings in the reeds.
                      No way to J-stroke
with an old board.
                    Delta, marsh, hummock,
bur-reeds and grasses, last year's cattails
like soft sculpture, wind-blown and torn.

                  From this end of the lake
you can see the whole of Mount San Angelo.
                        The small cedars
cone as if clipped, the taller cedars spread

and pyramid, staggered up the hill among pines.
Trucks on 29 audible but hidden, the pastures
rise toward the mansion, all but invisible
in hemlock, spruce, and the vast, domed
crown of the copper beech.
      The eye moves past
the elaborate, important landscape—an arboretum
reverting to wilderness, but held—
         past maple,
black walnut, redbud and Kentucky coffee-berry,
the eye reaches through ailanthus and dogwood and Paulonia
toward Bill and Juliana's house
        (a white splash
glimpsed in shades and levels of green)
         and falls
forward and down to the one man-made color, blue-green,
the boathouse settling, its peak already folding
toward the lake.

    Drifting now
the boat going broadside then turning on its skeg
bow to wind, stopping, spinning the lake
shore back the other way, swinging and eddying
each thing
     calling me swings my attention
like a great round weight at the end of a cable
each thing a summons
       the summons in the telephone
—parents, office, mechanic, student, lover—
the summons in the book I was reading
when the sunlight dimmed and went out and rain
came riding a black wind over the sill, the summons
at breakfast in the newspaper, too many summonses
to be in India or Paraguy, in London, Atlanta,
to go to the store, to appear in line at 9:30
at the Biograph, to see the paintings, to make
reservations, the summons at the door, through
the mailslot, through the open window across
the street and on the radio, the tiny summonses of
gnats falling at the base of my lamp and on my desk,
that summons, the letter calling to be read, reread,
and memorized,
     each thing taking the brush
of my attention, each thing passive, obdurate,

implacable, wilting, dropping petals, chilling
my shoulders, each thing insistent, nothing complete
completed ready finished dead to me no journey
completely made no book read or written each thing
a summons
                    to answer to come back,
to take up the board and head the boat
downwind to let it bear me
                              carry me toward the shoreline
where the Holsteins now are walking, toward the two
lakeside tulip poplars that rise and split and rise again,
toward the world there, cow-eyed and dawdling
but—yes—coming down to the causeway dam to meet us.

Thursday, July 6

Rounding the snowy blossoms on the mountain ash,
pushing through a gap in the lilacs
or hurrying up the lawn
past the wide flounces of a spruce

you come on them at dusk: wide-eyed,
startled, improbably large in the failing light.

MILTON KLONSKY

First Acquaintance with Poets

When W. H. Auden fell out of the sky I was just walking dully along West 4th St. in Greenwich Village late on Saturday night, returning home after picking up a copy of the Sunday *Times* at Sheridan Square, and as I got to Charles St., passing by the lamp post on the corner, I flipped the paper over to scan the headlines on the bottom half. There was his face—or rather what the years had made of it—as wrinkled and cracked and reticulated with deeply grooved crisscrossing lines as a dried creek bed, staring quizzically up at mine, as if curious to see my reaction, for above the photograph in large type was the news that he had died in Austria the day before. In a flash, of heart failure. The shock made me fumble and almost drop the paper, clutch for it and momentarily lose my balance, lurching sideways, so that I had to reach out and embrace the lamp post to steady myself. Right then, it so happened, as if meant to happen, by design, to complete the scene, two Saturday-night suburban-looking couples doing the Village came sailing by arm in arm and pointed me out to one another, gleefully, no doubt elated by what must have seemed to them something amazing yet also ludicrous and typically Villageois: a local drunk, or maybe a junkie, corkscrewed around a lamp post while reading the Sunday *Times.* Only who cared? Without budging, rapt and transfixed ("Now, now," I can hear him say in the nannyish tone he occasionally affected, "that's a bit over-*donne,* Milton, it won't do") beneath the lamp post, oblivious to the stares and double-takes of people hurrying by, I remained there for some time peering through the dim light at the small print of his obituary until my eyes started to blur, the words hazed over, when I broke off, looking about at the by now nearly deserted street, and reminded myself that while Auden's quest, his lifelong Icarian flight ("Now, now . . .") had ended,

and with scarcely a splash in the world-at-large, I still had somewhere to get to. . . .

That was on September 29, 1973, approximately thirty, though
it seems more like XXX, years after I first met him. But even
before then I had already encountered his poems and read and
reread them, to puzzle out their meaning, so closely that I got to
know many by heart, making them my own with the sort of
proprietary enthusiasm and exultation that can only be felt by an
adolescent bardling of sixteen or so, such as I was at the time,
for whom the discovery of a new poet speaking, in a manner of
speaking, his own language is also an act of self-discovery. Of all
the poets both English and American who had emerged during
the thirties, Auden, I thought, had the most original and prophetic voice. No matter that his early poems were so riddled
with secret passwords, personal references, double-entendres
and innuendoes intended exclusively for those already in the
know, that crucial lines and even whole passages despite all my
efforts to understand them seemed nothing but gibberish; for me
it was a delphic gibberish; and besides, as Coleridge tells us,
"Poetry gives most pleasure when only generally and not perfectly understood." What most pleased, and overawed me too,
was the voice itself, unlike any I had ever encountered before in
English poetry, the voice it seemed of an ancient Scandinavian
skald or tribal scop, terse and abrupt, elliptic, grunty with
Anglo-Saxon vocables, that might have issued from some auto-
chthonous source in the fjords of his own psyche. Despite that it
was no less modern, even à la mode, and fashionably Freudian
and communoidal as well, its grim prognostications of doom,
doom and death, "death of the grain, our death, / Death of the
old gang" in the coming of Marxist apocalypse set off by tom-
tom alliterative meters, slating atonal dissonances, half-rhymes
as surprising as puns. And at the time of which I was writing,
with Hitler dominant over Europe, it was just what I wanted to
hear.

In those days I was a sophomore at Brooklyn College, living at
home with my parents, and a timid contributor (an essay on e.e.
cummings, rejected derisively, and a Shelleyan love poem,
grudgingly accepted) to the undergraduate literary magazine, the
Observer, one of whose editors was the poet Chester Kallman. It
was through Chester that I later came to know Auden, but when
and where I first met Chester escapes me now. He seems to have
popped up present in my life without antecedence. One clue: he
was the cousin of a close friend of mine, Jack ("Yecky")
Freilicher, a precociously hip and talented jazz pianist with

whom in my earliest pubescent years, when I had just grown hair and self-conscious, I used to share a magical joint or two and discuss Sex, Art and Politics during midnight rambles on Brighton Beach, and chances are that "Yecky," who often mentioned his cousin the poet as someone I definitely ought to dig, would at least have tried to bring us together. But if he ever did somehow, I wonder, could I have forgotten?

Among the glumly solemn young Marxist literati who roosted on the staff of the *Observer,* Chester stood out like a tropical bird in a flock of jackdaws. He was then (as he describes himself in a poem looking back from middle age) "one of the handsome few," but perhaps "gorgeous" would be a mot more juste, with a ripe and finely carved mouth, heavy-lidded, dark-rimmed, liquid deep-blue eyes of the kind known as soulful, and wavy blond hair crested by a, suspiciously, blonder forelock trained to appear unruly and break and curl across his brow. While fairly tall and well built, there was nonetheless a Chaplinesque daintiness about him, a certain slight sway and flutter in his gestures and the way he moved that ineluctably spoke its name. Homosexual of course he was, and he flaunted it, but not *a* homosexual, for that wasn't the most substantive of all the things that made Chester Chester. It took some time, but once we broke through the psycho-socio barrier between us—he had told me from the start, *sotto voce* and gently, so as not to hurt my feelings, but to my immense relief, feigned to spare his, that I wasn't his "type," which made it easier—I came to see what a tough-minded bird he was under the fancy plumage, strong-willed and independent in his opinions, and with a range of experience, though in age we were scarcely a year apart, far wider than mine. My social and intellectual life was then almost entirely centered around the college; his, it seemed, began only when classes were over.

Those dark stripes under his eyes were earned. On several occasions, coming across each other by chance in the hallway or cafeteria, he'd greet me with the hassled, breathless air of someone late for an urgent appointment, pause and assume the sidewise stance of a relay runner waiting anxiously for the baton, his rear pivotal leg extended for a fast getaway and one arm stretched out to touch my fingertips, meanwhile straining himself apart inch by inch as he apologized for not being able to stay but promised to see me soon, asked how I was and what I was up to and if I was writing, all in one blurt. On his way to the exit, should he meet any of his many old friends, he might go through the same routine two or three times before taking off. Not to have known him, as they say in Latin, argued oneself unknown.

But of his private affairs, except that they kept him on the run, I knew hardly anything for months after we first became acquainted.

Then one afternoon, at an informal conference of *Observer* staff members and contributors held in the cafteria, at which he wasn't present, I heard the astonishing news, astonishing to me but an already well-gnawed and desiccated bone of gossip to everyone else, that "Wystan"—which I translated mentally into W. H. Auden, the way I invariably thought of him, an awesome surname preceded by those two Shakespearian initials stamped on the cover of a book—and Chester were intimate friends, more than just friends, lovers in fact, like Oscar & Bosie or Verlaine & Rimbaud, and had been inseparable ever since Auden arrived and settled in this country in 1939. Not willing to expose my own naivete, I remained silent while their relationship was knowingly discussed and bantered about at the table. Afterward, by asking around here and there, I heard the tale of how Chester and a friend of his, Harold Norse, similarly blond, homosexual and a poet, had attended a reading one night by Auden and Christopher Isherwood sponsored by the League of American Writers with the hope of later arranging an Anglo-American liaison. It was Norse who received an invitation from Isherwood to call at the hotel where they were staying but Chester, either through calculation or miscalculation, who took the card upon which Isherwood had written their address. When he arrived and knocked at the hotel door the next day, Auden is said to have opened it, stared at Chester, and exclaimed, "But it's the wrong blond!" But it was the right. Some three years later the affair thus started was still continuing and as fervent as ever.

Of homosexual love, in its physical aspects, nearly all I knew at that time was based on traditional street lore passed down from generation to generation and on what I could glean, furtively and guiltily, in the public library from the tomes of Kraft-Ebbing and Havelock Ellis, where the most interesting parts were curtained off in Latin. It baffled *(How can people do things like that?)* and somewhat embarrassed but did not morally offend me. As a private vice deserving public censure it fell somewhere, in my estimation, between stamp collecting and reading other people's mail. Nor did I feel either tempted or threatened by it. My own commitment to love between the sexes was exclusive and firm, never firmer than then, though I had little opportunity to prove it.

But that soon changed, and the course of my life as well, when I began my first "serious" affair, with a revolutionary blond sociology major named Rhoda Jaffe, whom I met one fall day sitting apart from the others at the Trotskyites' table in the cafeteria. It was she who approached me, getting up smiling from her place to ask me to sign a food-smudged and ink-bespattered petition (but it had the effect of a love philtre) against, I believe, war and fascism, which I did in a daze without reading it through (strains of the "Liebestod" sounding from afar), and one thing led to another. On my part it was both love and self-love, equally and reciprocally. I was then about nineteen. At the age of thirteen or so I would sometimes filch a couple of cigarettes from my father's open pack of Camels and go off on solitary walks at night along the tree-shrouded mall on Ocean Parkway in Brooklyn, smoking one going and one coming; and on an evening I've never forgotten a car pulled over to the curb and a man, seeing only the glow of my cigarette in the darkness, stuck his head through the window and shouted, "Hey, Mister! How do I get to the bridge?" That was the first time anyone had ever called me "Mister." And with Rhoda, at the commencement of our affair, I felt the same rush of instantaneous maturity and self-esteem. Greater even, for she had seen and selected me for herself in broad daylight, me, though she was obviously desirable, sexy, charming, beautiful enough to have had anyone else she pleased instead of me, a sophomore still living at home with his parents and dependent on them for pocket money.

A month before we had moved from Brighton Beach, where I grew up, to an apartment on Ocean Ave. and Ave. H. in Flatbush, only a couple of blocks from the college but a long trainride from my whilom stickball- and punchball-playing friends in the old neighborhood, so that I felt exiled and lonely. My romance with Rhoda changed all that; and surprisingly, though I couldn't imagine him ever playing stickball, it coincided with a growing friendship with Chester. Between them, each in his/her own way, they took charge of my worldly and sentimental education.

Chester was then living as Auden's guest in Brooklyn Heights at the now near legendary 7 Middagh Street—a dilapidated three-story building transformed into a sort of sixties-style commune of Olympian bohemians, and run as a boadinghouse, whose members at different times included Carson McCullers, Louis MacNeice, Gypsy Rose Lee, Golo Mann, Paul and Jane Bowles, Salvador Dali, Benjamin Britten; but whenever Auden left town to read his poems or lecture somewhere, which happened frequently, he'd come down from the Heights and stay with his father and grandmother at their house on Ave. J, within close walking distance from where I lived on Ave. H. As a result we saw each other more and more often, both on and off campus, passing by slow gradations from acquaintances to confidants.

Or rather I became Chester's. He had already, as said before, typed me as not his and thereby banished me in his mind to a sexual Limbo somewhat like Dante's, "where those without hope yet languish in desire." Knowing our circles would never intersect, and that whatever he told me would remain secret, he enjoyed setting me up as his heterosexual "straight" man and startling me with tall tales and inside stories of the Homintern (as he dubbed it), illuminating the darker recesses of the closet with flashbulb glimpses that left me momentarily wide-eyed. Over the years he had acquired a raunchy homoerotic nomenclature as extensive and subtly precise in its way as the working vocabulary of Eskimoes to distinguish among the manifold appearances of snow; no doubt for reasons similarly practical; but new to me, it served to heighten his sometimes stercoraceous revelations à la Jean Genet into a kind of poetry.

From the tales of his own romantic adventures, and there were plenty, I gathered the obvious inference that despite his ongoing affair with Auden, he had not forsaken all others. In the course of conversation he might remark, "Wystan thinks such-and-such" or "Wystan and I met so-and-so," at which I would at once clear my mind expectantly, hoping to hear more, but it hardly ever went further than that. Nor did I wish to embarrass myself and possibly disgust him with country bumpkin questions of the "Hast thou seen Auden plain?" variety. Chester, however, often asked me about Rhoda; but under the mistaken assumption that as a homosexual he would be antipathetic toward women, I was apprehensive about introducing them. Needlessly. By their second encounter, no later, they entered into a cosexual and sisterly intimacy, so much so that at times in their company it was I who felt like the third party.

The place where we all invariably met was- –had to be—the cafeteria. During that early wartime, with students and teachers abruptly dropping out from week to week to join the service, and classes subject to cancellation in midterm, the cafeteria was not merely a place to eat, the stomach, as 'twere, of the student body, but its social heart and intellectual brain center as well, a crowded, bustling, feud-ridden, volatile, and at times cacophonous place that had a continuous life of its own apart from that of the college itself. Dispersed among the undifferentiated mass of students, who sat anywhere and left soon after having lunch, there was: a jocks' table adjacent, by a mutually appreciated *discordia concors,* to a chess-players' table; a self-segregated Wasps' table, blacks' table, and Orthodox Jews' table; a Newman Club Catholics' table where all the prettiest girls, it seemed, wore tiny *noli me tangere* gold crosses trembling in the cashmere valleys of their bosoms; a Stalinists' table separated by the length of the room and the breadth of an ideological abyss from a Trotskyites' table; a plague-on-both-your-houses heretics' table of anarchists, socialists, Lovestoneites, Luddites, Shachtmanits, syndicalists, "Crullers" (Committee for Revolutionary Labor Action), and other such disgruntled utopians; a nonsectarian but perpetually squabbling and faction-ridden psychoanaloids' table; a jazz-oriented hipsters' and (conspiratorially secret but reekingly obvious) pot-smokers' table; and many others I suppose, concealed here and there in the throng, but whose *point d'appui* was unknown to me.

After I succeeded in wooing Rhoda away from the Trotskyites' table—which proved fairly easy, for, as she liked to say, she had always been a "democratic narcissist" at heart—we tried the heretics' then the psychoanaloids' and then went off to sit by ourselves at one of the anonymous free-for-all tables. There we'd remain through the afternoon, talking and smoking and talking and chain-drinking Cokes and coffee, as the hourly classroom bells rang out several shifts of scene and personae in the cafeteria, but break off at some point to find a secluded spot under the athletic field grandstand, if it wasn't too cold, or in an empty lab if it was, and return to the same table afterward. Occasionally we'd join or be joined by friends, chief among them Chester, for whom I kept an expectant eye cocked, as did Rhoda as well.

Whenever Chester made one of his entrances he'd pose, as if preoccupied, at the doorway for a moment, ruminating, while his eyes rapidly cruised up and down the cafeteria in search of an appealing or, failing that, familiar face, and then, having assessed all the possibilities, slowly insinuate himself through the crowded aisles, "the observed of all observers," bestowing as he went a nod here or a snub there, until he reached the table of his choice. As often as not, but most often if he had just written a poem he wanted to try out on me, or had had a romance he wished to confide to Rhoda, he'd join us. The welcome would always be warm.

As I envision them now, converging in memory as they lean across the table to embrace and greet each other with little yelps of affection, they seem as closely akin as Hansel and Gretel. If opposites, as they say, attract, it's astonishing that two people so much alike could have liked each other so much. Each, to begin with, through some genealogical fluke, was a natural blond, with the blond's distinctive chlorophyll, yet behind their eyes, and in a certain unerasable millennial palimpsest that came through beneath and shaded their features, both had to be Chosen. Their way of laughing and what, with almost equal frequency and decibels, they laughed at were also similar, Rhoda's laugh being rather low and throaty and Chester's a half-note higher than the norm, so that they met on approximately the same register. These physical traits aside, there was something else, even more important, that they shared only with each other and that drew them still closer: they had each at an early age lost their mothers, Rhoda and her two sisters as a consequence having been raised in foster homes and orphanages, and Chester, an only child, at home by his grandmother. It left them with a need to belong and be loved solely for being that could never quite be satisfied, as I see now; but steeped, and nearly smothered, in maternal schmaltz as I was then, I envied them instead their independence and freedom from family ties.

At the table Chester, if in an antic or a roguish mood, might continue aloud his assessment of the student body in the cafeteria, but this time tête-à-tête with Rhoda, offering critical comments on any of the male gender he found worthy, admiring some limbs and disparaging others, speculating as well on their inguinal attributes and sexual prowess, sometimes in imagery so graphic as to electrify anyone within earshot, his voice rising to an ecstatic coloratura trill of syllables poured forth in one breath and run pell-mell together *("Parlor-sizedbarelythatbututterly-utterlydiv* I-I-I-*ne"*—and perch for a long high moment on that sustained dieresis before slowly fluttering down—*"my dears!"*), all the while slyly encouraging Rhoda to express her own opinions. I'd sit there grinning stolidly. Rhoda, with reassuring knee-nudges under the table and side-glances in my direction, would always demur, or else modestly murmur something noncommittal, yet somehow I always had the feeling that if I weren't there her response would have been more wholehearted. Both of us well knew that what inspired Chester's performance was mischief not malice and, primarily, a desire to reaffirm with Rhoda their co-sexual and subcutaneous sistership. But to be jealous of Chester? It was absurd.

The aria over, and his hilarity having subsided, Chester would become aware of my glum silence and realize that he had ignored and possibly offended me as well; whereupon to make up for it, for unless carried away he was always gentle and tender towards others, he'd turn to me contritely and ask in a serious voice, "Have you been writing?" Which I took as a sure sign that he had, and I'd politely ask him the same. He'd hedge, I'd hedge, *à la manière* d'Alphonse et Gaston or of Abbott and Costello, until finally, after a few self-deprecating shrugs and sighs and disclaimers that it wasn't much and wasn't finished, "with sweet reluctant amorous delay" he'd yield, extracting from his inside coat pocket a much folded and refolded tattered sheet of paper scrawled all over with lines that had been scratched out several times, then rewritten and reassigned to distant corners of the page, with arrows pointing helter-skelter this way and that way to their new locations, out of which mess would emerge, like a nymph from a sewer, spruce and clean-limbed, a sonnet perhaps or a villanelle or even a sestina.

Since it was of course illegible, he'd consent to read, make that croon, the poem to us in a low, solemn Gregorian plain chant which he'd lower still more where required for dramatic emphasis, so that to hear him at all amid the babble of voices and clatter of dishes in the cafeteria we had to lean forward and listen intently. Throughout the recital I'd be ransacking my mind for something cogent or at least unstupid to say when it was over.

Chester was then under the spell of Thomas Campion's lyrics; but the violin-like phrasing and complex harmonies of that most musical of English poets were beyond his range. What his own youthful efforts evoked instead was the fin de siècle tinkling preciosity of Lionel Johnson's or Ernest Dowson's music box. Auden's influence was evident only in the avoidance and, possibly, in his predilection for traditional verse forms and elaborate stanzaic patterns. As a self-styled "courtly maker," Chester abhorred the lumpish "proletarian" free verse—precursor of the tub-thumping Beatnik type that erupted a generation later—in which left-wing political virtue tried to pass as poetry in those days, and I was with him there; yet for all their technical skill his own poems, most of them inspired by homosexual love, were evasively ambiguous, squeamish almost, and primly conventional in diction, with none of the pungency of his own natural speech. But how tell him that? I was so painfully aware of the pains taken in their composition that I was reluctant to seem ungrateful.

My comments at the table, offered apologetically and larded by admiration for the poem as a whole, would be confined to what I considered a tepid epithet here or a bumpy meter there.

Even so one ran a risk. Chester felt each critical pinprick like a wound in his own psyche, and would respond with scorn, implying that I was too obtuse, with a sensibility too obfuse, to appreciate what he was up to. As he went on to defend and explicate his work, pointing out shades of meaning thrice distilled and metaphorical nuances dimly pinnacled, I'd nod as if in agreement, while convinced more and more that he was describing some ideal Platonic poem existing only in his imagination rather than the one that lay bleeding before us.

At this point Rhoda, who loved a political but loathed a poetical wrangle, would remember a protest rally she had promised to attend, give each of us a neutral kiss and depart. Chester and I would then continue the discussion sometimes until deep into the afternoon—and on many such afternoons, conflated in my mind, so that they now, with a single exception, seem like one long afternoon and one long discussion—and remain there until the cafeteria employees started clearing the table of dirty dishes and sweeping rubbish around, and over, our feet, muttering to themselves meanwhile, when we too would have to leave.

On the afternoon that stands out from the rest, rather than break off the conversation then and there I decided to walk Chester home. It was a cold, windy day in November, and when we got to his place—a "private house" (as it used to be called), with a screened-in front porch, a kitchen large enough to serve as a dining room, a basement and even a back yard, of the sort that once lined the side streets of Flatbush but have since been torn down to make way for high-rise apartment buildings—he invited me inside to warm up. While we were sitting in the parlor Chester's grandmother, then well past eighty, shuffled into the room wearing a faded housecoat and floppy bedroom slippers and asked him, in Yiddish, *"Host du gegesen epes?"* ("Have you eaten anything?"), in a small, frail, quavering voice, pure as a mew, then shuffled out again and returned a minute later bearing within two trembly hands a plate with a smoking pair of blintzes covered with sour cream. As she set it down she offered me one too, which I refused because it was getting dark out and supper would be waiting for me at home, but either because she was hard of hearing or preferred not to hear, perhaps both, she brought me a plate anyway. Those blintzes were delicious. It must surely have been from her, come to think of it, that Chester acquired the culinary skills that made him in later years such a superb cook.

She enjoyed watching us while we ate, seating herself meekly in a corner of the room, and though Chester implored her,

"Please, Bubba, go lie down, rest," she paid no attention but kept following us with her eyes unto the last forkful, then got up to collect the plates. As she bent over the table she stroked Chester's hair, as she must have done a thousand times before, but by that one instinctive gesture, like the touch of a magic wand, he was suddenly transformed in front of me into a little boy again.

For most of his life she had raised Chester, as before him she had raised her own son, Chester's father, Dr. Edward Kallman, an orthodontist of some importance with a large practice in Manhattan, besides being an amateur landscape painter and, in those days, a reverential member of The Party. I had met him briefly on a couple of previous visits to the house, each time hurrying in and out with a different distaff comrade in tow, on his way most likely to a meeting at the local catacomb, when he would pause only long enough to say hello to me and exchange a few words with Chester. I had the impression, which deepened, that politics to him was merely periodontics on a world scale, and, having looked into the maw of capitalist society and found all its institutions too far gone in decay for any patchwork therapy, had concluded that the whole mouthful must be pulled, the sooner the better, and replaced it with a set of Marxist dentures. Perched on a buffet against the wall opposite me stood a framed picture of him, taken as a young man, looking earnest, normal, reliable, respectable and substantial, in sum a very *mensch,* and all the things that Chester was not, yet featured remarkably like him, with just a soupçon, a certain *je ne sais quoi,* of difference around the eyes and mouth. So go figure it. There must have been, I imagine, a clash in the beginning between father and son, between the rival claims of Homintern and Comintern, but during the years I knew them and observed them together they treated each other always with respect and affection.

It was getting dark out. I stood up to leave, but Chester, who had recently received a present of the 1936 Glyndebourne recording of *Don Giovanni,* with the superb baritone John Brownlee in the role of the cod-pieced "Dissoluto," insisted that I remain a while to hear one side—"Just one," he said—but one side and one aria led to another—"The last!" he'd promise—until finally I had to outshout his protestations and put on my coat. As we were standing in the foyer saying goodbye, the bell chimed outside and Chester opened the door.

In he, unmistakably and corporeally, like an idea personified, came, blowing his fingers and stamping his feet with cold, yet I couldn't have been more astonished if his mythological near namesake Odin had just entered the room. Embracing Chester, he was as yet unaware of my presence, so I had a chance to look him over unobserved. Though quite tall, about six feet, he was wearing a brown tweed overcoat at least two sizes too big that came down in symmetrical folds to his ankles and gave him the elongated appearance of a carved gothic apostle. His strong-featured, somewhat horsey face was then hardly furrowed; two prominent, cold-reddened ears poked out askew on either side of his head; and there (I looked for it, remembering the lines from his "Letter to Lord Byron," "Conspicuous . . . a large brown mole; / I think I don't dislike it as a whole.") it was on his right cheek, not so large as I had imagined, about blueberry-sized, but it held and focused my attention nonetheless.

Pretty soon he noticed me gazing at him, and Chester introduced us. As we shook hands he held mine a touch longer than usual, a flicker of recognition passing across his pale grey eyes while he tried to equate my image with what Chester must already have told him about me, then burst into a high-pitched neigh of Oxfordian vocables from which I could make out nothing but my own name repeated a couple of times. Flushed, I suppose, and mumbling how glad I was to meet him, I backed out the door into the street.

So that was Auden! I told myself. *W. H. Auden! and he knew who I was too!* Exultant at having met him at last, I started running home through the streets, but halfway there I stopped, deliberately, and slowed down to a walk, for what impelled me to run almost as much, as I realized in self-disgust, was the primordial childhood fear of being scolded for coming late to supper. Here I was nineteen already, going on twenty, and had just met the most famous modern poet in England, yet I was still living at home cribbed and confined and spied on by my parents. So far my mother knew nothing of my affair with Rhoda; but I had been staying out later and later with her at the small apartment she shared with another girl at East 84th St. in Yorkville, sometimes not getting home till 2 or 3 A.M., and even staying overnight a couple of times. Sooner or later, I knew, she'd begin asking questions.

And then there was the war. Several of my friends, anticipating America's entrance into the war, had already volunteered for some branch of the service—"Yecky," for instance, had learned to play the tuba in order to join the military band at West Point, where he was now blowing Sousa marches for the duration—and my own number in the draft might be called at any time. Rhoda's political weather vane, recently shifted toward pacifism, urged me to declare myself a conscientious objector, but to that, as a craven cop-out, since I fully supported the war against Hitler, I could, and did, conscientiously object. Within the past few weeks, however, suggesting it at first casually and, she insisted, solely as a means for me to get a deferment in order to finish school, then more and more zealously, she proposed that we get married. *Me?* I thought. *Barely nineteen? And married? No.* In a vision I saw parallel rails stretching ahead year by year through deserts of conjugal eternity. Appealing to her own political conscience, I reminded her of her oft expressed belief, which I shared, that love was free and needed neither state sanction nor religious sanctification; but our case was different, she replied, for we were using the state, not being used by it; and with the issue thus joined between us, there was hardly a time we were together, especially just before or after making love, sometimes during, when she did not raise it.

One thing, though, was sure: whatever decisions I made or were made for me, about both the army and marriage, the chrysalis in which I had lived as a child for so long was soon to be broken.

MILTON KLONSKY

Maxim Gorky in Coney Island

What may have been the first encounter between the American Puritan conscience and Russian Communist evangelism occurred nearly fifty years ago, in the Age of Innocence, when both were still tender and unworldly.

In the early spring of 1906, the eminent Russian novelist and revolutionary, Maxim Gorky, arrived in New York harbor on a mission to raise money in America for the Bolshevik cause. A large and enthusiastic crowd came to meet him at the pier. William Randolph Hearst's *American,* for which Gorky had written an article in 1905 on conditions in Russia, estimated the size of the crowd as "more than several thousand," while Gordon Bennet's *World,* engaged at the time in a circulation war with Hearst, figured it as "no more than a thousand." Accompanying Gorky as he disembarked, and sharing his bows, was a young and pretty actress from the Moscow Art Theatre, Maria Andreyeva, who was understood to be his wife.

Gorky could not have chosen a more favorable time to visit the country. The brutality with which the Czar had suppressed all opposition, the officially inspired pogroms, and the poverty and misery in Russia after the war with Japan had aroused the sympathies of the American public. A Committee to Help the Russian Revolutionists, consisting of William Dean Howells, Mark Twain, Arthur Brisbane, Robert Collier, Edwin Markham, Peter Finlay Dunne and Jane Addams, had arranged for Gorky's admission to America. Gorky assured the immigration authorities he was a Bolshevik, not an anarchist, and his purpose was to deliver lectures rather than throw bombs.

Once in New York, the literary lion of the Revolution was fed the raw meat of flattery and feted and petted until he purred. At a banquet held on the evening of his arrival, Arthur Brisbane dictated an editorial appeal for the Bolsheviks to be run in all

Hearst papers across the country. Symposia in honor of Gorky were sponsored by Charles Scribner of *Scribners,* Richard Watson Gilder of *The Century,* and W. C. Allen of *Harper's.* The most influential literary figures of the day came to his support. It was even rumored that an invitation had been sent him by President Theodore Roosevelt to dine at the White House.

H. G. Wells, who was present at one of these dinners, describes Gorky as "a big quiet figure with a curious power of appeal in his face and a large simplicity in his voice and gesture. He was dressed in peasant clothing, in a belted blue shirt, trousers in some shiny black material and boots. Save for a few common greetings, he had no language but Russian." A contemporary photograph reveals a face modelled in flat planes and angles like a cubist sculpture, with small, dark, indignant eyes set behind the high cheekbones; a wide, thin, mouth; and a pair of plump and luxuriant mustaches drooping down below the chin. The contrast with the pretty and fashionably dressed Maria Andreyeva, who was always at his side, must have been impressive.

From his suite in the Hotel Belleclaire, Gorky granted exclusive interviews to reporters from the *American* in which he attacked the Czar and appealed for aid for the exiled revolutionaries. A nationwide lecture tour, arranged by Professor John Dewey of Columbia, was expected to raise more than a million dollars. Faneuil Hall in Boston put in a bid for his first appearance outside New York, after which other cities as far west as San Francisco were to have their chance. And as Gorky's popularity rose higher and higher, the success of his mission seemed certain.

Then, all at once, the air was let out of the balloon. The Imperial Russian Embassy, dismayed by his reception in New York, informed the editors of the *World* that Gorky was not only living in sin with Maria Andreyeva, but already had a wife and child somewhere in Russia. The *World* pounced on this opportunity to embarrass Hearst by exposing his pet Bolshevik. Gordon Bennet, who was then, coincidentally, living in Paris with a young Russian countess, wired his paper to publish this exposure of Gorky. The next day the *World* came out with a grisly, heart breaking description of Gorky's wife and child out there in the frozen tundra, cold, hungry, and abandoned, while Gorky himself, grown fat on capitalist royalties, sported all over the world with his mistress. On the front page was a recent photograph of Gorky and Maria Andreyeva next to one of his wife and child.

Reverberations of moral indignation in the American press,

pulpit and parlor were instantaneous. For his part in the Gorky affair, the expulsion of Professor John Dewey from Columbia was demanded. The banquets were cancelled, the committees disbanded, the lecture tours postponed indefinitely. The manager of the Hotel Belleclaire requested that Gorky and his mistress leave the premises. They departed for the Hotel Lafayette-Brevoort in Greenwich Village and again they were forced to pack up and move, this time to the old and decrepit Hotel Rhinelander across the street. The pair then left to attend a socialist meeting and, on returning after midnight, found all their luggage piled up on the sidewalk in the rain. If not for the intervention of Mr. and Mrs. John Wilson, who invited them to their house in Staten Island, they would have been forced to spend the night in Washington Square Park.

Hearst's *American,* in a belated attempt to answer the *World,* asserted that Gorky was really married to Maria Andreyeva all the time, but could not reveal the details of his divorce from his first wife "without endangering the lives of scores and perhaps thousands of his countrymen." The newspaper took that chance, anyway. "It is here made known for the first time that there exists in Russia today a provisional government with a set of laws. . . . Gorky received his divorce under these laws." But no one, not even Gorky, was convinced by this explanation. And though his first wife, hearing the news, cabled the *World* that she and Gorky had parted by mutual consent and she was now happily remarried, it had little effect. Only five days after his arrival, Gorky learned that the Puritan conscience might tolerate political revolution in Russia but not sexual immorality in America.

Aleksei Maximovitch Pyeshkov—Gorky, meaning "The Bitter One," was his pen name—was especially bitter over the failure of Mark Twain to come to his aid. He had literacy affinities with Twain, since the boy from Nishni-Novgorod and the boy from Hannibal, Missouri, both made use of folk material drawn from their childhood and wrote in a vernacular style; and they even resembled one another, superficially, in appearance, since they wore the same flourishing handlebar mustachios—though Twain's had already turned white while Gorky's was a rich brown. Now the "Russian Twain," as he was called, felt that the "American Gorky" had betrayed him. When Twain was informed of these feelings of his former friend, he replied, "Gorky has made an awful mistake. He might just as well have come over in his shirttails." And, he added, "Certainly there can be but one wise thing for a visiting stranger to do—find out what the country's customs are and refrain from offending them. Custom is custom—it is built of brass, boiler iron, granite." But Gorky, on his side, felt that Twain had joined an international capitalist conspiracy against him.

The writer and his mistress spent the next few weeks in Staten Island and then moved out to the Wilson's cabin in the Adirondacks. There he began his most famous novel, *Mother,* and, except for occasional visits from the faithful John Dewey and H. G. Wells, remained in seclusion. The furor caused by the exposure of his private life in the *World* had almost subsided when, in August, an article by Gorky appeared in *Appleton's Magazine* called "The City of Mammon." In the doom-heavy tones of a biblical prophet come down from the Urals to judge New York, he delivered himself of the following fulmination:

> It is the first time I have seen such a monstrous city and never before have people seemed so insignificant, so enslaved. Yet at the same time I have never seen them so tragi-comically self-satisfied. There are many energetic faces among them, but in each face you notice before anything else its teeth. No inner freedom, freedom of the spirit, shines in their eyes. . . . Theirs is the freedom of blind tools in the hands of the Yellow Devil—Gold. . . .

As if to prevent any misunderstanding, he also sent a telegram to the I.W.W. leaders, Charles Moyer and "Big Bill" Heywood, who were then in jail awaiting trial for the assassination of the governor of Idaho.

"Greetings to you my brother Socialists. Courage! The day of justice and deliverance for the oppressed of the world is at hand. Gorky." The newspapers published this telegram and excerpts from his article, "The City of Mammon," renewing their demands that the Russian Bolshevik, novelist, and adulterer be deported. Whatever support Gorky still had in high and literary places now left him. Ambrose Bierce, whose stories on the Civil War Gorky had admired and recommended to Tolstoy, wrote of the incident to his friend George Sterling:

> Having been but a few weeks in the land, whose language he knows not a word of, he knows all about us and tells it in generalities of vituperation. . . . He is a dandy bomb thrower but he handles the stink pot indifferently well.

Even Hearst's *American* felt that Gorky had stayed too long in the United States. Without waiting to be asked by the immigration authorities, Gorky made plans to leave for Europe with Maria Andreyeva on an early steamer.

It was about this time that Gorky's remaining friends, in an effort to show him the American Dream from the inside, took him to "that happy island of illusion," (as the Guide Book called it) "where the sweltering masses of the monster city may forget the dry realities of work-a-day life and steep themselves in harmless frivolities amid the cooling breezes of the eternal sea."

Coney Island—then pronounced "Cooney"—had undergone a great transformation by 1906. Right after the Civil War it had been the headquarters for gangs of smugglers and rum-runners operating off Norton's Point, a center of gambling, skullduggery, and prostitution, and a kind of Casbah for criminals on the lam. (Boss Tweed was able to hide there for two weeks after his conviction before taking a boat for Spain.) The lowest and toughest dives in Texas and Colorado were sometimes called The Coney Island; and, so infamous had the name become in the 1870s, that a reform movement in Brooklyn seriously proposed to change it to Surf Island "without the peculiar and somewhat embarrassing associations of the old." But all this was over when Gorky made his visit in the late summer of 1906. "The long bare unfrequented shore," recalled nostalgically by Walt Whitman, "that I had all to myself and where I loved to race up and down after bathing," was then the playground for more than 300,000 people who came every day by steamboat, horse and buggy, and trolley car.

> A trip up the Hudson or down the Bay,
> A trolley to Coney or Far Rockaway,
> On a Sunday afternoon—

was a favorite song, the strains of which Gorky might have heard as he travelled to Coney on the Culver Line.

The trippers had already begun to come in increasing numbers in the 1880s when Coney's reputation improved and ocean bathing became popular. "A Day at Coney Island," written in heroic blank verse by Tad (J. P. Sweet), in 1880, celebrates the resort of those days:

> We hail with joy that geologic morn
> When Coney Island from the sea was born.
> As time sped on, with each succeeding year,
> The Oceanic's widening sand appear;
> This near the day when Caesar entered Rome—
> Then thy beach, Brighton! rose above the foam.

134

The poet goes on to describe the crowd on the beach—"The maiden whose sweet frizzes hang / In tufts inverted fashionable Bang," "the athlete ponderous with the brawny limb," "the spruce Apollo with his parted hair," "the ancient hay-bag," "the country rustic and the city swell / The western beauty and the city belle," "the Jersey farmer with his honest face." "It was" (as another writer described it) "the ordinary American crowd, the best natured, best dressed and best smelling crowd in the world." Gorky, of course, saw a much larger and more heterogenous throng pushing through the Midway and lying on the beach in their rented bathing costumes. Tens of thousands of recent immigrants out of Germany, Russia, Poland, Austria, Sweden, Italy, many still speaking their native languages and wearing Old World clothing, mingled with this "ordinary American crowd," even absorbed it, and shared the communal sun and the great mechanical toys of Coney Island.

Steeplechase, Luna Park, and Dreamland, the three amusement parks on the island, were then almost brand-new and in their hey-day. The use of quantities of electric lights for display had recently been developed. From the Chicago Columbian Exposition of 1893, in which impermanent structures of steel and plaster were shown molded into various shapes, Coney Island adopted its own timeless style of architecture. Entrances to all the rides and exhibits were built to resemble Egyptian pylons, Malmein pagodas, Arabian minarets, Babylonian ziggurats, all white-washed, with their weird forms outlined and festooned at night with thousands of electric bulbs. Luna Park, constructed in 1902 at a cost of 2 million dollars, had 250,000 electric lights; while Dreamland—the park Gorky visited—built in 1904 at a cost of 3.5 million dollars and intended to be two times bigger and better than Luna, employed over 500,000 bulbs as well as many beacons and towers of light. The 1906 Guide Book states:

> Dreamland at night glows and sparkles with an electric radiance. . . . For thirty miles at sea, the tall beacon tower may be seen like a gleaming finger. It is a marvelous fact that with all the profuse use of fire in electrical form, the element has never escaped from the control of the corps of experts in charge.

As for the rides, they were among the most Rube Goldbergish and ingenious contrivances of nineteenth-century mechanical science. There were "feeler" rides like The Old Mill, in which long narrow boats filled with couples floated through mysterious

135

tunnels of love; "tickler" rides like the Virginia Reel, invented by H. E. Riehl in 1890, in which round cars revolved and twisted downwards in a circular descent like pinballs; "round" rides like the carrousel, or the Airship Swing in which a series of steel arms lifted gondolas faster and faster and higher and higher in ever widening circles; and "gravity" rides, such as the switchback railway invented by Lamarchus A. Thompson in 1884, in which cars rolled down on their own momentum from peak to lesser peak and around curves unbanked to swing the couples together, until, the momentum exhausted, all the passengers got out while the motorman switched the car to another peak.

One of the many variations of the "gravity" ride was the famous Loop-the-Loop, a roller coaster which made a 360 degree turn inside a bow in the center, passengers being held in place by centripetal force; and, another, The Dragon's Gorge in Luna Park, with forty-eight hundred feet of track, where—says the Guide Book—"the passengers start from the North Pole and visit in rapid succession Havana, Port Arthur in winter, the Rocky Mountains, the bottom of the sea, and caverns of the lower regions besides experiencing a dash under a great cataract." A topsy-turvy take off on the "round" ride was the Ferris Wheel, a wheel of light turning sixty feet in the air, which dominated the Coney Island skyline. And, in a class by itself, was the colossus of all sliding ponds—Captain Roynton's Shoot the Chutes. Of all the rides on the island this was, truly, a Russian invention, having been first devised as an artificial incline for tobogganing during the winter fairs of Moscow. In 1823, it was brought to Sadler's Wells in London as "The Celebrated and Extensive Russian Mountains," and then, seventy-five years later, to Luna Park. There the ride was Americanized by sending, each night, a live elephant "sliding down the steep incline with frightful rapidity toward the lagoon in the center of the Plaza." Dreamland built two Shoot the Chutes, each one more jumbo than Luna's, with two elephants crashing down "with frightful rapidity" two times a night.

Other shows, rides, exhibitions, and spectacles offered by Luna and Dreamland were: Lilliputian Buildings, a fifteenth-century German town in miniature inhabited by dwarves; The Great Deep Rift, a section of a coal mine in operation; The Creation, a cycloramic presentation in which "the waters part, the earth arises, inanimate and human life appear," and its sequel, The End of the World, "according to a dream of Dante"; a Snake Dance by a tribe of Moki Indians; Le Voyage on l'Air, in which "the passenger, with the aid of ingenious mechanical and electrical devices, gains the impression of an air flight over the skyscrapers of New York . . . made possible by photographs taken originally by two daring aeronauts"; The Great Train Robbery, a cycloramic spectacle later made into one of the earliest movies; Twenty Thousand Leagues Under the Sea, a submarine excusion à la Jules Verne; A Trip to the Moon, a sort of scenic railway from which Luna Park derived its name; The Streets of Delhi, an oriental pageant with elephants, maharajahs and dancing girls; and that wasn't all for the hundreds of thousands of Ladies and Gentlemen who came each day to Coney Island.

On the Bowery, a midway barred to wheeled traffic, were all the fire-eaters, sword swallowers, rope dancers, jugglers and freaks—with huge "valentines," portraits of the Monster-osities, framed in electric light. A section of the Bowery between West First and West Third Street, called The Gut, was the original Tin Pan Alley of New York. Occasionally, important boxing matches, such as the Fitzsimmon-Jeffries fight for the Heavyweight Championship, were held on the commons. There were cabarets, dance halls, vaudeville, and kinetoscope shows on the side streets. Except for the smells of hot dogs, hot corn, hot fries, the swarming crowds, and the untuned and interfering clamor of barkers, hawkers, and pitchmen, a walk down the radiant alleyways of Coney Island was like walking up and down and in and out of the channels of a TV set.

The author of an article on Coney Island for *Munsey's Magazine* in 1907, Lionel Denison, commented on "the disposition of people to make their amusements so like their daily life." He continues:

> Like the circus horse driven around the ring from left to right, every day, on Sunday to rest himself went around from right to left. . . . So these city people, tired by the jar and noise and glare and crowds of the street, go for recreation where all these are intensified. The switch-backs, scenic railways, and toy trains are merely trolley cars a little more uneven in roadbed, jerky in motion and cramped in the seat than ordinary trains, but not much. . . . The Ferris Wheel and gigantic see-saw are but exaggerations of the ordinary elevator, and the towers are not unlike office buildings.

Nelson's *Views of Coney Island,* one of the many guide books of the time, takes an opposite position:

> It is no use to criticize the Island; it exists and will continue to exist because it offers to all, gentle and simple, poor and rich, a rare feast of fantastic illusions and wonders, complete enough to quench the

mysterious thirst for active excitement as an alternative to monotonous work. . . .

But the essence of the Midway, perhaps, lies between. The normal, the upright, the average—made freakish in the crazy mirrors of Coney Island and upset and unbalanced by all sorts of mechanical contraptions—was, after all, straightened out and reaffirmed for the great American middle class.

> Look into the pewter pot
> To see the world as the world's not,

as an old English rhyme of the sixteenth-century expressed it.

A few weeks before Gorky's own pilgrimage, Mr. Albert Bigelow Paine, a magazine writer in the genteel tradition and a close rhyming friend and biographer of Gorky's enemy, Mark Twain, came to inspect the playground of the masses. His article, entitled "The New Coney Island," was published in *The Century* magazine that summer.

Paine was pleased to find that the old, disreputable Coney Island, with its leagues of gamblers, thugs and prostitutes, was no more. He recognized the difference even on the trolley car going over. "There was a crowd of people; and the fact that in numerous cases the ladies were given seats while the men held on to straps, was evidence that Coney had changed." And as the trolley approached Surf Avenue, Paine heard the "undercurrent of excitement."

> A number of passengers were making their first trip, though these were inclined to speak in whispers as the wonder of the spectacle gradually lifted before them. . . . First came the chariots where the tickets were sold; then a row of entrance gates; and beyond them an enchanted story book land of trellises, columns, domes, minarets, lagoons and lofty aerial flights. And everywhere was life—a pageant of happy people; and everywhere was color—a wide harmony of orange and white and gold under a cloudless blue. It was a world removed—shut away from the sordid clatter and turmoil of the streets.
>
> Of course, it was still a whirl of noise and exhibition and refreshment—but the noise was within the limits of law and order and the exhibition and refreshment were more wholesome. Kinetoscope shows of a gay but harmless variety seemed to prevail where once painted and bedizened creatures attracted half-sotted audiences with vulgarity and display.

138

Among the lawful noises he heard on the Midway was the barker's "*Hu*-rry! *Hu*-rry! *Hu*-rry! Step-right-up-Ladies-and-Gentlemen!" and the pitchman's "Ve tell your name! Ve tell your age! Ve do not know you! Ve nevare saw you!"; and the hullaballoo of booths where "the passerby was incited to hit the colored man whose face decorated the center of the curtains to get thereby a good cigar"; and the clanking machinery and diminishing screams of passengers on "innumerable gravity railroads and chutes and whirling air-ship swings . . . [which] the appetite of the American people for rapid motion has produced." Paine himself was tempted to take a ride on the dangerous Loop-the-Loop, but thought better of it in time. He left well-satisfied with the afternoon and glad to recommend Coney Island to all the readers of *The Century*.

To Carthage then came Gorky, burning, burning, burning and brooding over the failure of his mission, exposure of his private life in the newspapers, betrayal by friends—and prepared to see what he wanted to see. He saw it; and then sailed two weeks later with his mistress for Capri. There, in a small, seaside villa on the ancient pleasure island of the Emperor Tiberius, he wrote his impressions of the American playground of the masses and the way of life it represented. The article, entitled "Boredom," appeared in the *Independent* magazine in the summer of 1907.

Gorky took the trolley to Coney at night when the great electrical display could be seen. Like those jewelled birds on the golden tree and the two gold lions in the throne room of Byzantium, which would warble and roar on the approach of an ambassador, the myriads of brilliant electric lights at Coney were intended to overwhelm and dazzle the eyes of any observer. The ambassador from Russia to Dreamland was suitably impressed.

> With the advent of night a fantastic city all of fire suddenly rises from the ocean into the sky. Thousands of ruddy sparks glimmer in the darkness, limning in fine sensitive outline on the black background of the sky, shapely towers of miraculous castles, palaces and temples. . . . Fabulous beyond conceiving, ineffably beautiful, is this fiery scintillation. It burns but does not consume.

But after this propitiatory hymn to electricity is over, Gorky invokes that "Yellow Devil—Gold" once more, and says what he really thinks of Coney Island and New York.

> The City hums with the insatiate, hungry roar—the ceaseless bellow of iron, the melancholy wail of Life driven by the power of gold,

the cold, cynical whistle of the Yellow Devil scare the people away from the turmoil of the earth burdened and besmirched by the ill-smelling body of the city. And the people go forth to the shore of the sea, where the beautiful white buildings stand and promise respite and tranquillity.

And Gorky tells what they find when they get there.

> The amusements are without number. Boats fly in the air around the top of a tower, another keeps turning about and impels some sort of iron balloon. Everything rocks and roars and bellows and turns the heads of the people. They are filled with contented ennui, their nerves are racked by an intricate maze of motion and dazzling fire. . . . The ennui which issues from under the pressures of self-disgust seems to turn and turn in a slow circle of agony. It drags tens of thousands of uniformly dark people into a sombre dance and sweeps them into a heap as the wind sweeps the rubbish of the street. Then it scatters them apart and sweeps them together again. . . .
>
> They swarm into the cages like black flies. Children walk about, silent with gaping mouths and dazzled eyes. They look around with such intensity, such seriousness, that the sight of them feeding their little souls upon this hideousness, which they mistake for beauty, inspires a pained sense of pity. The men's faces, shaved even to the mustache, are grave and immobile. They enjoy the tinsel, but too serious to betray their pleasure, they keep their thin lips pressed together and look from the corners of their eyes, like people whom nothing can astonish. The men with serious faces seat themselves on the backs of the wooden horses and elephants of the merry-go-round. With a whoop they dart to the top, with a whistle they descend again. After this stirring journey, they draw their skin tight on their faces again and go to taste of new pleasures.

Then Gorky, drifting along with the crowd in his own search for pleasure, found himself inside an exhibition called "Hell." This was an old-style morality play, stern, solemn, and ceremonial, which attempted to show the consequences of sin. As an attraction, it was just as popular as any other in Dreamland. P. T. Barnum had discovered in the nineteenth-century that the American public liked their circuses with a touch of revivalism, and their revival meetings with a touch of the circus; and so, even in his advertisements, the old master huckster never failed to mollify the Puritan conscience and to adopt biblical words and references wherever possible.

While Gorky watched the performance of "Hell," he seemed to see the hand of that Puritanism which had pinned the scarlet letter on him and Maria Andreyeva only a few months before. This was his chance to even the score.

Hell is constructed of papier mâché and painted dark red. Everything in it is on fire—paper fire—and it is filled with the thick, dirty odor of grease. On one of the stones sits Satan. He rubs his hands contentedly like a man who is doing a good business. He must be very uncomfortable on this porch, a paper stone, which cracks and rocks. But he pretends not to notice his discomfort, and looks down at the evil demons busying themselves with the sinners. The atmosphere in Hell is stifling. The demons are insignificant looking and feeble. Apparently, they are exhausted by their work and irritated by its sameness and evident futility.

A girl is there who has bought a new hat. She is trying it on before a mirror, happy and contented. But a pair of little fiends seize her under the armpits and put her into a long smooth trough which descends tightly into a pit in the middle of the cave.

The same treatment is given a man who has drunk a glass of whiskey and a girl who has stolen money from a companion's purse.

The audience looks on these horrors in silence with serious faces. The hall is dark. Some sturdy fellow with curly hair holds forth to the audience in a lugubrious voice while he draws the moral. He says that if the people do not want to be the victims of Satan with the red garments and the crooked legs, they should not kiss girls to whom they are not married because the girls might become bad women. Women outcasts ought not to steal money from the pockets of their companions and people should not drink whiskey or beer or other liquors that arouse the passions, they should not visit saloons, but the churches, for churches are not only better but cheaper.

At the conclusion, a nauseatingly beautiful angel appears on a wire holding a wooden trumpet pasted over with gilt paper between his lips. On catching sight of him, Satan dives into the pit after the sinners.

Gorky then proceeds to draw his own Bolshevik moral from this Puritan morality play.

Everywhere the one commandment is repeated: "Don't!" For it helps to crush the spirit of the majority of the working people. . . . On the right, they are intimidated by the terrors of eternal torture. "Do not sin," they are warned, "Sin is dangerous." On the left, in the spacious dancing hall, women waltz about, and here everything cries out to them: "Sin! For sin is pleasant."

Not far from the orchestra is a cage with bears. One of them, a

141

stout brown bear with little shrewd eyes stands in the middle of the cage and shakes his head deliberately. All this is sensible only if it's contrived to blind, deafen and mutilate the people. Then, of course, the end justifies the means. But if people come here to be amused, I have no faith in their sanity.

To conclude, Gorky himself, like that "nauseatingly beautiful angel" in Hell, places the "wooden trumpet pasted over with gilt paper" between his own lips and blows a call for revolution—an event as near and far for him then as the Day of Judgment.

> One thing alone is good in this garish city. You can drink in hatred to your soul's content—hatred of the power of stupidity. . . . Mean panderers to debased tastes unfold the disgusting nakedness of their falsehood, the naivete of their shrewdness, the hypocricy and insatiable force of their greed. The cold glare of the dead fire bares the stupidity of it all. Its pompous glitter rests upon everything round about the people. The soul is seized with a desire for a living, beautiful fire, a sublime fire, which should free the people from the slavery of a varied boredom.

Gorky's essay against our own Coney Island followed a long tradition of similar jeremiads against other and older Coneys, throughout history, by poets, preachers, and prophets. William Langland's "Vision of Piers Plowman," with it's "feeld ful of fok," was a take-off on the great Winchester Fair in Fourteenth-century England; the fair at Sturbridge in the Eighteenth-century was the model for "Vanity Fair" in Bunyan's allegory "Pilgrim's Progress"; and William Wordsworth's description in "The Prelude" of Bartholomew Fair—the spiritual progenitor of our Coney Island—seems almost to have taken the words out of Gorky's mouth:

> All out-o' -the-way, far-fetched, perverted things,
> All freaks of nature, all Promothean thoughts
> Of man, his dullness, madness, and their feats
> All jumbled up together, to compose
> A Parliament of Monsters. Tents and booths
> Meanwhile as if the whole were one vast mill,
> All vomiting, receiving on all sides . . .
> O blank confusion! true epitome
> Of what the mighty City is herself
> To thousands upon thousands of her sons,
> Living amid the same perpetual whirl
> Of trivial objects, melted and reduced

To one identity, by differences
That have no law, no meaning, and no end . . .

But all these were inspired by a desire for moral and spiritual uplift and a religious regeneration of the masses; while Gorky's indignation was directed at the American people for wasting their time at such low and trivial pleasures when they should be attending meetings and demonstrating against the government.

The editor of the *Independent* inserted the following comment on his article:

> To most people Coney Island, the playground of the metropolis, seems a place of gayety and comparatively innocent though somewhat vulgar amusements. But to the man who has assumed the name of "Gorky," The Bitter One, it only affords further evidence of the stupidity and depravity of the human race and of the tyranny of capital. When Maxim Gorky was in this country last summer he seemed to find life and its conditions everywhere as bad as in darkest Russia. Finally, to cheer him up, his friends took him to Coney Island and this is the impression it made on his sensitive mind. After reading it one knows better how to interpret his pictures of Russian life.

When Gorky and Maria Andreyeva left America for Italy, he was interviewed on shipboard by reporters from the newspapers. In answer to a question on the kind of activity he regarded as necessary for social advancement, he replied:

> Circulate cheap editions of classics, the great histories, novels, poems, dramas, provide picture exhibitions for the wage earners and lectures on natural science. Already your workmen have a plethora of material goods; their souls are stuffed with fatness; they, like the rest of America, have no souls.

But more than twenty years later, with the USSR already a reality and the first Five Year Plan for the industrialization of Russia about to begin, he changed his mind about the American "plethora of material goods." Confronted with his own criticisms of America while he was here, he said, simply: "I was a Russian rustic then." In 1928, Gorky was persuaded to return to Stalin's Dreamland as the chief literary figure of the Revolution. He lived luxuriously in a mansion overlooking Moscow, once inhabited by Napoleon during his Russian campaign.

Dreamland in Coney Island was destroyed in 1911, when that "element" which the proprietors boasted had "never escaped from the control of the corps of experts in charge" broke out one night due to a short circuit in a ride called "Hell Gate" and burned the playground of the masses to the ground. Gorky himself died in 1936, also as a result of fire, and under weird circumstances.

As the best-known Soviet writer of his time, he had held on stubbornly to his faith in the Revolution and continued to believe in the "sublime lie" of communism (as he called it) rather than the "petty truths" of Western democracy. Except for various official speeches and articles, his literary output was nil. Then, in 1936, rumors began to reach his friends in Europe that Gorky was trying to escape from the Workers' Paradise and, that same year, his death by bronchial pneumonia was announced dolefully over the Moscow radio. Two years later, his decease was called murder by the Soviet government and became the pretext for the famous Moscow Trials, with their sinister overtones of medieval trials for witchcraft. Under cross-examination by the chief prosecutor, Andrei Vishinsky, a certain Dr. Levine made this "confession":

> Gorky's great passion was fire. He loved the flames and we exploited this passion. . . . We lit a fire for him in the open air, at a time when he was fatigued and weak. Gorky stood next to the hot fire and this was very bad for his lungs, resulting in his death.

Almost all of Gorky's old pre-Revolutionary friends—called "assassins, spies, deviationists and wreckers" by Vishinsky—were made to confess in torture chambers and sent to the firing squad. In a wax museum in Coney Island today, there is a replica of one of those Russian torture chambers.

EDITH KONECKY

Eric and Max and Julius and Ethics

Eric Golden came home from college in June and made straight for his grandparents' apartment on Park Avenue. He was tired and apathetic and, though he would have liked to believe that he had mononucleosis, something definite and subject to medical prescription, he was pretty sure it was some kind of emotional crisis he was having, something to do with identity: who he was sick of being, who he was going to have to become.

It had been a hard year. He'd sat in, sat down, marched on, carried placards, shouted, wept, jeered, sung, and been beaten up. Violently nonviolent, he himself had not laid a hand on anyone. Committed and alienated, he'd rested up in coffee houses, listening to protest songs, feeling as bitter as the espresso. He'd made love to girls with long hair and dark glasses, and squatted in a desert with Indians, chewing peyote and having visions. He'd walked away unscratched from the scattered wreck of a Honda, defying his mother's monotonous forebodings relayed to him weekly by airmail. Still, he'd managed to get to class often enough to pass everything.

One more year and he'd be a bachelor of arts complete with diploma, nontransferable, nonnegotiable, good for absolutely nothing. He hadn't a clue about what he wanted to do with his life.

He declined invitations from his mother, abroad on sabbatical, and his father, who was in Chicago with a new wife, making another new start. On impulse, he wrote to his grandparents asking if he could stay with them. Their New York apartment had an extra bedroom that doubled as a "den." "Come, come," Grandma Tess wrote by return mail. "The pleasure is ours."

He had planned to sleep for two weeks straight but the tele-

145

phone woke him the first morning before eight. He opened his eyes to see his grandfather stride into the room to the desk, a few feet from where Eric lay, and take charge of the telephone. A den was supposed to be a private place where you could repair to lick your wounds, but Eric saw that he was not going to have any privacy and that his borrowed chamber was not a den but an office.

"Two o'clock this afternoon, Fortunoff," his grandfather bellowed, swivelling in the chair and looking at Eric with distaste. "They'll come to your office."

Those big feet, must be a thirteen at least, sticking out of the sheets, hanging off the end of the sofa bed. Eric. How he had loved that kid! Pink-cheeked, big-eyed dynamo, exploding with energy, full of importance. Smart. Two years old and he could tell you the name of every car on the street, though he couldn't read. "Ford, Pontiac, Chevrolet," he would chant, mispronouncing as the cars went by. "Plymouth, Dodge, Cadillac." He went wild at the sight of a Cadillac. Of course, cars were easier in those days, but still. And look how he'd turned out, this overgrown galoot with the beard and the long hair, looking like some kind of half-breed. And sleeping in his underwear.

"In addition to the usual, I want to know what percent if any their business fell off since the new motel opened across the throughway. Listen, Fortunoff, you know what I want, I don't have to tell you." He slammed the receiver down.

"I thought you were retired, Grandpa," Eric said, pulling himself to a sitting position and planting his feet on the carpet. "Christ, the carpet's softer than the bed. How come you sleep on rocks?" Their health. They thought a lot about health. "No kidding, Grandpa, I thought you retired years ago."

He'd been a manufacturer of ladies' ready-to-wear almost all his life. Five years ago he decided he'd had enough. He wanted to spend his declining years in play, sport, and travel. But cards bored him, golf made him angry, and although he loved to dance and did so crossing a variety of oceans, travel finally made him restless. Once you got there, what was there to do but look at *shvartzes* with baskets on their heads, eat food that gave you gas, or run with Tess to shops and watch her buy junk she didn't need or really want. In Leningrad he never even got out of the bus; he could see that they were all slaves and that the guide was trained to tell only lies.

He stayed home, looking for a hobby. He found one. He took to knocking down beautiful old estates and building on their ruins drab garden apartments which he subsequently sold, taking back mortgages. He had expected his fortune to diminish

146

with his retirement but instead it kept growing and he was faced with the problem of investing his new money. He formed corporations and acquired partners, men like himself who also did not know where to put their money, but he was the manager. He had never allowed anyone to make a decision for him, although he liked to think of himself as "open to suggestions." Before long, what with scouting investment possibilities, exploring all the angles, figuring on long pads of multilined green paper, talking to lawyers, accountants, builders, and bankers, and keeping his partners abreast, he was busier than he'd ever been.

"You don't sound retired," Eric said. "Why don't you play golf?"

"Put some clothes on," Grandpa Max barked. "What are you going to do, lay there all day like a lox?"

"I'm up, I'm up. Seriously, Grandpa, you've got more money now than you can use. How come you don't take it easy?"

"Responsibilities," Max said, pushing his anger down. "But what would you know about responsibilities, your generation?"

Why get angry with a kid? Some kid! Six three, two hundred twenty pounds. What did they need them so big for with the world getting so crowded. Big and sloppy, all that hair. Tess said, "Even so, he's beautiful." Leave it to a grandmother to find beauty. Furthermore, this kid was some kind of an anarchist. "*I* worked hard all my life. *I* slaved. One year of high school was all the education *I* got." A trust fund for their education. But he had been glad to send him to school, proud. "I sent him to school to get educated, not arrested. The trust fund is for tuition, not bail." Tess said, "They're all getting arrested nowadays. It's nothing to be ashamed of. It's a stage."

A stage. A phase. When I was his age, who had time for stages? I was already in business for myself. I worked fifteen, sixteen hours a day. I slept on the cutting room tables, too tired to go home at night. My mother came to The Place with hot soup in a jar. I knew what I had to do, I was in a rage to do it. Nineteen years old, working all my life, but now it was the real thing. Other people's money rode on my back. Five hundred dollars from Mama from the store, fifteen hundred from Tante Etta's hocked jewelry. And I paid them back in a year. One year. With interest.

"What do you mean, Grandpa? If you already have all the money you need. What kind of responsibilities?"

"You think the money just sits there? You have to invest it. That way, the money works for you. You use the income and you still have the principal."

Eric nodded.

"It's a lot of work, finding where to invest it. A safe investment, a good return. It's not easy, even with money getting so tight."

Eric grinned. "Grandpa, I feel sorry for you."

"What would you know!" He was angry again. "When I was your age, I didn't have time to lay around all day in my underwear."

"It's not even nine o'clock," Eric said, getting to his feet and scratching his chest. "I'm tired. Maybe I've got mono."

"Mono?" Max said. "What's mono?"

"It's a disease, Grandpa. Mononucleosis. Makes you tired all the time."

They even had new diseases, this generation. Fancy names for laziness. In my day if you were sick by God you knew it: TB, pneumonia, influenza, they didn't kid around with sicknesses.

He picked up the phone and dialed the garage, watching Eric lumber toward the bathroom.

In the shower, Eric shampooed his hair and beard, feeling the weariness in his arms. What if he really did have something slow and serious? Imagine having to languish, perhaps die, in a Castro convertible! And it would take more than his dying to keep the old man away from that desk. He would die listening to the old man shouting into the telephone about amortization and interest rates. Who was Grandpa Max to treat Eric's health so lightly, just because he was big, as if size had anything to do with disease, except that there was more of him vulnerable to attack? Both his grandparents were always saying, "The most important thing is your health." They had lived a long time and they had measured. The medicine chest was crammed with pills, the faintest symptom sent Grandpa to a specialist, and both he and Grandma made regular trips to spas where they dieted, took the baths, were massaged. They were both proud of how much younger than their years they looked. It was one of Grandpa's great pleasures to tell new acquaintances his age and then listen to their disbelief. Grandma, more modest, claimed it was all facade and that inside things were going to pieces right on schedule.

When he came out of the bathroom, Eric could hear his grandfather still on the phone, and he could smell coffee. He made for the kitchen. Grandma, dressed and finishing her breakfast, gave him a bright smile.

"Good morning, Sweetie pie," she said. "Did you sleep well?"

"Yes," he lied, pouring himself orange juice.

"Would you like to come to the club with me and play golf?"

Their club was in upper Westchester and, weather permitting,

148

Grandma was there every day, a calm, steady, dependable golfer who never made a spectacular shot or score, but never lost a ball, either. She had her good days and her bad days but only she could tell which was which.

Eric declined. "Maybe in a day or two. When I've had a chance to rest up." Why worry her with his fears about his health? He sat on, finishing his coffee when she was gone, listening to Grandpa's voice rising and falling in the next room. He suddenly felt happy. It was the first time in months that he had absolutely nothing to do, nothing to think about. He pushed away the empty coffee cup and stretched, then wandered into the living room. The windows overlooked Park Avenue and he stood for a while watching the traffic course uptown and down, separated by an island of tulips. He heard the doorbell ring and, knowing that Grandpa would not hear it over the sound of his own voice explaining and explaining into the telephone, he went to answer it. A small dapper old man stood there.

"Where's Max?" the man said, striding into the foyer. "Who are you?"

Eric told him.

"The grandson! I remember you when you were an infant. How old are you?"

"Twenty."

"Frances is fifteen, my grandaughter. A terror, fat." He fixed Eric with a sharp, calculating eye, daring him to deny it. "I sent her last summer to a fat girls' camp. Special. Two thousand dollars, laundry and transportation extra. Camp Sparrow Dell, you heard of it?"

"No," Eric said.

"She dropped sixty-five pounds, thirty dollars per pound. She gets mad at me, she eats Hershey bars. Already she put back twenty-two pounds, all spite. Six hundred and sixty dollars!"

"Hello, Julius," Grandpa Max said, coming into the room. "Eric, this is my uncle Julius." Eric nodded. He had seen Uncle Julius years ago, but his memory was not of such a small and ugly man.

"Is there coffee, Eric?" Max asked. "You'll have coffee, Julius?"

"I don't mind."

Eric went into the kitchen and lit the burner under the coffee. He found cups and saucers and brought them out to the dining alcove.

"In my day, believe me, I've hated plenty of people, but never like I hate that *shmuck* Weill," Julius was saying.

"You shouldn't let him bother you," Grandpa said.

"A know-it-all who don't know beans. Every time I have to talk to him it rubs me the wrong way. Let's get rid of him."

"He's a partner," Max said. "We can't get rid of him. You don't have to talk to him, I'll do the talking."

"Telling me, 'They don't do things like that today.' What does he think, I don't know how they do things today? I didn't get where I am laying in a stupor while time marched on."

"Ignore him."

"Inherited money, third generation money, is what he's got. If he had to go out and actually make a dollar he'd be dead. All he's ever had to do is be a big shot on boards. Temples, homes for the aged, hospitals. He makes me sick."

Eric brought in the coffee and poured it. He poured himself another cup, too.

"And while we're on the subject of sick," Julius said, "I'm going into the hospital this afternoon."

"Why?"

"Gall bladder. They're gonna cut tomorrow."

"I didn't know you had a condition."

"Neither did I. It never bothered me."

"So why are they cutting?"

Julius spooned sugar into his coffee and stirred it. "The condition showed up when I went last week for my regular routine checkup. I use Shapiro. You know him?"

"No."

"Tops, the best! I've been using him for years. I say to him, 'Shapiro, what's the difference if it never bothered me?' He says, 'Julius, you're not a young man, you're eighty-two, suppose it starts to act up two, three years from now?' 'So I'll have time to worry two, three years from now, Shapiro,' I say. 'By then it may be too late,' he says. 'At that age it might be too dangerous to operate, but it's your decision, Julius.' I say, 'Shapiro, if you advise, then what's to decide? You're the doctor.' "

"You're sure you're doing the right thing?" Max said, shaking his head.

"You think I want trouble, special diets, when I'm an old man?"

"You're not exactly a spring chicken now, Julius."

"I'm in the pink." He finished his coffee and pushed back his chair. "Keep me advised. Physician's Hospital." He got up.

"Let me know if there's anything I can do," Max said. "I'll come see you in the hospital."

"Thanks for the coffee," Julius said to Eric. "Why don't you get a haircut?"

150

Max walked him to the door. "I almost forgot what I came to tell you, Max. I made you my executor."

Max looked as though Julius had made him a declaration of love. Embarrassed, he coughed. "You'll outlive us all," he said. "You're too stingy to die."

"I didn't know he was a partner," Eric said when the door had closed behind Julius. "I thought nobody talked to him."

The break had come years ago when Max's mother, Anna, had loaned Julius, her baby brother, five thousand dollars, "a fortune in those days," in return for an IOU which her husband, Jacob, had put, they thought, in the vault with the other papers. Jacob, a soft-spoken, gentle, trusting soul who left all practical matters to his hard-headed wife, ran errands, offered fruit to the company, and studied the Talmud with his buddies. He was careless with papers and records, believing them to be superfluous. He carried promises in his heart and stuffed IOUs, deeds, and other trivia in his sweater pocket. After his death, the box in the vault was found to contain nothing but birth certificates, a marriage license, and an expired fire insurance policy. Julius was prospering by then and Anna, aging and supported by her sons, asked Julius if he couldn't find it in his heart to begin paying back the loan. Julius knew that there was no IOU and, therefore, no legal claim on him. He insisted that he had repaid the loan.

"What? When?" Anna gasped. "Not one cent!"

He had given it, he swore, to Jake.

"Jake? Who ever gave money to Jake?" Anna screamed. "Money fell from his hands like oats. Nobody ever gave money to Jake."

Julius stuck to his story. Anna clutched at her breast, promising to die on the spot.

"God should strike me dead," Julius lied.

"Help, I'm dying," Anna moaned, swooning on the sofa. "Somebody get the salts."

It had been a terrific scene. Max had leaped to his mother's side and offered to punch Julius in the nose. Anna, her voice never stronger, bellowed, "Don't hit him, Max, he's your flesh and blood, I'm dying." Max, who had never hit anyone in his life, restrained himself with relief, Julius departed, Anna got up off the sofa, and a little while later everyone went in to dinner.

"We didn't talk to him for years," Max said. "You think he cared?" Then five years ago when Grandma and I took that South American cruise, who should be on the ship sitting at the very next table? He sent over a bottle of champagne. What could I do, ignore him?"

"Bygones are bygones," Julius had coaxed. "Flesh and blood

are thicker than water."

"They live upstairs," Max said. "They just moved in, a ten-room duplex penthouse apartment. They're spending a fortune decorating."

"I thought he was divorced."

"Sophie. His second wife. Come on, the car should be downstairs by now."

"Where are we going?"

"There's a piece of property I want to look at in Briarcliff. I was up half the night with heartburn and I don't feel like driving."

Eric had never driven a Cadillac but Max showed him what was where and then, surprisingly, sat back and trusted him.

"I hope nobody I know sees me," Eric mumbled.

"What's the matter, you ashamed to be seen in a Caddie? I don't know what's with your generation. You have no values."

It was a beautiful day, one of those rare days when the New York sky is really blue and the river, even bluer, defies you to believe it is polluted. Max lapsed into silence, except for an occasional sigh. When they were well out of the city, the soft, early-summer countryside began to heal him.

"Who needs it!" he said.

"Needs what?" In spite of himself, Eric was enjoying the feel of the car. It was like driving a cloud.

"Not that I didn't have plenty of aggravation in the dress business," Max mused. "But there, at least, I was my own boss, the whole *shmear.* I made a decision and that was that. But with all these partners I have to be a diplomat, a nursemaid, a psychiatrist."

Max shrugged. "Force of habit. I've worked all my life. I had my first job at the age of five. Did I ever tell you that? Carrying pots of *cholent* to the bakery oven for the neighbors."

"What's *cholent?*"

"A stew. A piece of meat, carrots, potatoes, beans, cooked very slow for hours, the longer the better. Where we lived on the lower East Side, most of the Jews were Orthodox. They couldn't light matches on the *shabbis,* so they couldn't light the stove to cook. A baker in the neighborhood let them use his oven. They'd fix a big pot of *cholent* and it would sit in the baker's oven overnight. I had a regular *cholent* route, a nickel a round trip. Those pots nearly broke my back." He laughed. "And every nickel I made, I gave my mother. I was paying my own way and even at the age of five it made me feel like a *mensch.*"

Eric had grown up in New Rochelle. He thought of his friend

Lenny who delivered the evening papers. In bad weather his stylish blonde mother drove him in the family Lincoln Continental, pausing in front of each house long enough for Lenny to hurl the papers through the car window.

"A couple of years later I could write," Max said. "I could write not only English but Hebrew and Yiddish, so I invested in some stationery, got a folding chair and an orange crate, painted a sign, and set up shop on Second Avenue. I wrote letters for the immigrants to their people in the old country." His customers were mostly prostitutes, faded beauties with tears in their eyes, dictating in Yiddish to Max, assuring the old people that everything was hunky-dory in America, and enclosing a dollar. "I got three cents for a short letter, a nickel if it went over a page. I was seven years old and I wasn't a laborer any more, I was a white-collar worker."

Eric thought of the lemonade stands of his own childhood. Frozen lemonade and paper cups supplied by his mother. Ten cents a cup and the proceeds were clear profit, spent almost at once at the local toy store.

"I had all kinds of jobs in my day," Max said, motioning Eric to turn off the parkway at the next exit. "When I was twelve I spent a whole summer delivering orders for Julius. He had a delicatessen then. I worked fourteen, fifteen hours a day, mostly for tips. It wasn't easy to get tips in those days. Most of the time you didn't see the people you were delivering to. You sent the orders up in the dumbwaiter." He chuckled. "I used to send up notes with the orders. Little Poems. I hope the pastrami brings you joy, but don't forget to tip the boy."

Eric laughed.

"That summer was the first time I kept any of the money I earned. I kept half. I wanted a bicycle."

"Did you get it?"

"I did and I didn't," Max said. He was silent for a moment, remembering. "By the end of the summer I had enough money. The bike I wanted was in a store way over on the West Side. A beauty, I'll never forget it. I rushed over after work and bought it. I'd never ridden a bike but it didn't look hard. The minute I got on it, I fell off. It took me hours to get home because I'd made up my mind to ride the bike the whole way, not to walk it one step. I must have fallen a hundred times but by the time I got to my street I'd learned how to ride, though I was still wobbly and the streetcar tracks kept getting in my way. I was late getting home and my mother was worried. She was hanging out of the window looking for me and when she saw me she gave a yell you

153

could have heard in Canarsie. I guess I looked terrible, my knees bloody, my clothes torn and dirty. She took the bike away and I never saw it again. Later, I found out she'd sold it. I never saw the money, either."

Though it was hard to believe that Grandpa Max had ever been a little boy, Eric was moved almost to tears. "She must have been a terrible woman, Great-grandma Anna," he said.

"She feared for my life," Max said, making allowances. "I was her firstborn, the oldest son. My father wasn't going to be able to provide for their old age so it was up to me. Turn here. It's just ahead."

They spent the next hour looking at a piece of land, most of it covered by a sprawling motel. Since he owned the motel, Max must have been familiar with the property, which was leased to the people who operated it, but still they circled it slowly three or four times.

"How come you own the motel and not the land?" Eric said. "What good is the land if someone else owns what's on it?"

"The people who run the motel pay rent for the land, but we should have it for protection. If I can pick it up at the right price, it should yield eleven, twelve percent. A very safe investment."

They drove from there to a bank in the village where Max talked for twenty minutes with the bank president, an austerely solemn man, as suavely self-effacing as a funeral director. By contrast, Eric noted, his grandfather's vitality seemed like an act of aggression, inexplicable since Max was as conservatively dressed, as neatly barbered, his voice only a fraction more carrying. The atmosphere of the bank, ignoring the trend toward chumminess, was hushed and forbidding, but Max was not at all intimidated by it as Eric might have been, and although his grandfather had said he had come for information, as far as Eric could see, it was Max who did all the talking. Through some mysterious process, however, he came away in full possession of the facts he wanted.

Julius was operated on the following day. He nearly died. Eric went with Max to see him a few days later, by which time he was very much alive. The operation had shrunk him somewhat, but there were spots of color on his cheeks and his eyes were beady with anger. His wife Sophie was at his bedside. Much younger than Julius, she was a small woman of fading prettiness with graying fair hair. She seemed stupefied with weariness.

"He's impossible," she groaned to Max. "Everybody in the hospital is his enemy. He thinks they're all out to kill him."

154

"You saw with your own eyes," Julius rasped. "They turned me over like I was a bag of sand."

"If you weren't such a bastard maybe they'd treat you more gently."

"It's their bounden duty to treat me gently no matter what kind of bastard I am. They took an oath."

"It's your imagination."

"And the food is poison."

"It's the best food in any hospital. As good as a hotel."

"They wake me up all hours of the night with their thermometers and their blood pressures and their specimens. What's the matter they can't take care of those items in the daytime? I'm a sick man, I need my rest."

"*Im*-possible. The doctor says it's a good sign." Sophie sighed. Clearly, if she had ever had the stamina for Julius, it had long since drained away.

Max changed the subject. He told Julius he had gone to see the motel land and that he thought they should try to buy it.

"So buy it," Julius said.

"I talked to Higginbottom at the bank," Max said. "Six people own the land jointly and they're all willing to sell except one, a woman named Scribner. They're trying to come to some kind of terms with her."

"Go see her," Julius said. "Talk to her."

"Let's wait and see how her partners make out with her. We don't want to be too anxious."

"Sophie, show Max the card from that *shmuck* Weill," Julius said, his anger coming to a boil again.

Sophie shuffled through a handful of cards on the bedside table and handed one of them to Max. Eric, peering over his grandfather's shoulder, saw a crude cartoon of a man lolling in splendor and luxury, surrounded by a harem of shapely nurses, sipping a highball through a straw. The message read: "We're slaving in the market / While you have yourself a ball / You may have lost the bladder / But you haven't lost the gall."

Eric and Max laughed.

"Give it to me," Julius snapped, thrusting forth a naked, gnarled arm. He grabbed the card and tore it to shreds.

Without Eric quite knowing how, the days slipped by, assuming a pattern entirely unplanned by him. Max had appropriated him. There was never any discussion about it, nor any official recognition, but after that first day he had become a sort of factotum to Max, making phone calls for him, typing letters, sorting mail, chauffering him, running errands. Though he knew he wasn't really of much use, Max seemed to like having him about, a perpetual eye and ear, to heighten his sense of himself. Perhaps he was lonely. He had, after all, spent half a century surrounded by a small army of employees, many of whom had been with him throughout his career. Eric fell into his role with no resistance, partly because Max's energy had infected him, and partly because he was becoming fascinated by a way of life, of seeing it and living it, that, though it had spawned him, and though he would finally bury it, was entirely alien to him. He grew increasingly more curious, amused, puzzled, and, in a way he couldn't define, uneasy.

About a week after Julius came out of the hospital, Grandma Tess asked him and Sophie to dinner. Julius seemed fully recovered, but Sophie looked even more frayed than she had at the hospital, and there were dark circles under her eyes. She had two stiff drinks before dinner.

"He's still convalescing," she confided. She had a peculiarly flat voice, devoid of all energy. "It's awful having him in the house all day. With the painters and the carpenters and all kinds of mechanics in and out for him to holler at, I'm going out of my mind."

"It'll be over soon," Grandma Tess consoled. "He looks marvelous."

Eric tried to imagine how Sophie would have been acting at that moment if Julius had died. He could see nothing in their attitude toward each other that faintly resembled what he thought of as love. He had assumed that what bound Sophie to Julius was his money, but Max had told him that only a fraction of Julius's fortune would go to her, not enough to keep her for more than a year or two, and that Sophie knew it. Max, shocked when he'd learned this, had told Julius that it was shameful, but Julius had been adamant. "It's not like she's my own flesh and blood," Julius had said. "When I met her she was a total stranger."

"You've been married more than twelve years," Max reminded him.

"If I leave her my money how do I know she won't marry some gigolo, some young son of a bitch who'll take it away?" The thought of the unknown adventurer, handsome and gentile, racing his Jaguar through perfumed nights to gambling casinos where he would lose, drinking champagne and seducing beautiful starlets, courtesy of Julius by way of the foolish Sophie, made Julius livid. "Nothing doing!" he screamed.

"You have to trust *some*body," Max said.

"Why? Human nature is human nature, even Sophie's."

Julius dominated the conversation at dinner. He'd had his first outing since the operation that morning, just a brief one to try out his strength. His man, Benjamin, had driven him in the chocolate and mocha Rolls to the chiropodist.

"He couldn't believe my feet," Julius said, deftly spooning grapefruit. "'Just to look at your feet,' the chiropodist says to me, "you could be a boy of fifteen. Not a bunion, not a corn, not even a callous.'"

"A nice topic for the dinner table," Sophie said.

"Then why do you go to a chiropodist?" Eric asked.

"Maintenance."

"Weill thinks he knows the Scribner woman," Max said. "He's going to talk to her about selling the motel property."

"*Weill*," Julius said, his eyes glazing with hate. "You know I can't stand him. If he's in on the deal, count me out."

"Of course he's in on it," Max said. "It's the corporation that's buying the property."

"The least said about that Weill the better," Julius muttered.

It must have been then that Julius resolved to do what he did the very next morning, though they didn't find out about it until the end of the week when Max had Eric dial Higginbottom at the Briarcliff bank.

"Higginbottom?" Max said into the phone when Eric handed it to him. "They making any headway with the Scribner woman on the Open Arms property?" There was a brief pause and then Max barked, "What do you mean, *sold? Sold?* . . . When? . . . Why didn't you call me? You knew I . . . What do you mean you thought I knew? Who? . . . Impossible! . . . That dirty lowdown . . . What do you mean, for *me?* . . . No, naturally I didn't know." There was a longer pause while Max's face turned from pale to purple. His eyes were wild but he was silent, listening. At one point he pounded his fist on the desk with such force that all the pencils and paper clips jumped. Eric jumped, too. Max began to bellow and his anger was so naked, so pure, that it scared Eric out of the room. He tried to disappear into a corner of the living room sofa but in a few minutes Max stormed in and began to pace back and forth.

"Take it easy, Grandpa," Eric said. "You'll have a heart attack."

"That dirty double-crossing son of a bitch!"

"Calm down. Think of your health."

Max's hand went to the heart side of his chest.

"You're right. Nothing's worth that." He stopped pacing and sat down across the room from Eric, breathing heavily. "The bastard. He pulled the whole deal off in about three hours. First he saw Mrs. Scribner. It took him about half an hour to convince her. She thought he was charming."

"Julius?"

"Some people are charmed by snakes. Then he rounded up the other partners, the lawyers, had the contract drawn and signed and gave them a check. The crook!" Eric thought he detected a hint of admiration buried in the anger in Max's voice. "What's more, he paid eighteen thousand less than we offered."

"Can he do that?" Eric asked.

"What do you mean, can he do it? He did it."

"I mean, aren't there any ethics in business? Can people in the same corporation bid against each other?"

A light came into Max's eyes. "Ethics," he said, and the word was like a revelation to him. "Ethics. You know, Eric, I think you might have something there. Go fix me an Alka-Seltzer."

By the time Eric had the bromide fizzing, Max was on the phone with his lawyer. He took the glass from Eric and drained it. "Sorry, Irving," he said, turning aside to burp. "Go ahead, Irving. You were saying?"

What Irving was saying was that the corporation could sue Julius and had an excellent chance of winning, but was Max sure that he wanted to sue his own uncle? He most certainly was. Full speed ahead.

"We'll get that bastard," he said when he'd hung up.

"It's a game," Eric said, seeing it all clearly.

"This time he really went too far. He thought he could put one over on me. Well, I've got the same blood in my veins."

"It's Monopoly," Eric said.

"What are you talking about?"

Blacks were being slaughtered, babies napalmed, good men assassinated. The air was foul, fish were dying, chemicals were slowly poisoning them all. Thousands of people were drowning in tidal waves, being sucked into earthquakes, suffocating under mountains, starving in arid lands, being held hostage in airplanes or gunned down in airports by desperate men, while Julius and Max played Monopoly over a piece of land that wasn't even there.

"Listen, Grandpa. This business . . . all this with money, buying and selling and being shrewd, it's just a game to you, isn't it?"

"A game?" Max shouted. "What are you, crazy?"

But even so, Eric thought, was it any less valid than anything else? Money, power, philosophy, glass beads? What difference did it make? Once you had gotten through the business of arranging the conditions of your life, your survival, weren't you stuck with the game? Perhaps the means swallowed the end. Perhaps there was no end.

A few days later, Julius's mail brought him the word that he was being sued. The complainant was the corporation but it was at Max's door that he instantly presented himself, his little monkey face distorted with suppressed rage.

"What's this all about?"

"It speaks for itself," Max said.

"I want to hear it from your own mouth."

Max shrugged. "As a private party, you bid against your own corporation. It's unethical. The corporation is suing you. A, B, C!"

"You're actually suing me?"

"The corporation."

"Your own uncle?"

"You're a double-crosser."

"After all I did for you?"

"What did you do for me?"

"I gave you a job, you were just a little snotnose kid."

"*I* worked for *you*," Max yelled. "Like a horse, fifteen hours a day, delivering your lousy delicatessen, sweeping your floors. For practically nothing."

"It wasn't easy to get jobs those days, especially for little kids."

"My feet were already bigger than yours. You were wearing my outgrown shoes."

"I gave you advice. I was like a father to you, a big brother. I taught you."

"You robbed my mother, your own sister. Now me. You'd rob yourself if you could figure a way to make a buck out of it."

Julius hunched his shoulders, then composed his face and said, "Listen, Max, let's be reasonable. Bygones are bygones. I only wanted to cut out Weill. I bought that land for you, too, fifty-fifty."

"I don't want it," Max shouted. "You think I could take it?"

"All right, suit yourself," Julius said. "I can't stand here and argue all day. I'm a convalescent."

"Why don't you just sell it back to the corporation," Max said, his voice a little calmer. "Save us all a lot of heartache."

"Over my dead body. Why don't you just drop the suit and

forget it?"

"I'm managing a corporation," Max said. "I have to consider the best interests of that corporation."

"Okay, Max, okay. I'll see you in court." He began, briskly, to leave. "By the way, Max," he said, pausing at the door, "how much is two and a half percent of three million dollars?"

"Seventy-five thousand," Max, the computer, said. "Why?"

"If I'm not mistaken, two and a half percent is the standard executor's fee," Julius said, closing the door behind him. Max swore at the closed door.

"What did that mean?" Eric asked.

"He was telling me that if I sue I'm no longer executor of his estate and that I'm out seventy-five thousand dollars. He was trying to bribe me."

Slowly, the mills of the law began to grind. The days went by. Max had a new proposition, a shopping center that took him and Eric to New Jersey several times a week. Then, late one afternoon, Sophie appeared hesitantly at their door.

"I want you all to come to dinner tomorrow night," she said firmly.

Max just as firmly refused. He and Julius were no longer on speaking terms. Sophie persisted. Tears came to her eyes. "I can't do a thing with him, God knows," she said, "but I can't allow this to happen." Tess, too, coaxed Max.

"How can I have dinner with someone I'm suing?" Max said.

"Be big."

"To celebrate the apartment," Sophie said. "Here we have all this beautiful new furniture, it cost a fortune, and who can we invite?"

There was no mistaking that the apartment had cost a fortune; every penny of it showed. Eric wiped his feet on the doormat for a long time before allowing himself to cross the threshold. The walls were either paneled or antique-mirrored, the floors ankle deep from wall to wall, and there was a fireplace with a real fire in it though air-conditioners throbbed away to make it bearable.

"Welcome to my humble home," Julius said.

The first awkward moments were passed touring the rooms with Julius as guide detailing origins, ingredients, even prices. Eric, stumbling along in his grandparents' wake, was overcome by a sense of unreality, as though he had wandered out of his own life, whatever that was, onto the set of a 1940s movie. He listened while Max and Tess politely admired everything, but was relieved when Max finally took exception to the mammoth white Steinway grand.

160

"What do you *need* it for?" Max said. "Nobody plays."

"Need, shmeed," Julius said. "At my stage of life, a man doesn't have to need."

During dinner, which was simple but good, Eric could sense beneath the small talk the growing tension, and he waited hopefully for the obligatory scene. It came with the blueberry pie and coffee when, with the solemnity of a carefully planned moment, Sophie nervously said, "Listen, Julius. Max. I want you to iron out your differences."

"Mind your business," Julius said.

"Whose business is it if not mine?" Sophie said. "They're my family, too, Who've we got, God knows?"

"So why should I be any different?" Max asked. "*Nobody* talks to Julius. Not even his own daughter, I hear."

"Shhh!" Tess said.

"It's no accident," Max said. "What does he care about friends or family? He only cares about being rich. He's not a nice man. Even you have to admit it, Sophie. What he lacks, he has no *ethics.*"

"*Ethics?*" Julius snorted.

"You think that's not important?" Eric felt called upon to say. It was he who had supplied the word to define the issue. "If people have no ethics, no morals, they might as well be animals." Julius turned to look at him briefly, as though trying to remember who he was.

"Ethics," he said again, turning back to Max. "Where your mother and I came from, Max, they didn't have much in the line of ethics. Pogroms they had. Dogs attacking us they had."

"That was a long time ago. It was a different world."

"Maybe for you it was a different world. For me it was my world. When I came to this country, just a little kid, I was over three weeks in the hold of a stinking ship like cattle herded together, pigs in a pen. And I was hungry all the time." He held up his hands to stave off interruption. "If I didn't steal I'd have starved to death on that ship. You know how I made it? I went where I smelled vomit, that's how. From that person, who was too sick to need it, to care, I stole food. I *had* to steal because nobody gave, not even to a little kid and believe me scared. Your Mama came here first, Max, two years before. She sent me the ticket and the fifty cents to take the taxi wagon from the boat and the address written on a piece of paper to show the wagon driver. With her new name. Because when they got to Castle Gardens and your Papa gave his name to the officer to fill out the papers, the officer didn't have the time to listen so good so he wrote out some other name. You know that, Max? You know that you haven't even got your own name?"

"I know, I know," Max nodded. "So what's in a name?"

"Ethics! Dozens of people crowded scared to death in a taxi wagon with their scraps of paper and their fifty centses and not a word of English and all of us dumped like a load of garbage practically in the same block. The streets were supposed to be paved with gold but right away I saw they were paved with *dreck*. It was a jungle. And what was I? A little *shtunk*, weak and ugly. If I walked in the next street they threw rocks at me and beat me up and called me *kike* and *sheeny*. What did I have to fight my way out of that jungle with? Ethics?"

He paused and looked lovingly around the room at the gleaming crystal chandelier, at the silver glowing behind the leaded glass panes of the cherrywood breakfront.

"Others came out," Eric said, frightened. "They came out decent."

"It was a jungle for me, too," Max said.

"Listen, Max," Julius said. "I am what I am. I'm eighty-two years old. I'm on top of the world. You know what you can do with your ethics."

In the end, there was no lawsuit. The corporation bought Julius out, but he kept the land beneath the motel and he reverted to what he had always been and should have remained, a lone operator unencumbered by partners or affiliates. As Max said, "A hawk doesn't fly in flocks."

When the summer was over, Eric went back to school. Though he still didn't have any idea who he was, he was beginning to understand why.

Doggedly, he went on with the search for his own life.

DOUGLAS LAWDER

Lake Light

You wake up with wet-light spilling from limbs—this lake shimmer
filling the room, the ceiling water-
rippled, walls of shine.

The kitchen's a chamber of light:
the coffee pot struck with a water gong,
bright clatter of spoons,
light shaking through the faucet's flow
—a flame in sun shine,
cellophane burning.

The broad lake's squarred
to the living room mirror, now
made perfectly round and deep
as a well by the glass top table.

It's a day when fish
flick at the window pane
or hang in the pooled light
of the polished floor.
Bubbles breaking ride up the wall
—a bright chain of small moons.

It's a dream of watery light descending,
of evening's long reach,
its slow flutter of shine on the far wall
like water thinning and thinning.
A shiver of doused light.
A splashing through shallows
into the darker and
darker layers of sleep

Beginnings

With first snow light
that's never been inside before
comes through windows.
From off miles and miles of fields outside a snow shine pours
through pure as paper
and there's a line
of icicles hanging from the roof
—bright possibilities—like new nails.
Now walls seem to fall away,
the ceiling rising like a dome
and these typewriter keys
are rounded in white
like small incipient suns.

DAVID MCALEAVEY

For My Mother

Old low mountains, gorges, water
falling, steel footbridges stained
& rusted by rust-filled mist—

in my childhood album, a two-snapshot
day: one, ore ships loading
below a Michigan bluff, the other

a meadow where you kneel
giving documentation
to a wildflower unusually early

or large or out of habitat. You'd
posed for my father, at first
reluctantly, but then happily,

conceding that you & the flower
were a flower, that you & he were
a special flower not to be caught

except slyly, kiddingly, through
a photo of the flower you
point to, smiling, in summer sun.

I took you too, not with his large
Argus, not in color, but with
my clumsy Kodak, wanting to share

the moment, to declare in one
wordless sentence a boy's bursting
black-&-white gladness,
the primrose, the iron hills.

Night Hill Walk

1.

we walk up the hill at night
lit the modern rural way
high-watt yard lamps on barns & tall poles
sideways flashes from the highway below us
pale overturned bowls of scattered towns

2.

fireflies so profuse sight
tricks us till we conceive a screen, on which play
intelligent Brownian worms transforming the whole
surrounding wall of woods into a rebus
that shows us as we are: aliens, clowns

or we are not clowns, are right
to test the world's malevolence, right to play
at fear like shocked opossums who'll
never get used to fuss
or eeriness—before which we too keep our heads down

3.

into the wind you recite
words about vanity as if to say
the universe has a hollow core or is a coal
burned & burning & to be burned, is an abyss
eating itself & its surround

overhead & across the fields the lights
of cars & trucks sweep & sway
on & by our nearly hidden figures on this knoll
demarking us
whose consciousness is always in its bounds

166

vulnerabilities in me quiver here despite
my words, & yours, which in the day
amuse me—now these swooping beams rake & troll
the hillside, blind calamitous
hooks which do not mean to but which do astound

4.

from the hill we see close by a white
spire ringed by spotlights, one aimed away
arcing off wide & high making an infinite accidental hole
towards what is beyond us
& past all creeds & gowns

we cannot draw any closer tonight
tho I see your face deep-wrinkled your temples gray
even in this light & know: if love could make whole
what ages or bleeds . . .—it has
never been so hard just to stand still on the ground

5.

I lean my head back to face the stars, trite
tired unhappy with the way mind repays
the senses by holding back, holding out to be sole
arbiter of things & then gets scared & deserts us
deserting too the sweet of new-cut hay souring down

6.

midnight
a long Amtrak sashays
through, sounding different rackets as it tolls
the looser ties over culverts, blows its tattoos
& leaves a new silence all around

and in the quiet
beside a tree we say
hello, hello to the moles and voles
crickets & toads, interrupting them yes with our tremendous
human voice but also comforting the spiders tending their
    nets among ivy & creeper on the warm summer ground

Illuminations

We found a cool clean room in Bonn
with a louvered skylight where we saw
fine snow fall as we dropped off to sleep.

In the melting clear morning
we saw through it again, though
only depthlessness, blue sky.

Downstairs someone part sang,
part hummed one tune, phrase by idiot
phrase without progression. From out of

earthly monotonies streaking clarities
may pierce even the hardest headed;
but reckoning love to be no vision

& unattached to place or private wish
(mere wish), we turned to each other,
under eiderdown, in that pine-scented
room, to make what is only between us.

PETER MEINKE

Ruby Lemons

"Ruby Lemons," Jack gushed all at once, turning from his
typewriter. "High ruby lemons." He smiled his crazy smile at
Mr. Mason and nodded his head wildly up and down. The monkey leaped from his lap to the top of the china closet without
seeming to touch anything else. Three plates with pictures of
churches on them were balanced on top of the closet and, leaning precariously against the wall, rolled back and forth as the
monkey paced swiftly in front of them, from one side to the
other.

"Pesky, get down here!" Aunt Dodo cried. "He means high
bilirubins. Jack has *always* had a high bilirubin count and they
don't know what to do about it." They all turned to Jack for
approval and he shuffled his feet vigorously.

"He never gets it right," continued Aunt Dodo, while Aunt
Lottie and Aunt Gussie smiled at Jack and he smiled hugely
back. "But it always comes out like real words. He's a pet, is
what he is." Jack all but nodded his head off his thin shoulders.
"Poetry," he said.

"You know what Jack calls Miss Pennyfeather? Mrs. Ferry
Weather!" said Aunt Gussie. The three grey-haired sisters
laughed and Jack joined them with an explosive snort. "Ferry
Weather!" he said, and turned back to his typing. Mr. Mason
tried to smile, too. The monkey swung back down and settled in
Jack's lap again, leaving the cups in the china closet swaying in
unison on their hooks, like a line of chorus girls in hoop skirts.

Two of the sisters *had* been chorus girls, if only briefly, and
Aunt Lottie had been a lead singer in church groups and little
theatres; they all were musical, even in their sixties and
seventies. They liked nothing more than to gather around the
small black spinet and "sing the old songs again," with Aunt
Lottie playing and Jack providing a surprisingly good, if erratic,

male tenor. Jack suffered from cerebral palsy but for some unknown reason music seemed to clear the blocked roadways of his brain and he could follow along perfectly, though he had a tendency to go on after the others had stopped, repeating, soulfully, "alive alive-o" at the end of "Cockles and Mussles" four or five times before realizing the music was over.

They lived in a tall grey skinny house in St. Paul, somewhat isolated because of vacant lots on either side and a practice field in the back that belonged to nearby Hamline University. In the summer several huge lilac bushes gave it a festive air but in the long winter the wind banged the house so hard that its curtains blew as if the ancient windows were open. There were three small bedrooms upstairs, one for each sister; the downstairs was a classic example of "shotgun" architecture: from the front, four rooms lined up in a row—the living room (with the piano), dining room, kitchen, and, in the back, Jack's bedroom. He liked to sit at his window and watch the college girls run back and forth, awkwardly flailing their field hockey sticks at the bounding ball.

"Hole!" he would shout when one of the girls scored, as elated as she was.

Jack was twenty-seven and his interest in girls was as much a topic of conversation in the house as the high number of bilirubins in his blood. In fact, Uncle Frank used to say, when he caught Jack watching the girls, "Your bilirubins are a little randy today, eh Jack boy?" The sisters were more sedate and circumspect, though they tried to interest some of the girls to come play checkers with Jack, because he enjoyed their company so much, and the sisters thought it was healthy, "someone close to his own age." But one of the girls had got frightened, over nothing at all, and this had brought Miss Pennyfeather and the shadowy disturbance of the State into their lives.

Aunt Gussie, at sixty-four the smallest and youngest of the sisters, worked as a part-time librarian at Hamline, and the last girl she had brought home, a petite brunette sophomore named Thelma Freese, had been nervous from the start. Gussie had explained about the cerebral palsy and how Jack loved to play checkers and needed the company of young people; but his appearance had clearly startled her and, to be honest, Jack had been in one of his more manic moods. He had been one of those children who couldn't swallow, the muscles of his tongue and throat working backward to propel the food out instead of in, and he still looked starved: when animated, his thin, twisted body jerked about like an emaciated puppet.

Most of the girls had been big tough farm girls from Min-

170

nesota, who took his looks in stride and who could squeeze energetically back when Jack surprised them with his powerful left-handed shake (although he could type with his right hand he had difficulty raising it). As Aunt Lottie would say, these girls didn't know diddly about checkers and didn't expect to win, taking pleasure in Jack's gleeful capture of their pieces. And when they said good-by, after tea and homemade honey buns, the tears in Jack's eyes were so genuine that they forgot their embarrassment at not understanding what he was saying, as he talked faster and faster, trying to hold them. Each one was beautiful to him, said Aunt Dodo, he fell in love at every single checker game he ever had, which is why they had to ration them severely, as he was upset and moody for days afterward, mooning at his window, searching out his love among the strong-limbed panting girls galloping back and forth across the hockey field.

But Thelma got scared, or repelled, right away, forgetting to put out her left hand as Aunt Gussie had instructed her, then wincing with pain as Jack squeezed her hand backward.

"Jack's been typing package labels and addresses for almost eight years now," Aunt Dodo explained. "He works for a mail-order company and makes very good money." This was not entirely true, as the pay was pitiful, but the sisters were proud of Jack's job and constantly praised him for it. He was a slow typist, but faultless, a perfectionist: every address centered, every letter correct. And over the years his hands and fingers had grown strong, at least compared to the rest of his underweight and undersized body. His large pale head wavered unevenly on a stalk of a neck; beneath a high forehead his blue eyes were long-lashed and intelligent, with an upsetting ability to enlarge enormously at moments of excitement or frustration.

"Do you like chickens?" Jack asked, in a rush. When he smiled, the gold in his teeth glinted richly. Any other girl, said Aunt Dodo, would have known he was talking about checkers, but Thelma seemed unable to make the tiniest leap of imagination, and this in turn made Jack self-conscious and nervous. Some of the other girls had put him so at ease that he was able to talk very well; long, complicated sentences came tumbling out of him, only slightly garbled. At times he was so pleased with what he said that he'd have to excuse himself, and go look in the mirror, tilting his head as if thinking, *So that's what I looked like when I said that!* But Thelma just looked puzzled no matter what he said, and turned helplessly toward the sisters.

Perhaps to control herself, she played checkers with grim determination and intensity, growing more and more angry as Jack mirthfully marched across the board, moving very fast and without apparent thought. Although Thelma was small, she had prominent breasts and Jack stared at them constantly. This was a trait, the sisters claimed, that he picked up from Uncle Frank who, as he headed into his sixties, would sit on the porch watching the college girls go by on their bicycles. When a particularly pretty one would pass, he would stomp his feet and bang his head on the porch railing.

Thelma's face had turned a deep red and it was hard to say which emotion was causing it. In the third game, when she had jumped one of Jack's pieces only to suffer a double-jump in return, she cried, "Stop looking at me like that!" so startling Jack that his arm twitched, sweeping the pieces off the board, and they clattered and rolled on the parquet floor. The monkey leaped off his lap with a shriek and began scooping up the checkers with his long black clever fingers, carrying them to the top of the china closet. In the confusion, Jack began to cry, his head on the table, his body racked with convulsive sobs. Aunt Dodo wrapped her arms consolingly around him, but he only sobbed louder. Thelma jumped up, ran out of the house, and—Aunt Gussie found out later, when she returned Thelma's abandoned jacket—complained to the Dean about "that madhouse" on the edge of campus. The Dean had his secretary get in touch with the proper social service organization, and the end result had been the initial visit of Miss Pennyfeather, which had not been an unqualified success.

She was really quite nice, though it was difficult to explain to her what Jack was doing in a house with three old ladies to whom he was not related, and who had not adopted him. Wasn't he dangerous? Miss Pennyfeather wanted to know; he had apparently badly frightened Miss Freese.

"She frightened *him*," Aunt Dodo said heatedly. "No one has spoken to him like that since he picked up Frank's revolver five years ago!"

"What?" said Miss Pennyfeather.

Lottie's husband had been a policeman, Aunt Dodo explained, pointing to the pair of handcuffs hanging from a hook on the side of the china closet, and one time Jack had picked up Frank's service revolver. It was empty, of course, not like the time Lottie herself had picked one up, but when Jack playfully pointed it at him, Frank had walked up to the boy and slapped him across the face for his own good. Jack had cried for weeks, it seemed, but he eventually got over it because basically he understood that Frank had hit him because he loved him. And no one had spoken sharply to Jack since that time.

"We think Jack understands *everything*," Aunt Dodo concluded, "He just gets it bottled up inside him."

Jack was the son of another policeman who had joined the St. Paul force about twelve years ago. Uncle Frank was the man's immediate superior and quickly found out that the boy was a source of despair, financial and otherwise, for his parents. They began bringing Jack over on weekends to be watched by the three sisters, and then eventually during the week, too, where he was cared for by Aunt Dodo, the oldest, who had recently retired from teaching at the age of sixty-two because of a chronically goutish leg that made standing for long periods of time impossible. Aunt Dodo had taught typing, and she continued to do what came naturally to her: she taught Jack to type, to the great amazement of his parents, though not to Frank and her sisters. "She could teach the Pope to eat pork," said Uncle Frank, who had mixed-up notions of other religions' dietary practices.

It was a perfect arrangement, emotionally and practically. At the time, Aunt Dodo and Aunt Gussie, neither of whom had married, lived upstairs, and Uncle Frank and Aunt Lottie, childless, lived below. They were a passionate family, fond of music, politics, pinochle, checkers, and cribbage, not to mention the monkey, Pesky, whom they had acquired when Lottie shot the organ grinder. There had been burglaries in the neighborhood; Frank had been teaching her to use a small derringer when he was called to the phone, and the gun had gone off, according to Lottie, by some form of spontaneous combustion, shooting through the front window and slightly wounding a passing organ grinder named Ugo Pesti, whose name they thought to be Pesky until they saw it written down. They took him into the house for some first aid and saw him several times after that for the purpose of negotiation, the end result being a small settlement in cash and the purchase of Pesky, a stout capuchin monkey whose humorous expression and tonsured head gave him the look of a miniature Chaucerian friar. Frank had tried to protest.

"What do we want with some damned African monkey swinging through the house by his tail?" he said. "We'll all get fleas and start jibbering like Tarzan." Here he beat his chest, and the monkey, either thinking he was being called or because Frank was the only other man, promptly jumped on his shoulder and clasped him around the neck. It was the right move to make.

The monkey sipped at, but scarcely lowered, the great reser-

voir of affection and energy the sisters possessed, so when Jack
came into their lives he stepped into a void aching to be filled.
Aunt Dodo, in particular, couldn't get enough of him and Jack
throve under her constant care. He had tended to be sickly,
subject to fits and other disorders, but his health improved steadily as she increased her time with him. Conversely, when Jack
moved into the spare bedroom upstairs (ostensibly so his mother
could get a full-time job), his parents' marriage broke apart almost immediately, as if he had been the cement that held it
together. After a while they divorced and moved to other cities,
leaving Jack behind, though scarcely anything was said and certainly no papers were ever signed: Jack was in his twenties, after
all. Shortly thereafter, Uncle Frank suddenly died, within a week
of retirement ("They gave us his watch, anyway," said Aunt
Lottie). And now, three years after that, the sisters lived on a
combination of social security and small pensions, plus Gussie's
half-time salary. "But the house is paid for," they said, seeing
Miss Pennyfeather's frown, "and Jack has a steady job, too."

Miss Pennyfeather pressed her pretty lips together and shook
her head, causing Jack to imitate her, which he did quite well,
narrowing his eyes like someone who knows there's a mouse in
the soup.

"It's not the money I'm mainly worried about, at least not
yet," she said, looking at the three grey heads lined up on the
couch. "We could even help you on that score." Miss Pennyfeather was sitting in an old black rocker and Jack was in his
chair at the typewriter, Pesky sprawled on his lap. She began to
explain but Aunt Dodo covered her ears, so she stopped.

Aunt Lottie covered her eyes.

Aunt Gussie covered her mouth.

There was a silence while Miss Pennyfeather considered what
to say. Jack broke the spell by turning red and guffawing, bang-
ing his left hand on his knee so that Pesky leaped up to the china
closet.

"Get down here!" Aunt Dodo said, as the sisters lowered their
hands. "Frank used to tell us it looked like three more monkeys
in the house when we sat on the couch together, so we used to do
that to tease him. I'm Hear No Evil," she added somewhat
redundantly.

"Jack loves us to do it, so we try to do it at least once a day,"
said Lottie. Jack was smiling, covering his eyes with his left
hand.

Miss Pennyfeather decided her best resource was her natural
dignity. "What I worry about, frankly, are your ages. *Is* your

174

ages." She hesitated, grammatically puzzled. "What will happen to Jack when you're gone? He's become dependent on you. What if you get sick? It seems to me you have very little leeway for emergencies. Who would you contact?"

The sisters had no idea where Jack's parents were. The mother had gone to St. Louis, Aunt Gussie thought. "But she didn't even like Jack," she whispered as Jack typed. "She was afraid of him. She didn't think he could learn anything."

"When we taught him to play pinochle, she didn't believe us," Aunt Lottie remembered, indignantly. "So we invited her over to watch. But *she* didn't know how to play pinochle herself—can you imagine?—and insisted we were just throwing cards in a pile."

"Jack was so nervous and proud he kept droppir.g the cards," Aunt Dodo put in. "Frank said he was doing it on purpose to throw us off our games."

"Well," said Miss Pennyfeather, "I think we could find the parents. Maybe that's the thing to do. It seems you've done an excellent job with him," she smiled, standing up, "and Miss Freese was just a little overexcited. We just want to do what's best for Jack, the same as you. What I'll do now—I'm just what is called a Preliminary Field Reporter—is to make a report, and you'll be hearing from someone in the agency fairly soon. Thank you very much for the honey buns, they were delicious." As she awkwardly backed out the door the three sisters stared at her without smiling. Jack's hands were frozen above his typewriter and even Pesky seemed to be pointing an accusatory finger.

Mr. Mason, the man from the agency, didn't show up for almost four months, so they had almost talked themselves into believing that he was never going to come. But he came, finally, early in January: snow banked high against the house, and the wind pressed relentlessly against the doors and windows, so that they were sitting inside with heavy sweaters on, drinking tea and playing cards in the kitchen, which was the warmest room in the house. Jack was typing at the table set up between the dining and living rooms, wearing a long stocking cap that Pesky occasionally took a swing at. The Christmas decorations were still up. On the front door hung a lopsided circle of pine cones strung together.

"Jack did that," said Aunt Lottie, letting Mr. Mason in. A large heavyset man with a melancholy air about him, he shivered and kept his long dark coat on as the sisters settled on the couch, shifting and fluttering like birds in a nest. "He did a *lot* of the decorations." The tree had no electric lights but had clumps of tinsel, cutouts of angels and stars, brightly colored paper chains, and a few ornate, obviously aged, Christmas balls.

Mr. Mason had several reports: one from Jack's doctor about the high bilirubin level in Jack's blood, one from Miss Penny-feather, and one from the agency reporting that Jack's mother had still not been found, and that Jack's father didn't know where she was. *He* was a night watchman in Chicago, had re-married, and his new wife had three young children. Jack's father was perfectly happy with the situation as it was; and no wonder, said Mr. Mason.

Aunt Lottie burped loudly. "Cucumbers and radishes always repeat on me," she said. Mr. Mason wasn't sure the sisters had been paying attention. They were waiting for the bottom line. "What we're concerned about," he said slowly, looking at each sister in turn, "is that Jack be protected in case of emergencies. Suppose he starts having seizures again? This is always possible, with a high bilirubin count like his. And you don't even have a car. Another problem is, is he realizing all of his potential? I know," he went on hastily, as the three old women stiffened as one, "that you have done wonders with him and have taught him a great deal. But we aren't quite sure how much he knows or how much he can do."

"He's good at cards," said Aunt Gussie, "and nobody can beat him at checkers! Would you like to try?"

"Chickens," blurted Jack from the typing table.

"No, no," said Mr. Mason, waving his hand. "Not now. I know how good you have been for him, but I have the feeling he would learn even more in a more"—he paused, searching—"*educational* environment."

There was a stunned silence. The sisters looked as if they had been simultaneously slapped. Jack's typewriter stopped.

"Goddam it to hell," cried Aunt Dodo, suddenly, her thin, white hair flying in the draft. "How can you talk like that? If you try to take that boy you'll have to take me, too!" She stood up, lurching on her bad leg, and roughly grabbed Jack's motionless hand. While Jack's eyes bulged until they almost blew out of his head, she snatched Uncle Frank's handcuffs off the china closet and snapped them over his corded twisted wrist and her mottled brittle one. She waved the key in her other hand.

"I'll swallow the key," she shouted, her old voice cracking with fierceness. "I'm ready!"

"Go to it, Dodo," said Aunt Lottie, although the key looked entirely too large to go down without strangling her.

Mr. Mason was not an unreasonable man. He looked nervously at Jack, who was changing color every few seconds. He was thinking many things at once. One was that maybe Jack was keeping these old harridans alive and would continue to do so. Another was, well, he could always keep track of them by a phone call every few months. The last, somewhat ungenerous, one was, simply, if they want him so much, they can have him. Save the State money. He would figure something out, temporarily.

"Very well then," he said, with as much formality as he could muster. "Keep working with him. I'm going to send you some forms and I will expect a report every few weeks." Gussie got up and opened the door for him without saying anything. The icy wind ruffled the Christmas tree, the drying needles dropping off and drifting across the floor. Mr. Mason stepped out into the world.

Gussie pulled the door to, and walked over to the typewriter, where Aunt Dodo and Jack clustered in a state of shock. She took the key, opened the handcuffs, and hung them back on the china closet. Jack put his head against Aunt Dodo's withered breast and they stayed there, the truest lovers in the world. Aunt Lottie sat down at the spinet; it was going to be a night for singing.

"Lily robins," Jack said quietly. "Goddam it to hell."

"Listen to him," said Aunt Dodo. "Finally he gets something right."

TAYLOR MORRIS

Fires

My life seems to be a series of dreams from which I continually wake up, sigh gratefully "Thank God," get out of bed to march off and dream again. Recently, however, my luck seemed to take a different turn. The New England Colony for Creative Artists, in southern Maine near a little town called Limerick, had accepted me for a three and a half month stay, from March 15 till June 30. I had obtained a full fellowship; meals, lodging and working studio free and at my disposal for the above period.

A friend of mine, a painter, had returned less than a year before and his description of the place was not quite believable. "Absolute privacy," said he. "In fact . . . no one can come to your studio unless he or she is invited. A basket lunch is *brought* to you and left at your door. Yes," he went on, "it may be one of the few places in the world where the artist's wishes are deferred to, totally—where the artist is treated as he should be."

I racked my brains to remember what I had put down on that simple application but could remember very little. "If accepted," it asked, "what do you intend to work on while at the colony?"

And I had answered, "A seven volume poem-novel."

By far the most ambitious plan I had ever conceived, and perhaps for that reason. . . .

Well, and what *did* I work on while there? It would be easier to begin with what it wasn't—yes, perhaps the length, breadth, depth of my ambition was one reason for the odd turn which my work did take—and no, it wasn't any seven volume poem-novel.

Did I feel any guilt about my pledge to do a certain major project when, in fact, I didn't even begin it? After all there are many and *many* young creators; deserving, aspiring young artists out in the world looking for exactly my situation. I had time, a beautiful studio, punctual meals and even a basket lunch brought to the door of my lovely wood cottage (made of maple, pine and oak, I believe, not poplar), a quarter of a mile from the nearest similar studio—separated further by oak trees, sugar maples, ash, pine, beech, birch and poplar (the last named, I might as well tell you now, does not burn readily). And the studio had sparkling windows, two work tables (wood, of course), a bunk bed and even a typewriter. From the beginning the typewriter haunted me.

I realize that this does not answer the question about "guilt," but I'm on the track. Did I feel "guilt"? As I was saying, the typewriter haunted me (for a week anyway) but I did take good care of it—until the fire, that is. And the fire (the big one) wasn't really my fault. I could even say it was the raccoon's fault. At any rate the typewriter, or the word mileage on that typewriter, remained essentially the same as on the day I got it, and I did take good care of it . . . until the fire.

The word does something to me. And who'll know how much it costs me to admit it? My studio, as most, had a fireplace which was blocked by a big oil burner. Out on the back porch there was a load of stacked wood—big fat logs, sticks, kindling, squat fat hunks of wood, wedges, sawed-off telephone poles unpainted. A load? Seventeen loads of wood, direct from the world's storehouse. And more where that came from. No questions asked, said an old colonist, they'll just stack the porch full again.

Guilt? Conscience? No, I don't have a conscience either. I could never have done half of what I did accomplish if I had been burdened with a conscience. What am I even talking about the word, wasting time with it for? If I'd had a conscience I would never have learned about fires. I would have done what I told them I was going to do. And who needs a seven volume poem-novel?

The oil burner was removed from my studio by Chester, the big muscle-man—I suppose there's one in every similar place—with many grunts and "gawd damn the gawd damned thing," while I stood by in artistic . . . well, autistic silence. I didn't care a rap about him and his gawd damned back. The artist wanted wood heat. And he couldn't work without it. So, out with the oil heater. And out it went. Gawd damnit.

Actually it was more complicated than that. The fire in the oil burner had gone out and it was nineteen degrees—Maine is very cold at the end of March *or* April. I left a note in the office that the heater had gone out, to please have someone come and relight it or else take it out, that I could do very nicely with the

179

wood-fire. That's when Chester came over with his by gawd and he's gawd damned sure gonna take it out. Now it was up to me. He was gone and the fireplace was waiting.

I studied those neat piles of logs out on the back porch and I felt rich. Ash. Huge birch logs. Poplar. Rock maple in jointy squarish stumps. Oak. Beech. And, of course, pine—not excellent firewood but full of sizzling sap, pops and explosions.

I hauled in enough for the fire and a few more logs for insurance and it was the way I felt toward the "insurance" which might have tipped me off—like an alcoholic toward his bottle on the night table, just to have it, not to drink from of course. Since then I have thought long and often of how innocent we are before ourselves. Yes, that fire excited me to an unusual degree, but I had a lot to learn. My work was still that seven volume poem-novel. Fire was for heat.

My first hazard was smoke. Not much heat? Well, just move the andirons out into the room farther. There, the smoke is still being sucked up the chimney, and it is very snug here creating my own heat. Suddenly I found I had created a huge fire and about half of the smoke was coming back into the room. I adjusted the andirons and burning logs for another fifteen minutes. Opened windows for the smoke to clear out. Back to the desk for another few minutes. Fire. Desk. Fire and more wood. Poke around. Check smoke. Open windows. Desk. Freezing. Close windows. Wait. Okay, and to the desk for a few more words. Well, it *looks* warm—about eight logs are burning fiercely.

Suddenly I decide, with despair, that I am different from most people. Everyone else knows so much; studies, learns, seems to know what's good fer 'em; "Better learn that, man, might need it . . . good word for scrabble." They remember. Know ways to get to Boston. Know when to take the oil heater out. Or San Diego. You just take 107 till you hit 803, at 803 there's a little junction. But how do they remember it? I might find the junction, and take the right turn (or the wrong one) but that's it forever. Even if I have to do it the following week. "How's that again?"

Now the andirons are in far enough and for the first time there is enough heat without smoke. Still I couldn't stop (another sign); I had to go over and poke, fix, adjust, get it snapping hot. The old stoker, face gleaming red in the light, making his own heat. Me, against the frozen northland and the wolves out there. As a matter of fact I did see a fox on those early days—a skinny, shy creature who disappeared so quickly that I could hardly believe I'd seen it—and someone at table, in the big lodge where we ate the evening meal communally, said he had seen a fox. I felt better. It was at one of these early meals that I asked about our studio-privacy and was, again, advised (almost warned) by an absolutely round-headed and perfectly bald composer that no one, *no one,* could visit another studio without "express invitation." I was oddly relieved.

At first I admitted that I was playing around a great deal with my fires. The typewriter and the neat little table it sat on watched me, followed me everywhere, like a picture with eyes. Occasionally our eyes met, but never for long. The blank paper hanging out of the black machine seemed jaunty for a day or two and then began to wilt. I never did take the paper out. . . . I was afraid to touch machine or paper. Even the table I approached hesitantly but I did, finally, move it into the corner.

My fireplace was wide, at least six feet across, very deep, with a couple of very large pieces of granite across the inside top of the fireplace. There were seven layers of brick and above the seven layers was a stone mantel.

Very soon I settled into a routine. Early to bed because even before buying the axe and wedges I was foraging for kindling wood and rotten logs and was exhausted by evening, and even on those first days I knew something was happening to me but since I was inside of it, it was difficult to see. I was getting up before breakfast in order to get to my studio to build a fire to warm it so as to be able to "work"; that's the way I thought of it. After the first week or ten days I got up early in order to start "work" early. Warmth of the studio was a by-product.

All right, I will build fires.

When did I give in? The exact time of a decision is difficult to pinpoint but I do remember one afternoon when I, with some ceremony, covered the typewriter and the table it sat on with a faded, holey, woolen blanket of uninteresting brown and gray squares. I did it with some solemnity and it was, in a way, a sort of burial. Was it a sad performance? Well, it was something like a New Orleans funeral for an important member of the black community, sad on the way to the graveyard, happy on leaving it.

And each day thereafter I grew farther away from my fellow artists until, soon enough, I became contemptuous of even the most hard-working. What did they know of art? Real art? Near the end of my stay I changed again but that was a journey many fire days and nights away.

I must stop and explain something about myself. I have not mentioned my special trait. I am very strong. *Very* strong. I can sit for hours, days, weeks and literally do nothing. That takes a certain strength. I have it. Well, safely behind me were the days

when I would build a fire and then say, "Now I can get to work."
No, it was all very direct now; I got to work building the fire and
then, my other phase, sitting and watching.

I tested the heat and strength of the fire by holding my hand
along the layers of brick above the fireplace. So, after the fire
had been blazing for three hours or more, while I sat in a daze
watching it, I'd hold my hand to the bricks and discover which
layer I could no longer suffer my hand to. The day of the burial I
built such a happy, roaring fire that I could not keep my hand on
the third layer of bricks.

White birch is probably the most often pictured firewood. Because I have so often seen it pictured and because I had a good
deal of birch I decided to make an all-birch fire. I was going to do
white birch only but I discovered later that I had probably used
some gray birch as well. Birch begins spectacularly; it catches
fast and makes a fine licking and crackers-crunching sound, but
after the bark has been devoured it is a silent hot fire. It is hot
and fast and the flames go straight up. In fact birch flames are
almost puritanical; not at all playful, they reach straight for the
chimney in a frantic way and have the most ordinary flame colors—no blues, purples or reds. When the life is burned out of
birch logs there is a quiet but powerful hussssssssss while the
birch coals glow and breathe, coals as bright as fire. Glow
glow   glow the living ripples—heat but life-changing vibrations
as well—then down to goldfish-colored goldfish-sized flickers.

This morning I heard from the eminent playwright, Dr.
Fluegel, who spoke about India.

"Death. Poverty. Destruction!" said the doctor. "That is India!" He looked around daring anyone to contradict but, alas, no
one else at our little table had been there. That was his first
word, his second and his last on the subject.

"Doctor"?   And how was it that his was the only title at a
place which included equally famous painters, composers and
writers? A mystery. The doctor has a little dog, a tiny dog (I
mean to say an insect) who simply twinkles to keep up with long-
striding though short, skinny Dr. Fluegel who has the deepest,
most melodious voice (and most irritating) I've ever heard. Dr.
Fluegel rarely talks, but when something stirs him from his creative slumbers he gives speeches for both tables (or all three). He
even banged the table to make sure no one could see anything
else in India, and dared anyone to doubt him—*or* to go. I ate my
eggs.

"When will the mud dry?" says poor blinking Edward, composer, musician. It is breakfast early one April morn.

"The Mud Will Never Dry," I tell him. "That's the title of my next novel." He thinks I make fun of him. If he only knew. I adore this biblical character who wears a black overcoat six inches off the ground, whose Orthodox Jewish background is so apparent, in his walk, his ways, his set speeches. I'm sure that it is a pure music that comes from him.

One day at evening meal Edward showed everyone his new pants which he had bought at a rummage sale in the little town just two miles from the colony. When he turned for us it was plain to see that they were, at least, six inches too big in the waist, and they were all bunched at the back. "What are you laughing at?" Edward asked in his careful and well-modulated voice.

No one would quite answer him but, finally, someone asked, "How much did you pay for them?"

"Fifty cents," said he, lofting the words out to us on a very high serving tray. Ah, my god; with a bunch of pants in back, his dignified stance, and fifty cents. I was changing toward them. There was the Polish sculptor with whom I played ping-pong one evening. The fierceness which he brought to the game was startling. In my mind I could see him attacking a wall of stone. Mountains. Nevermind.

Log cabins.

Secure and alone I scrunch up paper balls, lay a bed of kindling, then set two same sized logs across, two crossing those, two across. Finally I put half of a big pine chunk across the very top of my cabin. That piece is not wet but the sap is still inside and it sizzles. Pow! Pop! Crack!

Through quiet. Rain. Or spring storms outside. For the first time since I've arrived I am fully engrossed in my work. Lost in it. Wood is hissing away. The hiss beside the rumpling ruffling of the flames themselves. Outside the birds chirrup pleasantly, make nests, make birds, look for food. I heap logs on my fire and watch. We all have our work in this world. They make nests and sing. I make fires and watch. . . . Now I watch fingers of yellow leap up hysterically, shouting silently. Heat shoots eight feet into the room. The world is unmoving.

Flowers bloom-fade-die, but fire is living-dying.

When my log cabin was down to a hot bed of coals and broken logs, I placed one stick of applewood in the middle, to watch it from beginning to end. First there was a fury of smoke. Then, suddenly, behind it, from some indistinguishable piece of wood, came a one-bodied, majestic gold flame twisting up, dancing with grace, even dignity. The apple hisses. Yes, it is the apple

. . . I am in there with it, eyes listening, ears watching. Now its underside is caught. Flames are unsteady, of course, but each piece and each kind of wood has its own rhythm destiny, its vibration rate, its own quality, and inherent in every grain of its composition exists, well before it turns to fire, just *how* it will burn.

No doubt any longer, the apple is burning. Dark orange . . . and still the hiss. Blue flickers jump out—air changes to blue flickers—gone. Blue again. Applewood hisses out the sound of blue, the color of hisssss. Now flames burst out and hug just that apple, hug from both sides. Ah, it smells. Essence of the best of pungent fire-eaten wood. Behind and to the left is a pocket of green blue orange yellow all-in-a-flame. Gone. Suddenly it's back . . . and stays. Gone. Pops out breath-taking blue-green blue-green-yellow. And a slower, lower, waving flame. Its ends are not fingers, they simply break off, disappear.

Gradually the apple sinks into fire. Settles, almost seems to decide yes, perhaps, well, I will be fire.

That little cabin in the woods, all mine, and inside of it I'm up to my eyes and ears in smoke, fire, heat, and burning log cabins. That night I came to supper in a daze.

"Well, how's it going?"

"Great!"

I guess they had visions of my huge poem-novel. I don't know, but my eyes were full of logs splitting open, streamers of flame, popping pine logs, and the smells of maple and ash, beech, oak and applewood. Lengths of time for different kinds to catch, how long in the burning, how far out I could build fires before I was smoked out of my log and brick cabin and how hot I could get it up those seven layers.

Would I ever be able to build such a fire that I couldn't hold my hand on the seventh layer of bricks? Ha! The seventh volume.

How long my parents had worried themselves sick—and me too—over when I would discover what I was going to BE!! How close they must have come with all of their hopes and questions to snuffing out the flame. There they stand, these good parents, just aft of all their crazy ambitions for us, their offspring, their chance to continue in this dream life, parents whose very own discoveries—and the fact that they never figured out what the hell they're doing here on earth either, regardless of their years and whether they're called DOCTOR, LAWYER or even FIRE-MAN—were wrecked, perhaps, on the reefs of their hopes-through-children for that one, if only one, who would know and

184

really know. Well now, if one of them would come to me, in my delirium, in my ecstasy, oh with what fervor I could answer. "I . . . I . . ." hear it right, "I . . . am a Fire man."

To go that far in the imaginary conversation made me know it would never take place.

"But son, you . . . I mean, it doesn't pay very much."

"No, dad, it doesn't pay at *all!*"

"Well, then, I don't understand . . . no, I simply don't understand."

"You asked me what I *am—*"

"But . . ."

No, a secret not to be shared. Them, mother and father, screaming at my craziness about how brave Popeye was; "I am what I yam and tha's all I am." No, couldn't tell them that either; about Popeye. They'd have strokes in each others' arms. No, for any real discoveries we're doomed to be secretive. Even doctors can't tell. Who know they're not doctors.

Back in the evenings after some nutty "urgent" talk about "art" at the table. Sculptors, composers, painters and writers of all kinds, jumping in or agreeing vehemently. Then back to the studio to tend the muse, to my tranquility; sssssssss, the nearly constant juice-wood hiss with blue flames licking. Watched as if it were my sacred job to watch. To watch it down to glowing orange and a lower hiss before poking to make ready for a new layer, waiting again for those first hopes, the young flickering puffs of light or a bursting into light combustion.

Puifffff goes the mystery. Ungraspable as the wind, only a little more visible. Ungraspable as the wind, brighter than moon, faster than flowers bloom-die.

I slept eleven hours a day for the first week. I had a lot to catch up with from my fire-less city life. I was getting well. And the well-er I got the less sleep I needed, and the less compulsion to do poem-novels, seven volumes *or* one.

"You're looking healthy!" Someone dared to tell me.

"I thrive on hard work," I told him, feeling the joy rise in me. Lying's not the problem. The problem is we don't lie with joy.

Just as suddenly I was dashed to the ground by a young girl painter who caught me between the eyes and, "I'd like to see some of your work," she said, and followed my long hesitation with, "I think we ought to share things. Don't you?"

I lied without joy.

Another time someone asked how I stood the cold, now that my oil heater had been removed and I had only my wood fire to keep warm by. I smiled and looked at him in my crooked-fixed way. Then someone else took it up, "I tried that one year, but I found that the fire was very distracting. . . . I was fussing with it all the time. . . . I would spend an hour with the fire to every hour of painting."

No, I didn't laugh, not at all. But later I watched him. Of course he . . . *he* had turned back to painting. How different our stories were, how close to being the same.

Morning. The coals were sun-yellow and the flames off the coals were sun rays. I put a big half stump on and got almost a furnace effect. It was somewhat more than half of a mighty log of white maple. Behind it I wedged a piece of pine, blackened and heated through from bark to center; then, diagonally and crossing the right andiron, I put a round log of beech, smooth-skinned beech. That day I was studying beech and white maple flames.

I must stop and discuss something else about my stay there. I had brought very little money with me because I had very little, but I decided that it wasn't enough for the colony to furnish my wood, enough wood or enough of an effort, so I went to town and bought a two-edged Tru-Temper axe, a wedge and a log splitter. I had been planning to sneak back but decided I'd walk back proudly, just like a sculptor with his tools; better than a sculptor; a wood-carver, a fire musician, a fire painter, a worker in air-castles who, best of all, had nothing to show for his efforts. Nothing. I wouldn't be one of those artists who said I don't care if people see my work. I was one whose work would *never* be seen. All of it up in smoke, every day. Only I saw, only *I* loved.

"I burned some paintings today!"

You headstrong young fool! I burn 'em all, *every* day.

So, with the purchase of tools began my logging operation. I not only stole wood from others' studios for my sacred work but with my trusty Tru-Temper (honed and sharpened down in the cellar of the main dwelling place late at night—of course late at night) ranged deep into the woods and learned about logging, clearing, hacking out dead trees and spacing live ones out of no book. No, I turned pages in my head; looked, thought, watched, checked it over, chopped and, twice, was almost crushed. Every day I was chopping down trees, hacking them into logs, logging them to my studio. Birch trees were my natural prey because they grow in copses and need thinning and because they burn easily without aging. Birch is serviceable, and burns obediently, like a good child; unlike applewood, exotic apple, whose flames are full of surprises and more devilish twists and turns than any.

At some interruption I was in the middle of my work . . . ah yes, my morning that fire, my fire that morning, was at the stage less than halfway through its potential but the bed was burning solid red hot and those big logs were ready to crack. Beech gives lovely fast-flickering flames with more purple than orange. More purple even than apple, although the apple colors are more varied.

But *there* is a contrast of flames; purple beech flames to the side of white maple. White maple flames are fluid, slow, yellower and bluer than beech—an almost opaque wall of yellow-blue. I added another tough log of beech and placed a cut of poplar from a ten to twelve-year-old tree riding high on my fire. But, oh, poplar burns hard! Build your house of poplar if you're afraid of fire. It sizzles, pops, shoots sparks above a fire whose flames jump out, around, even nestling, hugging the very top of the log which will soon enough be the base for the next buildup.

The flames jumped, danced and died to their own music—feeding/licking/gone/replaced. What trick of air-wood-heat plus what secret joined them? And the juncture: at the very death of wood came birth of fire and the very point at which it all changed—like the change to steam the change for wood firing it changed and blossomed as it became the secret, the death-secret.

Match gives to paper, paper gives to branches, branches give to logs, and logs pass it on for the rest of the day, until they crack, split, crack. Lower flames join coals, coals become ash and the secret has slipped away.

Damn, it has been a good day, full of making and appreciating. And, to my surprise, the fourth layer of bricks was so hot I could barely hold my hand there. Let's say three-and-one-half layers.

It is springtime and cold. Sixteen days left. Rain somehow turns to snow and I'm walking through the changes. Thick flakes among raindrops and then solid flakes. Later they are smaller, tinier, steady. No matter. Snow. I speak to you. Come on down.

I'm walking back from the studio for breakfast. By now I don't have a shirt, a pair of pants, or even a sock that doesn't smell of fires—mark of my trade. One other person (finally, I'm too far into it, no longer talk of artists, just me, her, them, all of us), another one of us has been working early and, eventually, we join at the steps of the lodge for food, for fuel, wood for fires. She's been up till 1:30, slept in her studio, stretching canvas, getting ready. I understand perfectly, for haven't I been piling logs this morning out in the early cold? Splitting them? Canvases for my day's work?

Despite my earlier hesitancy I am beginning to talk to others; my façade is slipping. Dangerous time, although I don't socialize much because, despite their friendliness, know they couldn't or wouldn't understand what I'm doing. I see them passing manuscripts around, at times showing slides in the evenings, asking us all to come to their studios to see sculpture, paintings, to hear music.

No, it's too much to ask of them. I feel happy, secure, and bereft all at the same time, for what can I show? Three and a half volumes of a poem-novel in air. Sad and happy, glorious, hammered air ideas in green grey blue yellows; symphonies and red jungles mountains yellow rivers purple tongues entire orange dreams I couldn't show or they couldn't see unless they sat down in the very rocking chairs of my mind.

Twelve days left when someone asked me about the seven volumes, and would I finish them. I could hardly answer him and perhaps I didn't. How did I feel? Desperate, full, tender, caring. Twelve days.

I construct slowly, carefully, puffs of paper bunched everywhere. Kindling woven to my pattern, each piece placed after waiting to see how I'd be guided. Criss. Cross. Big decisions but it was not the mind, my dear, no not the mind, the mind would have to follow and give the simple commands to hands and fingers down the ends of arms. I, or *it,* constructed a building with foundation supports of birch (with delicate flying buttresses braced against the rear of the fireplace itself) then I arranged seven good-sized hunks of apple over the birch. Soon it is applewood over birch coals. Within minutes the fire has taken on darker orange hints and the flames are slower, sweeter, more sinuous, dancing. Within the flames are purples, greens, much more red and . . . a different life to the flames—a sweet sinuousness, a hard sweetness, still wistful. That is apple giving up its life. Its fingers are less distinct and less frantic; they don't reach out they simply disappear. Apple fire. Blue orange purple. But *red* coals. Yes, *red.* It speaks. ffffsssss ssssffffffff and smells of fields, of rocks and hills, bees and microscopic flowers.

I began missing meals because these people, my fellows, who scattered to their various fortresses over the three hundred acres and did their assorted, lonely tasks, had become first names, then people, then human beings. Almost as human as I. It was frightening. I was not so important, I was only another, an other—all of us legitimate, all phoney, all flesh all blood, all fuel burning each in his own way, or still waiting for flames, working, waiting, dying a little.

I had also used up a hell of a lot of wood. Mainly because until I lost that first wildness I was concentrating on huge fires. How

188

high up those layers of bricks? How many hours would my fire last?

But the only complainant was Chester, the guy who brought wood, and since he was a big muscle-man I figured he too might thrive on hard work. I overheard him speaking of me once to the emaciated, gentle cook, a Mrs. Sprockett: "I don't know what *else* he does, all I know is he *sure* burns up a lot of wood!"

I left my lunch-basket on the counter and pretended to have heard nothing while answers ricocheted from one side of my brain to the other: "But that *is* my work! That's what I do, you dolt! I burn wood!"

That remark I overheard during the middle of my stay, after my big fires period, soon after which I had begun to follow my mood—the second phase, a time of change and simplification—when my eyes were adjusting, when my mind did not seize on things but was more willing to float, was more patient, when the very meat of my body was becoming less dense, more porous. I was still playing games but the games were different. Once I even had a desolate little fire. I was an old tramp, alone in some hobo jungle. Didn't have no smokes. No money, course. Didn't have no eats. Didn't even have no more wood, just these little sticks left. I almost cried for myself, for the beautiful loneliness of my situation, and the fact that no one in the whole world knew of it.

But there were changes, even in my little world. The weather was warm enough for "work" without any heat. I had to open the windows (even the door at times) to cool my studio. I had also gone back to big fires but there were differences. My fires were first big with anger, and a misdirected wildness, a feeling that I wanted all of it (sevenfoldness) all of the world in flames. My last fires were also huge but different. After all of my careful small fires and the long contemplation of beds of coals, to throw on logs, then one mighty log and see the leap of a big joyous blaze made everything right again. I was poor but I was rich. *Look* what I had! These were occasions. I had not at all changed about showing my work—if they could just share, just *see*—but I had despaired of the change and rarely thought of it any more.

The tenth day before I left was a day of raging fires; I was stoker on the Mississippi River Queen and the big race was ready to begin.

"Charley, you're our only stoker today, it all depends on you, boy. Give it all you got!"

"Don't worry, skipper!"

And I meant it. My clothes were thrown in the corner and I

was as naked as the day I first came on the scene. I forced six and a half foot logs in, kicked, wedged them against the sides. I crammed and pried so many logs in there that I was collapsing from the effort. I was inside of the fireplace poking, forcing, breaking, kicking. When did I stop? What was "enough"? Blake said it, only after you know "too much" will you know "enough."

Even when I could not get another stick in I was itching itching to put more on. I finally realized that the only way would be to get up on the roof and drop logs into the chimney. I hesitated, wondering how best it could be done.

But even without that I almost burned the skin off my hand on the fourth layer of bricks. And, of course, we won.

The skipper's face appeared in the doorway (I mean the hatch) above the boiler room. He was looking down at me and . . . how can I describe that old riverboat pilot's look, his tone, the love and pride in that crusty old man's voice: "Charley!" That was me. "Charley! Charley!" He was almost croaking, "We beat the shit out of 'em!"

I smiled. No, I must have beamed . . . touched my cap and, out loud, in my own forested boiler room, next to a still-raging fire, modestly exclaimed, "I just done my job."

As I uttered those words—"out loud" is the expression we use—a very strange feeling came over me. To break the speaking silence at that time was to break a different kind of barrier. It was the very gangplank from imaginary to real.

What was the difference between myself and a madman? I'm not the one to say if there was *any*. But I like to think there was some—even a vital difference. Although the word "artist" might not apply in my case, it seemed to me that the difference between a madman and an artist was the same difference as between myself (a fire-man) and a pyromaniac. My disappearing art. Art that disappears as fast as it's seen. How defensive I felt about it.

I mentioned that I was seeing things in a different way; old boundaries were coming down, frames off pictures, sculpture in a field included more. Even historic bronze personages in parks became art because of trees and pigeon shit. A bronze boat with a bronze George Washington in the bow, dramatically pointing to the other side of the Delaware suddenly becomes worthy when a sparrow settles on the very end of his long arm and scratches mites.

I meet John, a sculptor. One night we're alone at a table having coffee. He asks me to come with him, help him lug some

190

stone out to the field and set it up. He wants to see if it "works." The "piece" is two slabs of marble in the trailer behind his jeep. Why did he ask me? this sculptor I've never even talked to before? He asks and I agree.

Into the jeep. He bends down, fiddles for a second and suddenly it started. He wheels it around and right out across the lush, heavy, wet field full of dew and shining long grass in waves. Like a boat we're cleaving a path through waves of yellow-lighted grass dew sparkling, a fine field in daylight but on a bright though cloud-filled night with the low headlights yellow lancing across these grasses a stunning field, a field's field. A perfect stew of greens and field flowers.

Fifty yards from the lodge we're stopped, turned across it, his back red lights are on and blinking. Blink blink to red and dewy tall grasses; the motor is idling and we grunt over hundreds of pounds of slab marble in clouds of smoke-white, smoke-red, smoke-white blinked and colored warm air hitting cold turning to vapor clouds as we wrestle with those gravestone slabs—one a square cylinder one almost flat, and down goes the cylinder, then we muscle the slab across it; a primitive marble "T."

Which is the sculpture?

It is cold damp spring bright darkness.

Long yellow lights are drowned in clouds of tiny field flowers; exhaust and vapour clouds alternately red and white hover over the back of the jeep and two working figures. To the side and for our work area we have a lamp-lantern for lighting the slabs we work over in that greeny field-sea of bent-over wet grasses. That scene below is not framed, however; for over it all stands the huge washerwoman with her mighty arms at both ends of a mountain-sized gray-white towel ready to start wringing it out.

The trailer behind his jeep, which coughs out smoke in magical quantities and lights everything with its powdery red blinker, contains mattresses for those precious slabs to lie on; marble chips and rolling logs all visible only at ON intervals.

"I just want to leave it here and see if it works." The words cut through an ever-renewed cloud around us; he looks at the "piece" while my look has broken the frames, veers to long yellow lights over green jade in hills and valleys . . . jade spears and buds, sparkling slivers of jade green—stand in exhaust clouds of red winking lights dim yellow and look. "Works"? *Works?*

Lights, field, clouds and grey skylight, a million tiny flowers in lavender, white, red, blue. That or a couple of stone slabs, one on top of the other. Which is it, John?

In ten more seconds one piece disintegrates. The jeep engine gurgle-guts us out. Lights swing over grasses, tires chew mud-grass, we're on the road again and the field's dark.

My Polish ping-pong playing sculptor is leaving today. "My" sculptor? The Polish sculptor is leaving. He leaves this morning for New York and then, possibly, back to Poland, for his stay in the U.S. is over with. He dreads leaving but swallows it, smiling. He ruffles Barbara's hair and laughs, telling her that he is so sorry not to dance next time with her. What? Never mind, it's better than English-English the way he does it. He goes stumbling on, "No . . . no . . . nex' time? Nother time again with *you*." Ahhh, now she understands. They're full of laughs, hair flying, smiles and glances just caught or just missed. It is a gentle and real goodbye. They are more people than artists. I stood not so in awe of them . . . more in awe than ever.

He was going to do a last "very small" show in New York before leaving for Poland, and the frostiness in his voice as he said the word was more effective than any warning. His Poland is a place I never want to see. But where was I going? What did my future hold? No show, not even a very small one. No fireplace in New York for all of us to sit around and just watch. No shows no showplace for my work. No shows no people no money for fire-painters, for fire-wood sculptors. First place it wasn't, or was it, art? No matter how deep the concentration, sitting or lying at floor level watching, studying, I knew it wasn't. With a sinking heart I knew that but, somehow, everywhere around it, deep in the caves of purple air overglowing underglowing orange it was *in* there and I was very close to it, flying just over the ground because of it.

He is gone. Others would replace him. Ahh, it's strange here. We're a little like ghosts, coming-going, and what are we all doing? We struggle, some of us, maybe all of us, and on all sorts of levels. In eight days I too would have to pack my Tru-Temper, my wedges and go. Such is life at the colony.

"You gonna finish those seven volumes?"

Was he laughing at me.

"I'm not sure . . . depends."

Rock maple (along with ash) is the hardest, longest burning of all the woods I worked with. I set aside four good-sized chunks and started a fire with newspaper rolls lined along the bottom, rotten pine branches, assorted sticks of birch, then the first logs of rock maple. Touch a match to the bottom and all of the news is in flames. I turn my back, sitting close enough to feel and listen but not allowing my eyes any of it: the early conflagration, first quick hot blaze of paper, the slower glowing heat of the smaller pieces, longer period of cooking wood after the settling down, the period of doubt, then bark then logs were blazing steadily before I turned and saw purple close to the logs and full voluptuous flames above. I watched till the fire was gone and there was only a glowing city left.

What is it to say "orange"? To say red-orange-yellow does not help. Nor that it glows, ripples, still lives, that it is a color so deep that a seer could use it, a prophetess, even an amateur with the insane courage necessary could read the history of the world past and still to come in that glow over coals, let alone his own future.

Tea leaves settle in the bottom of a cup; why just that placement? "I see . . . that you're in just a little bit of trouble now . . . and . . . it will get worse before it clears up." Throw the coins and one's touch has what to do with how they land?

Fling wood into the fire cavity at random. Random? We are waylaid by such word outposts, spend the night there and by morning don't remember where we were going. "Accident," "chance"—conveniences we settle for—part of the word conspiracy, mirages which keep us from continuing on to see there is no random, are no accidents, no coincidences.

Now it has settled even more, aged fire with half a black birch ready to crush an orange-ash city. I poke, push, level the city with great care, looking everywhere over it, an old witch spreading his gravel-coals three inches deep of rough red-orange gravel looking over the ruins, searching for the secret, scratching, searching. The smile took me by surprise, and a sweeter taste than anything I've ever known. I already had the secret; it lived in instants and could not be explained or passed on.

The very next morning I was waylaid—by water, of all things.

The spring rains had, at last, washed away all of the snow. During that great melting period rivers were going over their banks, little streams became rushing rivers, puddles were lakes. It was a fascinating sight and, true to my nature, I stopped my work and began playing dams and floods. For one or two mad hours I decided that maybe I wasn't a fire man after all, that maybe, *maybe* I was a water man. I built a huge network of channels, levees, spillways, lakes and industrial canals with chips-of-wood boats, bridges, loading docks, rock cities and canal locks at different levels before finally sitting down to watch over it. Suddenly I was overwhelmed. I was juggling six balls— play, work, direction, aims, guilt, duty—and I couldn't tell one from another. I decided on one glorious flood before getting back to, yes, maybe one glorious last fire. Yes, I must stop playing with water. There's work to be done.

I kicked down dams, levees, broke barriers holding back lakes of water, and smiled at the rush. Four days more.

There were some decisions coming up. For one day, while I thought about them, I did not build even the tiniest fire. I gathered wood. I split logs, chopped birches, lugged old pine logs over and, very simply, worked harder than any mule. But I didn't even strike a match.

You gonna finish those seven volumes?

Was it the same voice as before? The same person?

"It depends . . . I don't know." I didn't look up then either.

It's time to talk of the raccoon. And chance again. How can I blame the raccoon for burning down an entire studio? How can such a claim be made?

Let's go backward. First place I am not an animal lover. I am not a raccoon man. There is nothing about raccoons that would cause me to alter plans. But I've not seen many raccoons, since I've lived in cities most of my life. Let's just say I was distracted by a raccoon, or, well, that it was a coincidence.

I was into the very last four days of my stay. Three and a half days, really. I was going through the pain of realizing, or trying to realize, that "my" studio was not really *my* studio at all. That someone else was scheduled for it even on the day I was supposed to leave. Now try living in a place, and do special things in that place, very special and very private things in that place for a couple of months, and then ask yourself to give it up just because the newspapers and all the calendars say that it is such-and-such a day.

Hey!   Looka that raccoon!

Just a minute. It was the second to last day. I had collected an impossible amount of wood. Well, almost impossible. I mean that I had a regular mountain of wood in piles front and back. I even fussed around, wasted half the morning before laying a bed of papers, then a bed of little sticks, then a layer of medium-sized logs. Carefully. For this fire, the whole thing, from beginning to ashes, was going to include everything, and that would take some doing. The "biggest"? My feelings by this time were not nearly so simple. It was the desire not so much for bigness as it was for all-ness. My show.

Besides, there was all of that firewood. How could I leave when there was firewood to be fired? I have always been a person with a sense of decorum and in my way have always been obedient, as I've come to understand the word. Even from childhood, ever since the incident of the toy fire engine when my mother hid me under the bed while she explained to the fire marshal. Well, but how could I get all of that wood burned? I would have to stoke from the roof. All the way. All-ness. Seven volumes.

I pulled the andirons farther out into the room than ever before and started three interconnected fires. Three huge fires; one to the right of the andirons, one in between and one to the left. More wood. Those little sticks underneath were screaming. Then I rigged up my rope sling around the chimney, put five logs in the sling, climbed up on the roof and pulled up my hoist. I hauled up three loads and I knew, although the smoke kept me from looking in, that not much more could fit. I climbed down, noting with pleasure that even the outside top of the chimney was good and hot.

Well, I climbed down and, just as I was thinking of going in . . .

Hey looka that raccoon!

No, wait! That's not when I saw it. I was walking, had turned to look at the studio, watching the smoke pour out of the chimney, and the windows so, in a sense, for a time, I was abandoning the studio, was just ambling along when

Looka that raccoon!

That's really a big raccoon. Let's see where he's going.

It seems silly to say that something similar to the incident in my childhood was about to happen all over again. I had gotten a toy fire engine for Christmas. A fire engine that really "worked." So, we loaded it up with water and set fire to some old awnings out in the garage and took a stroll around the block . . . just to see. We must have been diverted then too, climbing trees or something, because we were only halfway around the block when we heard fire engine bells and sirens.

Hey listena those fire engines!

Ting-a-ling!

It really must be close by!

Yes. It was just opposite my little toy fire engine.

Well, I lost the raccoon soon enough. But I wandered on.

Ting-a-ling!

What is that? Sweet little bells. I forgot to mention that out on the back porches of some studios there were little bells in case of emergencies. Little ting-a-ling bells. Sweet and pure. Ting-a-ling! Ting-a-ling-a-ling-a-ling!

Might as well get on back.

Ting-a-ling-a-ling!

Those are bells!! Now! How long have they been ringing? Voices!

Was I really astounded? Did I know? I was running, knowing,

fearful, excited, and worried that I had missed something.

Well, I had missed a part of it, the real beginning, but I got there and, oh yes, oh my God!

The seventh layer of bricks must have been ready to crack. In fact, the volunteer firemen from town had already abandoned the studio—they were chopping down trees near it in order to prevent a forest fire. I must confess that, for one split instant, I thought they were going to throw them on the fire.

I ran up screaming, yelling, as much in happiness as in total shock: "My God! My work! *My work!!*" I don't know whether I was putting them on, putting myself on or simply asking them to look, but I was grabbed and held by at least five other colonists. Hugged? congratulated? No, prevented, I guess they thought, from running into the fire to retrieve anything, while the steadiest explained and pleaded to have me understand that "everything" was gone. That it was impossible to salvage anything. All of this while I gasped at the realization of what was happening.

Flames roared, ripped up and out, caressed, devoured the studio. With one side of my mind I was identifying flames and wood, colors, smoke effects, the tantalizing tremendous dance of flame-ends and with another I was stunned at the SHOW.

I was like a painter who not only has been promised a show but finds the entire thing all set up and all of his friends and some strangers as well there to see it. Already invited and there. However, much more difficult. Imagine finding everything you've ever wanted, coupled with having to walk around as though you've lost everything. I had only isolated moments of sanity.

One kind-hearted person, a painter and a beautiful simple person who painted flowers because she loved flowers and had, much earlier, confessed, "I know it is not the mode, that I should be painting penises or something, but I just like flowers . . ." was talking very seriously to me, I was looking back trying to appear sane and serious (should be painting penises), but her words did get through—they knew not much about me but they knew, more or less, how I lived; that everything was in my studio, that I lived there, almost all of my clothes were there, my work, everything—asking about my work and if it was all in the studio or whether I had copies back in my room, asking me at least twice, and I answered, "No."

"All of your work is . . . was . . . in the studio?"

"Yes."

"All of it . . . is in flames!?" She could hardly bring herself to say it.

196

"Yes . . . all of it . . . everything." I said, daring her to read my mind, wishing she could, afraid she might. "Yes, it's in the flames," I yelled, perhaps hysterically, yes, definitely.

She couldn't face me, turned away, crying.

Once again my reason slipped gears when I was next to one of the new colonists, "Great . . . fire . . . the loss . . . I mean . . ." moment of pure madness but against the mad roar a licking-roar of the flames swirls of smoke now blowing over us, now clearing, words were hardly noticed, barely heard. I knew my eyes were bursting with the news but in such moments—I can still see Jackie Kennedy crawling across the back of that car—people are not held accountable. Tears . . . and laughter. They knew that I was hysterical, they just didn't know why.

But they were crushing me with their sorrow. Crushing me. For behind the sober mask forced on me by their bodily attitudes, their faces, I wanted to dance, sing, shout, "Look! Oh . . . beautiful!! Do you see??" And instead one, two, three, I guess, all at different times were crying on my shoulder. "Yes," I kept saying to them, "Yes," and "Yes!" Hugs in commiseration, in genuine and comradely sorrow to my "Yess!!! Yess!!!" Spirals, sprays, showers of flame, showers even cascades of sparks and the waterfall roar of the broadest strokes of a dark orange no tube, no paint can would ever contain.

Finally there were four or five of us together and I asked that they call others to come over, they did, and I asked them to watch with me, watch it go up in smoke; poems, flames, paintings, dreams, visions. I don't know what they got from it but, for me, there were all of the possibilities, as in a bound book I once saw, a book with an introduction which, in gentle language, asks the reader to consider the difference between the container and the content then presents the reader with a blooming flower— one hundred and fifty cool, clean, totally blank pages.

Well, if I was the content, the container was almost down to the ground. And no, my joy had not come out dancing, screaming, laughing. I had it with me.

The next hours were nightmarish. My work was done, the show was over. I can't say what happened at the evening meal, other than that I left early and went to my room, closed the door and actually had a deep and peaceful sleep. People had spoken in hushed tones to me and even at the other tables the talk was subdued.

Next morning I went to the studio, "my" studio. My still-smoking once studio had been almost totally transformed, had heated and entertained the area for a time and then disappeared up through those trees into sky, into the sky and mind, all swallowed up. Of course it remained in the memories of those artists whose names appeared on the wooden plaques inside of each studio, now erased by fire, dating back to 1921 or before.

I had gone back to the studio out of a force not of inertia exactly but almost to see what was left of the thoughts of a certain phase of my life. Whatever I might have discovered, however, was interrupted by a speeding pick-up truck which swung the corner and up the long dirt road to my tucked-away studio. I turned and remained quite still, for I felt stilled by the entire experience as if a vast inner wind had finally released me.

It was Chester and he pulled up, stopped abruptly, lowered his head as if he were going to butt me with it and, instead, delivered himself of the following: "Mr. Kenrad would like to see you . . . in the office!" Chester's eyes, his voice, were those of the tough kid in school who, somehow, in a reversal of roles, was also the messenger from the principal. The voice seemed full of hope that, at last, one of those "artists" would "get it." I rode back with Chester, empty and silent, and walked into the light and airy office of Mr. Kenrad, the manager, as blank of mind and as sober as ever in my life.

I don't remember his exact words, only that I could not believe his first sentences or was it that I could not hear them, or that I couldn't believe I was hearing correctly. The gist was the following: In order, he said, in some slight measure, to aid me at this time of irreparable loss, even this time of personal tragedy, not to mention the loss of personal effects due to the fire, and, although unable to extend my stay here, *because* of this terrible misfortune, he had been on the phone and had gained a two-month stay for me at a similar colony in upper New York state, the details and date he would include in a note which would be in my box in the main hall by that afternoon. He wanted me to know that he was in complete and total sympathy with my position and if there was anything further to be done he would *appreciate* it if I would let him know.

It was at this point that a little mosquito of a thought began to pester me. But, that aside, of course I could not refuse the very welcome offer and thanked him sincerely. We shook hands and, with a lowered head (and thinking briefly of Chester), I started for the door while this imp of a mosquito darted to and fro, buzzed insistently in my head—imp, mosquito or the devil himself—worm, gnat, a little something which had not quite been exorcized by the fire. Of course I was done with a phase of my life and yet the thought danced there, exactly like a mosquito, flitting, dancing, never quite lighting—or was it that I would not allow it to light—until after I had closed the door; but not until I had released the knob, and only then, did I allow myself to examine this buzzing insect of a thought, or question, really. It was about the studios at the next colony, yes, the imp prompted me, about the studios, and how they were heated.

HARVEY OXENHORN

Blue Walls

As usual, you can sleep.
Scant light climbs the blue walls.
Turned away, your scooped hip eclipses the dresser.
I know what is in each drawer—
amber earrings, suede skirt—
what you wear in which mood.
On the door, my shirt you said you'd patch
hangs by its tear. Tomorrow
I will put it on and go.
Round shadow, cooling girl,
I am the crescent of your curl,
waning.

MOLLY PEACOCK

World We Sleep In

There's no one to watch us and grin at us
as we scratch each other's bottoms and smalls
of backs in the blind way of sleep, phallus
breathing in the Y of the thighs, and walls
about us breathing, no one to look down,
like God, enjoying the view in His way,
curling His nostril and lip to frown
at the profane beauty of how we lay
in our bed of beds. The two college kids
who are not our children and who have not
come home for summer vacation making bids
for our attention by flinging open—"What?"
"Look at them."—the bedroom door, then stopping,
pleased only as our pleasure reflects on them,
are not watching us. Without God or popping
eyes of sophomores, no one lifts the hem
of our privacy. It is a godless,
childless world we sleep in, relieved that we
are relieved of faith and responsibility,
though that means there's no one to watch us
and therefore bless us. And so I clamber
through my eyes, then fly out from my head
to bless, if I can, our sheeted chamber
gawking from the ceiling at us in our bed.

The Burnt Lawn

The August lawn is overmown; it's tan,
almost, instead of green. It's dry, but not sad.
(It's not going to die.) Millions of bodies ran

through the lawn this summer: dogs, birds,
bare-footed kids, and the feet of women
and of men, strapped with tan marks from the sun.
The bare calves, fleecy heads, and lemon-
colored buttocks in the distance in the sun
of those two beautiful kids' bodies making
love rolled down the lawn while we watched with drinks
in our hands on the hill one day, taking
our time, taking all the world's time for the links
which would link you and me momentarily.
You noticed them first. I was talking too hurriedly.

Things To Do

Planning and worrying and waking up
in the morning with items on the list
clanking like quarters in the brain's tin cup,
this and that and what you might have missed
or who pissed you off, suspends you in a state
that wishes and hopes for its goal like some
little one wiggling in a chair who can't wait
for when her legs will reach the floor. The numb
knockings of anxiety are like the heels
of sturdy little shoes steadily beating
on upholstery. It's how anyone feels
having been put into a chair, meeting
responsibilities from a padded perch
too big for anyone's ass. As monarchs
we make ourselves small and govern in search
of what we'll grow into. Except we are
as big as we'll ever get, and we've gone as far.

North of the Eyes

Sure it's hard to have sympathy with a
healthy pair of arms and legs and hair
growing bountifully and a belly, a
belly on the oversized side, and a pair
of listening blue eyes over a mouth,

a smallish mouth, that is telling you it
can't go on. "I can't go on," it says. South
of the lips, the chin is firm. The eyes are lit
but not about to cry. North of the eyes
a hand with infinite gentleness smoothes
the skin across the brow as it removes
the strands of hair that fell into the eyes
which looked so clearly out at the world as
the mouth talked. That gentle hand is part
of the same body. It is hard to impart
sorrow from such clarity, since a face such as
this, wiping its own brow without a hope
of having it soothed, says it has such hope.

Those Paperweights with Snow Inside

Dad pushed my mother down the cellar stairs.
Gram had me name each plant in her garden.
My father got drunk. Ma went to country fairs.
The pet chameleon we had was warden
of the living room curtains where us kids
stood waiting for their headlights to turn in.
My mother took me to the library where ids
entered the Land of Faery or slipped in
the houses of the rich. A teacher told me
to brush my teeth. My sister ran away.
My father broke the kitchen table in half.
My mother went to work. Not to carry away
all this in the body's basket is not to see
how the heart and arms were formed on its behalf.
I can't put the burden down. It's what formed
the house I became as the glass ball stormed.

DAVID RAY

Jaipur

His tiny dogs have names of gods,
bark at peacocks and the mongoose
tethered near a burlap bag of cobras.
A monkey scampers on the wall
that's terra cotta, not the pink
most guidebooks persist in claiming.
And my friend Mohan Singh who sits
under his front verandah arch
looks out on terraces and trees
left by his Rajput ancestors
who built a high castle on the hill.

There women in a labyrinth
worked in turns to please just one king,
another Singh. Now tourists come
to crane their necks while a guide bobs
a candle to make ceilings skies
where twinkling stars in mirrors shine,
all this in darkness though mid-day.
Most bourgeois husbands want to know
where the harem thrived—its rooms form
a maze of walls viewed by standing
on a parapet. The roof's removed,
a beehive viewed in cutaway.

The king and eunuchs knew the way
and where they kept the *vish kanya,*
the favorite who sipped poison till
her own kiss was like the cobra's.
She was the gift for friend betrayed
or enemy deceived, her love
the final, facile, fatal trick.

But all that's past. My friend rents rooms
where the Japs sleep by paperbacks
or watch the lacquered Enfields glow,
crossed with black spears upon the wall
near lithographic battle scenes
of tigers fighting elephants.
We crack our peanuts, leave the shells
in Pan Am ashtrays travellers swipe
but then get bored with—thus they're left
on Singh's front porch, gauche trophies of
five-star hotels and London bars.

Two girls navigate the garden
in bright red saris laced with gold.
Their nose rings flash, mere diamond motes,
and the peacocks scatter, leaving
one tribute feather on the path.
Under the tamarinds the doors
of weekend cottages are flung
wide open. Wrinkled sheets attest
to last night's orgy or collapse
when sad-sack lovers just returned
from seeing Amber or the Taj
quarreled or wondered how they'd left
so many rupees in their wake.

The tour group's gone and we're alone
with old servants and Krishna,
eldest daughter, married but
flighty as a bird, dark as teak,
with eyes that gleam when she pours tea
from the trunk of an elephant.
We gaze out where old cannons face
the drive; they've got black barrels, red
wheels, and one's a true gatling gun
with twelve barrels tied together.

Outside these walls, those not so fair,
grim princesses of dust, lift pans
of heavy sand upon their heads
or whirl in groups of six to make
a machine of brooms, dancing girls
whose speed through gutters rivals wind,
a human cyclone flinging dust
and redistributing the earth.

I think of them now as I see
the fat coughing German approach
the pool. Last night he stood an hour
there at dusk with his Hindu friend,
a lady courted, compromised,
in public with him for a week.
I fear he'll leave for Hamburg soon
and leave her here, in grim disgrace.
Besides, it's clear he can't live long—
he's coughing out his bloody lungs.
And yet he came because he dreams
of a love that's perfect, that Taj
again, a pearl, a mosque, a tear
that drops off the earth's riven cheek.

Near us, a crow sits on a chair
and has it out with a peacock;
one simply squawks, the other yowls
like a giant cat, beautiful
with a neck of sapphire blue, yet
loud as an alley tom. And there's
another path where small green birds
flutter before my silver wheels
then whirl behind me like a cape.

The Ganges at Dawn

A black crow finds his chunk of skull,
eats it on a rocking boat. Girls
with clinging saris duck their heads,
shampoo, cup drinks before they rise,
give way to others. Two small dogs
lie within a bed of ashes,
last night's cremation fire.
They're curled so blissfully, pretzel-
boned, like netsuke, porcelain,
you'd think they had been fired to life
upon those kilns whose flames shot high:
thus souls of men rushed into dogs,
despite the ancient promise—all
who by the Ganges die or burn

go straight up to Hindu heaven.
We stood and watched the fires last night,
first one corpse, then another burned
while our rickshaw-wallah cautioned,
"No good to think at night, just day."
But still we gazed, and watched the Doams,
men of that caste who touch the dead.
With a burlap pad one threw a foot
back in the flames. Pale pelvic bones
of women take longest, as if
the work of love and birth drew forth
from earth some concentrate, hard wood.
It sputters in those hips, boils till
they break apart like sticks of Neem.
Hearts burn quickly, if not Shelley's.
And now at dawn, while thousands bathe
and the bridge fades in sudden fog
we watch the young pups nose through ash.
The yogas squat upon their ghats,
some on all fours, it seems, make love
to splendid women made of air.
They mumble prayers. We're off today
for Khajuraho, where temples
rise to Tantric love. Stone couples
tremble there at their passion's brink.
Two girls lift a third upon him
and all, the scholars say, to show
how we should kill the fiend Desire,
eschew most apples of our eyes.
First we leave the holy river,
buy eight flutes from a Hindu boy
who bargains poorly, drugged by fumes
and Ganges mist, forbidding greed.
We step past bodies, mummies wrapped
to wait their turn, to join the air
and swirl as smoke. Small babies, though,
are gently shoved out, with a stone.
A priest squats in a boat, lets go
this gift, small soul upon the waves,
transported to another life.
The mother bravely stands to watch.
There's no farewell my words can say.

MARK RICHARD

Ditch Water Cure

Coming into the channel me and Joey dropped about fifty
seagulls with the pump-action before we decided there wasn't
much sport to it. Already a school of blues was hitting at the bits
and wads of busted birds as our wake spread and folded over
itself. Up in the wheelhouse the Spook was sucking on his dentures and bumping the auto pilot in and out with the toe of his
bedroom slipper. He had the last pack of smokes aboard and was
selling them for fifty bucks apiece. I got one and told him to take
it out of my share. In the galley Tom Smith was snoring and
slobbering all over the table. I was bent over the stove getting a
light when we hit a brand new bar that had blown up in the
middle of the channel. We rolled with one outrigger in the water
and the other to the skyward. Tom Smith's body flew off the
table and pinned me against a locker, crushing my damn
cigarette all over my slicker. The starboard bunks emptied below
decks while the Spook punched the throttle and powered us off
the bar and back up the channel with water running off us
everywhere. Joey came busting in the aft cabin door soaked
down and all pissed off because the shotgun had gone over the
side and his brother would kick his ass for that.

The Spook sent me and Joey out to haul in the deltafin stabi-
lizers that planed the water from the outriggers. We had the last
handful of speed the Spook kept in a mayo jar in the wheelhouse.
It made you into kind of a zombie that saw things in the fringes
of the decklights at night and made you want to smack your best
friend in the head with a shovel for looking at you funny.

The Aussie came on deck slapping bottom sand out of his
gloves and blowing snot. He was gutshot homesick for the out-
back and Perth. I'd had to pull him out of the path swing of the
dredge more than once. Finishing a roach I passed him he picked
up a knockout hammer and beat an empty link bucket boom two

208

three, boom two three. Okay mates, he said, all together now, and he started in on Waltzing Matilda for about the five hundredth time.

Joey picked up a deck shovel and did a rubber boot waltz with it to the Aussie's tune. I cut in and whisked the shovel out of Joey's arms. Dirty bird-dogger, he said. I waltzed up the careening deck and rudely fondled the shovel's backside groove. Rain started to slice down on us again. Low lying marsh and fish houses darkened ahead on the horizon and I needed all the fortification the simple madnesses aboard could give. Water ran down the Aussie's face as he sang and beat the bucket boom two three, boom two three, boom two three.

Joey stood bareheaded in the downsweeps of rain and studied his hands. The speed had pushed his fingernails into his palms when he made a fist and he just noticed it. I had to go below and find the hiney bucket and toilet seat because I got a bad stomach to begin with. I sat comfortable in the roar and warm of the engine room. An oil filter rolled from behind the tool chest and dropped into the bilge. Over my head a light bulb on a cord swung in wild circles and I watched my shadow strike in aimless directions across the dirty floor.

To the dock after packing out the Spook dumped a couple of big yellow envelopes on the galley table that had twenty or so thousand dollars of share money in them. He and Jerry who'd been to college were sorting the bills into hundreds and fifties down to ones. I went to college for about twenty minutes before they found out who drove the tractor-trailer into the lake. My spot of education is like a horny little tattoo some women get on their breasts or inside their thigh. You usually don't see it unless you get friendly. When I'm in a crew of convicts and misfits I try to be like a ray that takes the color of the bottom he's on.

The skies had cleared and the rest of the crew was out on deck watching Joey and the cook beat the hell out of each other. I was up in the wheelhouse focusing the binoculars on a cabin cruiser coming down the waterway. On the bow was a tobacco-brunette who caught my eye like a quick slice of fin in the water. She was coiling a line backward and my mouth went stone dry. I hadn't seen a woman in three weeks and my underwear twisted tight.

Joey fell through the galley door with a split lip and said Give me something to kill that son of a bitch with. The Spook stuck a bluenail thumb into the bundle of hundreds he was counting and handed Joey a butcher knife out of a drawer.

Cut him long and deep, says the Spook, god-damn I hate greasy eggs too.

I hitchhiked down the beach road with my wad of share money and cut across the dunes on the leeward side of Vinnie Mancuso's beach house. Vinnie was watering some big potted plants with a hose and didn't see me come up but this goon on the porch who was protecting Vinnie pulled a rolled-up beach towel closer to him on the bench and I figured there was a gun in it. Vinnie, besides dealing coke, also inherited the Tubewash franchise from his old man Sid The Rat Mancuso up in Virginia Beach and at night they recycle stolen cars in the wash part of the building. During the day Vinnie brings in a busload of work-rehab guys from the Mental Corps. They don't have both feet on the curb but they don't ask a lot of questions. At night Vinnie's thugs put new paint and serial numbers on the cars. My friend Stebo says that around closing time it's hard to tell the loons from the goons.

Anyway, ever since old man Mancuso got shot up in a phone booth outside the Dunkin Donuts on Mercury Boulevard Vinnie has had this guy in ventilated shoes shadow him all over. The guy is built like a dinosaur. I go up to Vinnie and say Hey, Vinnie! and Vinnie is obviously trying to look happy to see me although he's not and he looks up at the goon real quick and back at me and smiles and something doesn't turn right in my chest. I'm about ready to forget the coke and head back over to the highway when Vinnie says I'm just in time to eat dinner with him and Elona.

I've known Elona ever since my friend Stebo started poking her every time Vinnie had to go to Virginia Beach on business. She's got great legs that sort of sting right out of a bathing suit. Vinnie is fat and a slob and doesn't treat her right. So things being how they are pretty soon I'd be sitting on Vinnie's front deck listening to the radio and watching for a glint of sunlight off the top of Vinnie's sedan way off over the dunes while Stebo would be inside playing hide the carrot with Elona.

So when I come inside Elona is in the kitchen and when she sees me her face rubbers up and she goes running out of the room crying and I hear a door slam way in the back of the house. I'm getting bad feelings right about that time and they get worse when another smaller dinosaur comes out of the bathroom tucking in his zipper. How come you'd buy a shirt with buzzards on it? he asks me. They're sea gulls I tell him. Fuckhead. He's dressed like he got his clothes off a dead clown.

Vinnie brings Elona out of the back bedroom by the elbow and makes her set another place at the table for me. She doesn't even look me in the face. We sit down at a big long table about a foot

thick. Vinnie's at the head and I'm sitting across from his two
goons. Elona is shaking as she lights the sterno under a fondue
pot. Every time one of Vinnie's boys leans over to drop a stick
with about fifty pieces of meat into the grease I can see pistol
grips under their coats. I try to get the conversation onto the
coke so I can get some and leave. The undertow in the room is so
strong I keep my chair pushed an extra hand's width from the
table. You don't fight a riptide. You let it pull you out past the
breakers before you make your move.

Vinnie tells me lots of things have changed while I'd been out
fishing. The guy in ventilated shoes says Yeah, I thought I
smelled something. Yeah, says Vinnie, I don't deal in no nickel
and dime oh zees any more. So I say Come on, Vinnie, me and
Stebo helped you out a lot.

Well, when I said Stebo's name something clicked on everyone's faces at the table and Elona acted like she'd hung a fish
bone in her throat. Nah, says Vinnie, I can't help you unless
you're interested in something like this, and in his showboating
style he pulls a kilo from his briefcase beside him and cradles it
onto the table. I'd hardly ever seen that much coke in all my life
but I tried to play heavy and pulled a phone up to my plate.
Maybe I can do something with you, I said, even though I was
only calling Stebo.

Frank, Stebo's brother, answered and right off I could hear
someone in the background talking up a fight. Frank, I say, let
me talk to your brother. Something ripped the goons' muscles
and they stopped chewing. I can't, says Frank. Get on over here.
That goddamn Vinnie Mancuso has broke both his legs this
afternoon and put him in the hospital.

Well, it was like being kicked in the stomach but I forced
myself to say When you hear from him tell him to get back to me
and hung up. I looked at Vinnie and said About all I can do for
you is this. I picked up the kilo and dropped it in the fondue pot
where it sizzled and boiled and popped and stank. Vinnie's lungs
seemed to seize up and he clawed his shirt pockets. The riptide
had a good suck on me but I was in the breakers. I guess it
wasn't every day the goons got to see sixty thousand dollars get
deep-fried because it took them a couple of seconds to go for
their guns but I used all those muscles I'd built up carrying
seventy-pound bushels of scallops across a rolling deck and
power-pressed the table over on them. Poor Elona rocked back
and forth in her chair screeching.

I bolted across the room and flung the sliding door back so
hard it shattered and glass plunked into an aquarium. On my way

out I turned and was going to say something sassy to Vinnie but the guy in ventilated shoes was crawling out from under the table with a Thousand Island splattered hand pointing a gun at me. There was a loud bang and a bullet split my cowlick. In a heartbeat I was over the porch railing and doing a forward roll toward the dunes.

It was still dusky out and after zigzagging over and around some dunes I lay still a minute. I could still faintly hear Elona screaming and Vinnie yelling Shoot to kill! The dinosaurs shot a couple of times way off to the left toward the bay but it was getting dark fast so I just sat there spitting grit and picking sand spurs out of the collar of my new shirt. After a while all you could hear was somebody's dog barking somewhere out over the dunes and the shadowy sound of sliding sand.

It was about midnight when I got to the trawler to get my pack. The Spook was passed out on the galley table face down in a plate of stew that a cat was eating from the edges of. There were two empty tequila bottles and a couple of coffee mugs and a .45 on the table. My good sense told me to stick the pistol in my belt but it belonged to the Spook. Some harbor whore was asleep under the table with the Spook's bedroom slippers under her head for a pillow. PU.

I sat in the crease of the bow and lit a joint. The lines creaked and drew hard on the pilings as the moon sucked the water from under the trawler. Yes, I thought, you've done it again. You drift along on the currents, just a throwaway between swells and when you run up on a shoal you let weird winds and random violence blow you back into deeper water. Not much to show for a life of dragging anchor except a chameleon skin and a heart as empty as the horizon you're so happy with. The reefer was making me think so hard I had to put it out.

Against the side of one of the fish houses I saw a girl standing in a pyramid of pay phone light. It was the one I'd watched through the binoculars. I drifted over to where she was and said Ought not walk these docks at night by yourself. I'd given her a start. She dragged a sleeve across her face and I could tell she'd been crying. Waiting for a call? I said. No, she said, do you want to use the phone? No, I said, I don't have anybody to call. I know the feeling, she said. There was a smell of tar and low tide in the breeze.

I made a circle in the sand with the point of my shoe. How far down the ditch ya'll going? I asked. She backed off a little, running me up and down. I mean, I was just wondering if maybe ya'll could get me down the coast a ways. I got plenty of money for some fuel, I said. She stepped closer and pushed her hair away from her face. I know the signals. Do you know the sound south of here? she asked. Shrimped it a lot, I said, feeling the bottom. My friend is down with a fever, she said, maybe you could take us through the sound and we could drop you off somewhere. I turned so the breeze raked my face and folded my hair back to give her a strong profile. I'd like to leave first light, I told her. Me too, she said. We shook hands and smiled. The phone rang and we let it. I walked her back to her boat. Nice shirt, she said as I left.

There was a mattress lashed to the trawler topside for catching tans off watch. I spread out on it and watched heat lightning, the kind that flashes too quick to cast a shadow. I smoked cigarettes until the lights in the cabin cruiser went out. I rolled over on my back and felt the tide turn.

We left at dawn and made fair time out Old House channel and down the sound. The girl, Sara, had a long tanned neck and copper eyes and she reminded me of a gazelle in a National Geographic I memorized in the forepeak on the last scalloping trip. She sat on the stern and read fashion magazines in the sun. Her lips moved as she read but I couldn't make out what she was saying. We hardly spoke. About noon we had corned beef sandwiches and then she went below for a few hours.

I headed us to a backwater spot I knew of where I'd packed fish a few winters back to lay up for the night and take on fuel. The tide was running out so I got the binoculars to pick my way amongst the hardwood stakes that marked the narrow channel to the dock. I scoped the seafood house shoreline and in the corner of the oyster-shell turnaround was parked a blue sedan that looked just like the one Vinnie's man in ventilated shoes drove. My bowels bubbled hot like I'd swallowed a rack of tiny depth charges that were finding their soundings and going off. I was so rattled that I kept the glasses fixed on the car and didn't see the fuel jockey step out of a shed and try to wave me around the other side of a fresh-cut stake. In no time at all I had run us hard aground.

I threw it into reverse and gave her some throttle. Sara's boyfriend came bleary-eyed up from below and immediately I was catching a major rag. He started screaming in my ear when I gassed it forward and he fell backward on his ass. The dockmaster was shouting and waving his arms but I had that feeling in the soles of my feet that we were aground at least for a tide and I wasn't too sure that I hadn't sheared the prop. I cut the engine just in time to hear someone on the shore finish a long sentence that ended in Ignoramus.

It was dark when all the ruckus was over. The boat listed as the tide ran out from under us. This guy Keith was a real fireball. I felt pretty bad. I piled up a couple of cushions on the stern and watched the stars come out. Below I could hear the rattle of mayo and mustard jar tops so I smoked a cigarette to numb my stomach. I rolled over on my belly when the big lights over the seafood house flickered on but I couldn't make out the blue sedan anymore. There were lots of spooky shadows moving in the trees along the shoreline and I'm not one to get the creeps all that much but I was getting them that night.

About an hour later I heard Keith giving Sara a hard time about bringing me on. It didn't sound like anything more than just relationship racket until I heard the hurtful clap of open hand against face. I sat up and felt the suck of the undertow. The hand struck again and I thought I heard Sara call out Nick. That's what I was calling myself then. Nick Starns was a great-uncle of my father's mother who checked out at the Alamo with his hometown buddy Jim Bowie. Nick tagged onto Jim toward Mexico after he had to kick a man to death in Sumrall, Mississippi. I can understand it. Mexico has plenty of fine open horizons.

I pushed open the plywood cabin door. Keith was standing naked in front of Sara with a backhand in the making. Sara sat on a bunk in just panties and a bulky sweater. There was a bright splash of red handprint across her face. The cabin was a wreck of dirty clothes and paperbacks and empty scotch bottles.

What's going on here? I asked. This isn't any of your goddamn business Keith said. I took a step inside. Get out shouted Keith and he shoved me back into the passageway. I rebounded with a rolled fist and my arm cocked for a roundhouse but he pulled a .38 from under a pillow and stuck it against my neck. No Keith, Sara pleaded but with his free arm he pushed her hard back onto the bunk. I looked at her and then I relaxed my arms and un-clenched my fist. Pull the trigger, asshole I said. For a heartbeat everybody thought he would.

You know how it goes when two neighborhood toms cross paths on your front porch and after the growling and hissing and slash or two they back off from each other an eighth of an inch at a time until they reach the invisible circle where one or both can slowly walk away with some honor still. Well, about midnight I was seriously thinking about swimming the way to shore and

214

taking my chances in the shadows when Sara comes up from below with a sandwich wrapped in a paper towel and a bottle of scotch. The sandwich was gone in three bites and when I opened the bottle she sat down beside me. There was just enough light to make out her pretty face but not enough to show the handprint.

I asked her why she stayed with Keith and she said that in all relationships you have to put up with stuff and take some shit and that sometimes you have to see just how much shit there is before you have to let go. I told her I thought that was a pretty fucked up way of looking at things. She turned away from me and I took a long pull off the bottle that scorched my stomach linings. She said she could see I didn't understand and I said all I understood was it seemed to me like a pretty good time to let go. She said if you let go all your life you end up with nothing. Maybe, I said. Then she said Is that all you have? That was a tough one.

We were quiet for a while. I offered her a drink and she said she didn't smoke or drink because she had a heart murmur. I asked her what it felt like and she took my hand and slid it under her sweater between her breasts. It's like a hiccup, she said. When my hand touched her skin blood flooded my heart like a storm tide with a wind behind it.

She kissed me full on the mouth and then went quietly below. I started making my way down into the bottle. Near the bottom I whistled Waltzing Matilda with my foot beating boom two three over the rail and then I sang what I know of Me and My Shadow so loud that my throat got raw and I happily threw up over the side.

I woke up to a grey mist and the feeling of the boat lifting free. There were a few people milling around the dock and no sign of the blue sedan so when I figured we'd clear I started the engine and backed off mud. The boat vibrated bad. When we got to the dock and tied up I went over the side in my underwear and felt where we'd lost a blade. By this time Keith and Sara were about so I got some money from my pack and hitched a ride on a fish truck into town.

I wasn't gone all that long and when I hauled the new propeller to the dock on a rope the dock-bastard laughed. He said They been gone a while. Yeah the feller what had the boat had a spare prop and my boy Ed hepped him put it on, said you'd pay Ed since 'twas you that run her aground to begin with, ha ha. Not only did they leave me but they took everything I owned including the share money in my pack. I gave Ed twenty bucks and ended up selling the prop for less than what I paid. The sun broke through the clouds and cast my shadow long and dark as I headed back down the dirt road.

Out on the highway I got picked up by a biker who was on his way to Daytona to murder two guys and a girl who had left him in a jam in Virginia Beach and when we pulled into a rest area to snort some crystal meth he showed me the dum-dum bullets he had made to do the job with. I envision their brains as my paint and a cheap motel wall my canvas the biker told me. I felt like I'd stuck my finger in a fuse box.

At Benny's Guns and Ammo Benny wouldn't sell me the twelve gauge or the Lone Star .357 I wanted because of me not having ID so I settled for a red metal flake-handled Bowie knife. In a twinge of crystal I got Benny's wife to inscribe No Prisoners on the blade. The high tin hum of the electric etching pencil was making the biker gnash his teeth. On the way out he ripped off a copy of the Intercoastal Waterway guide for me. As we hit ninety miles an hour I picked out a likely spot to ambush Keith and Sara just before the wind ripped the chart out of my hands and I nearly fell off the bike trying to reach back for it.

My eyes felt like two burnt holes in a blanket. Me and the biker pulled into a truckstop and I bought us a couple of ranch steak dinners and strawberry pie but my stomach was acting up so I ended giving mine to the biker and he ate them both. At the roadside I told him So long and good luck and I hiked to a draw where I figured Keith and Sara would have to pass. The keeper was watching a little black and white TV in his shack and I sat on a slab of concrete down by the canal holding my side which hurt right bad. About an hour before sunset I heard an air horn to open the draw and I saw the boat coming so I climbed up the bank and laid in some trees.

The drawkeeper came out of his shack feeling his pants pockets for a lighter. He looked at the boat coming up the waterway and then he checked the tide marker in the channel. Keith blew the air horn again. The keeper cupped his hands around his mouth and yelled Come on, you'll pass. Keith cut the throttle back and blew the horn again. The keeper shouted I said you'll pass, jackass, and he went back inside.

Another boat was coming up the channel behind Keith's. It was bearing down awful fast. A fat man with a bullhorn leaned over the rail and said Outta the way! Coming through! and he opened the throttle a little more.

Keith was looking anxious. He could either squeeze under the draw or get rammed astern. I pulled the knife out of my belt.

Keith turned the wheel and inched forward. I ran out of the trees and onto the bridge. Looking down I watched Keith's bow start to come through. It would be a hard drop but I figured to use Keith as a cushion. I buccaneer bit the blade, climbed over the rail and hunkered close to the girders ready to pounce. More of the boat passed below me. I started to loosen my grip on the railing until I saw Sara at the console shaking her head and waving me off. I didn't understand until the stern drifted through and Keith stood looking up at me laughing with my pack in one hand and his cocked and ready to go pistol in the other. I had forgotten to become invisible.

Keith heaved my pack overboard and took aim to shoot it but didn't. I felt sick at my stomach watching it roll over in his wake. The fat man's cruiser broke out below me fast and loud. In a clean motion he gaffed my pack aboard and blew me a kiss. His boat, the Sandy Bottom, almost sideswiped Keith and Sara as it passed and disappeared around a bend in the canal.

I made to pull the knife out of my teeth with a free hand and yell at the fat man but when I did I lost a toehold. The Bowie slipped and splashed the water and I almost pitched after it except that my left leg hung in the crotch of a draw brace. I dangled upside down over the water, my heart pounding in my ears like the marching tramp of a million Mexican feet.

I beat time down the ditch with a handful of one dollar bills and fine-tuned reptile reflexes. I had a hunger for gazelle and I lost the fear of Vinnie's man in ventilated shoes. I travelled day and night. I was nameless and dangerous. It was pure tide suck.

In two days I walked to the end of a dock at some piss-ass marina and jerked the fat man out of his vodka sleep by the lapels of his banlon shirt. Where's my goddamn pack? He squinted up at me and smiled. It's our hero at the bridge, he said.

I started to take the Sandy Bottom apart while the fat man poured two drinks. This is what you're looking for, he said. He kicked at a plastic bundle. Inside my clothes were soggy but all my money was there.

My name is Raymond Clay, he said, handing me a drink. I specialize in divorce boating. If you can throw a line and steer I can offer you a job.

I pulled on my drink and recounted my money. I don't want no job, I said. I gotta go. Also, said Raymond Clay, we're within a day either way of the boat you were so hot to jump. This isn't a murder story you're in, is it? Not yet, I said. All right, said Raymond, we're fueled up. Want to leave now?

I guess so, I said, but what's this divorce boating about? Hang around and you'll see, said Raymond. I threw off the lines and he eased the Sandy Bottom away from the dock. Where're we headed right now? I asked. We don't have a particular destination, said Raymond, spilling drink on his sneakers. We're just headed down the ditch. With any luck at all we'll never get where we're going.

Down through Florida Raymond kept the throttle pretty much wide open even in the No Wake zones. We drank all day and dropped anchor wherever we were when we were too drunk to see past the bow. I had a gut feeling we passed Keith and Sara. Once some people threw beer bottles at us for cutting so close and another boat shot a flare across our bow. Raymond got on the stern and hung them a moon.

Just outside of Marathon Key the engine burned up. It coughed and pooted a couple of times, then just quit. We were already into our fifth or sixth vodka. One of us hadn't cleaned up the anchor line from the day before so when Raymond threw the hook over, the twisted wad of tangled up line followed it to the bottom. While we argued over whose turn it'd been to secure the anchor the boat drifted toward a reef and pretty soon she was crunching all over the coral and we were a little too drunk to be effective.

We started taking water and by the time I could get my money out of my pack and Raymond could get a life jacket the Sandy Bottom sort of half sank and rolled over on her side. Raymond looked happy. The wind and current slipped us into deeper water and before she went under some bonefishermen came by and took us to a dock at Marathon. As we climbed out of the boat one of the rescuers said sarcastically to Raymond that he didn't look too upset for a man who had just lost a boat and Raymond said Another day another dollar.

I sat at one of those dockside tiki bars while Raymond called his client in Maryland. The bonefishermen walked past in the parking lot and pointed me out to some women they were with. They yucked it up. Raymond came back and ordered a vodka.

It looks like you and me might as well hang out here for a few days until we get our money, he says. I said You mean we still get paid? and he says You still don't get it, do you? Of course we get paid. The bartender brought Raymond his drink and he sucked it hard.

Look, says Raymond, this guy's wife is breaking his balls in a divorce and it looks like he's about to lose his boat. So he hires

218

me to run it to the Abacos out of the wife's reach. Divorce boating is always either or. Depending on court dates, I either get it down there or bust it up. It's insurance then. All business. Guy says today's last Tuesday for the insurance report and we get a bonus. Drink up. We're travelling back in time.

We drank so much that at closing time the bartender laid us out on the dock like a couple of trophy fish people leave to rot on the pier after the picture has been taken.

Me and Raymond rented us a bungalow near a marina in between a restaurant and a veterinary clinic that looked pretty much closed down except for a wino that read the Miami Herald on the front steps and juiced all day. Raymond hung out at the tiki bar with this older divorcée type who wore lots of jewelry and purple eye shadow. I killed time around the docks mending net and splicing cable for pocket money. The afternoon Keith and Sara tied up across the way I hid behind some oil drums and spied on Sara. Mostly she looked over the side into the water down and out daydreaming but I still got a lump in my throat and thought Gazelle Gazelle.

The next day our checks came in. Raymond told me to let it all go between me and Sara. Besides, he said, I got a lead on another divorce boat in Baltimore. I felt the tug and pull so we decided to get a couple of plane tickets and then go out to dinner. At the airport in line for a ticket is Keith. I don't let him see me. He's got a little duffle bag packed and Sara's nowhere around. I got so worked up I started having hot lava seizures in my guts. I told Raymond to find the tiki bar lady to go to dinner with and to meet me at Sara's boat in an hour so we could double date. He said fine and left while I felt my pockets for a dime to put in the pay toilet.

Somebody had left a *Key West Citizen* in the john and I tried to read it while my stomach cooled down and settled out. I was reading about a girls' softball game when I hear somebody put a dime in the lock on my door.

This one's occupied I said but they went ahead and turned the knob. Hey, now, I said as I folded the paper, this one's—and then I looked down and fear rolled in on me like a sunami. The pants legs beneath the door were wearing the evil ventilated shoes.

I stood up just as Vinnie's goon busted in and sliced down with a knife. I blocked the jab and kind of grabbed his shoulders and pulled him past me in the stall but on the way by his blade caught me good and sliced from my navel to my left nipple.

I tried to give him a Steve McQueen elbow to the temple but instead it just shoved him off balance and his foot slipped into the toilet. I bounced off the door and gave the back of his head a punch that popped his Foster Grants off. When he tried to pivot on the stuck foot he caught himself on the flush handle. The toilet sucked on his shoe and I grabbed him by the hair. He was too slow for close fighting. I beat his face against the tile wall until it colored red from his smashed-up nose. I gave his head three good last bashes and he went out cold. The toilet overflowed on his other shoe and I fell out of the john pulling up my pants and bleeding like a stuck pig.

The last plane had left for the day and the airport lobby was empty. I felt dizzy staggering across A1A but nobody seemed to notice. You see it all on that highway anyway. I didn't think I'd die or anything but just in case I headed to Sara's boat.

I fell into the stern and crawled into the cabin. My shirt and pants leg were soaked warm and sticky red. Sara was sprawled on a bunk asleep with an empty pill bottle beside her head. It didn't look too good. She looked one stripe above a crapper OD and the blood poured out of me faster than I'd hoped for my dockside drama. I was losing hope and conciousness. My anchor was churning up big clouds of sand as it dragged the bottom and I'd even started to rethink all the gazelle had said about not letting go. I passed out depressed.

Raymond and the woman from the tiki bar came around the boat ready to go eat when they saw the trail of blood. They came below and dragged us out. Raymond loaded me in a wheelbarrow they used around the dock to tote nets and took me to the veterinary clinic. The wino turned out to be Dr. Garcia who stitched me up pretty good between his dry heaves. Raymond and his date force-fed Sara black coffee with a handful of salt in it to bring up the sleeping pills. Dr. Garcia sent us home with a jar of antiseptic cream and a dog food sampler.

At the bungalow Raymond and the woman stripped our bloody and puke messed clothes off and laid us out on the big bed in the back. Raymond's date quick braided Sara's damp hair so she wouldn't smother in it, she said. Sara was mostly asleep through it all. I was groggy from losing blood and the half a horse pill Garcia had given me to sew me up. My side started to burn so the lady gave me a couple of Darvons out of her purse before she pulled the sheet up to our chins and tucked us in. Then she kissed us both on the forehead like she was our mom and closed the door quiet on her way out.

Later on I could hear her and Raymond in the kitchen drinking and every once in a while she'd say something like Raymond, take that life jacket off and put your pants back on for christsakes. It felt good to lie in the darkness next Sara and hear her breathing. I cleated her braid snugly through my fingers, an anchor line to swing from on the tide. In the morning I'd tell her my real name. I held her tight and put my head between her breasts. I drifted off nice, not letting go, listening to the boom two three boom two three of her murmuring heart.

J. W. RIVERS

from *When the Owl Cries, Indians Die*

Poems of Mexico and the Southwest

"For Norman Rosenfeld, with thanks"

from *Part I*—Father David of the Grayrobes

In the Olive Orchard

The landscape is wrapped
in sunlight and silence.
Riding piggyback on a jabalí
Father David dispatches roadrunners
to proclaim good news.

Arriving before empty adobe hovels
he cries, Behold the New Jerusalem,
hacienda of the Lord,
bride in waiting.
Behind these walls
the true world awaits us.

A light rain descends.
Heaven is happiest
when in tears, he says;
this rainy season refreshes us,
shriveled plants are fleshed.
The Lord deals with thirst
in overflowing grace.

A bare olive tree appears.

Beneath its branches
Father David genuflects,
then turns to the desert:

Bring your souls
to the tree at night, he says,
on the coming of the moon.
Bring them wrapped
in garments and rags.
Hang them from a branch,
the Lord will make them
into leaves and fruit.

Through many ears his message goes.
From far off, pigs and chickens,
lizards and falcons,
grizzlies and prospectors,
squaws and children appear.
They kneel beneath the tree.

Father David, Brother Sun and Sister Moon

Motionless,
arms strained to either side,
Father David stands bound
to the ribs of his mission door.
His hair is widely spaced, his eyes
are coffee beans in dry cups,
his teeth are loose as sand.

The sun witnesses his silence.
Are you on retreat? it says.

Brother Sun, says Father David,
his body as bright as a burning bush,
now we are a faith community of two.

I have no faith, the sun replies,
this journey saps my strength.
Heaven is boundless, I falter,
each day I faint at the end of the march.

Brother Sun, Father David says,
we travel together;
all things faint, to arise again, renewed.

The moon slips through a slit in the sky
to suckle stars,
her back in modesty toward the earth.
Patiently, Father David watches tiny stars
travel from far off—pale, slow sheep,
they await their turn,
and blink more brightly afterward.

Sister Moon, Father David softly says
when the nightly nursing is done,
Brother Sun has lost his faith
and this unsettles me.

Each night I mother him,
Sister Moon says with a smile.
His faith is nourished with my milk,
he will not stray from the fold.

Beaming still, she slips away,

and even dawn's bosom
is cream colored.

Resurrection

The bell tolls five times.

With a dry, grating sound
the mission door moves.
From pools of sand within,
five cats file out.

Father David in cruciform,
fastened with rawhide
to the ribs of the door,
stirs,
snaps his bonds,
steps down.

His eyes are pits, his flesh
is dried into his bones.

He kneels by a spiny cactus.

Lord, he says, where there is sand
let me moisten tongues,
where there is fever
let me bathe foreheads.
To this land of illusion
and thin air, where men,
nameless as grains of sand,
shrink into nothingness,
let me bring truth.
Let me sow joy
on the dead level dust of the desert.

He gets up and follows the cats
toward buttes
that dance in the distance.

Father David and Brother Wolf

Two are present in eating,
the eater and the eaten.

Pinna the Witch

Disguised as a dog,
the killer wolf sizes up the priest.
I see you travel lightly,
it says with a smile,
you carry a small bag of bones.

To expand one's flesh, the priest replies,
is to increase food for predators.

*You speak with patience in your voice
but thorns in your heart,* says the wolf.

Stinging hairs and prickles
are from a world which is not mine,
says the priest; patience
thins this bag of bones
that hold the marrow of the Lord.

Father, for all your fraternal charity
you mistrust my motives.

Brother Wolf, the priest replies,
you may fool me from afar,
but close up you fool yourself.
A wolf should smell its own hole first.

Sweet of voice, short on faith,
the wolf counts its teeth.
Father, it says, *men would kill me*
or put me in a cage.
Winter is cruel; hunger, crueler,
but men come straight from hell.

Peace, Brother Wolf,
trust in the Lord.
Eat herbs with me, and grass.
Follow me into town,
men will give you biscuits.

The eater of sheep and shepherds
senses good faith in this simple soul.
It sheds its dog's disguise
and goes with him to town.

*

Men arm themselves and leap like goats.
Women dissolve into shadows.
Children flee from fires
of Moloch in the monster's mouth.

Peace, my brothers and sisters,
Father David says. Come, pet

this simple beast who is our brother.
All creatures are mirrors of God.

Men put down their clubs and stones,
children return from their dreams.
Women flow from shadows
to prepare cornsilk tea
and hot blue biscuits
in the dead silence of the town.

from *Part II*—Tequistalpa, A Village

*Early morning in Tequistalpa. Bells toll Mass, stirring hundreds
of birds who occupy the church tower and roof. The stone walls
of the church, thought by some to have been built by Spaniards a
long time ago, are moss-covered, and ferns grow from crevices.
Walking among maguey plants and ocote trees, we men and
boys come wrapped in sarapes; women and girls, shrouded in
shawls. Inside the church, myriads of colored paper chains
stretching from rafter to rafter, and offerings of potted dahlias
placed before saints in their niches, attest to the piety of my
people. Once as bright as gold, the altar, and the baptismal font
off to the left, are greenish. We kneel, cross ourselves, then sit in
worm-eaten pews. Beeswax candles—the eyes of God—flicker on
the altar. Feet of squirming children mash sombreros respect-
fully laid on the dirt floor. Lean dogs settle down behind the
pews, and in the open doorway, to await their masters.*

The Mayordomo of Tequistalpa Waits at the Village Gate To Receive the New Priest

Church bells are ringing.
Those who ring them
are in the grave,
in the moist comfort of the soil.

The last priest who came

wore only his cross,
he shunned our petrified deer eyes,
would wear no wind pebbles around his neck.

He turned in his sleep
and whimpered like a dog,
confessed his sins
to the ocote tree

which wasted away and died.
We slit open
the soles of his feet
and told him to leave.

Here you will find nothing.
Maybe a wooden plow, a team
of oxen in the field.
While among us you will not see

the hidden life of the soil.
When you leave,
the soil beneath your feet
stays here.

Everyone is related,
there is little need for words.
We have no shoes,
but the soles of our feet are hard.

Valentín

Little Valentín is gathering
dark vanilla pods. At home,
his mother makes fritters
flavored with anise.

Valentín stops to watch men make pulque.
With long gourds they suck
juice from maguey plants.
They pour the sap from vat to vat
and sing, We praise the mystery
of the Holy Trinity.

Valentín's mother is cooking
a hairless dog for supper
on the Saint's Day of her son;
Valentín himself is crossing
the sands of the Hill of Time
to enlist in the army.

Children are eating tamarinds,
insects drowse in the shade
as Valentín fords the river
of fish that cannot be caught,
passes the jaguar who crouches low,
hears the sound
of monkeys peeling bananas.
In cold wind he reaches
the high range of the owl.

Staring toward the Hill,
children talk in low tones.
Valentín is headed home
with boots, a uniform,
a gun with bullets.
Surrounded by cold wind,
he approaches the jaguar
who crouches to spring
at the stir of movement
in the gathering night.

At home, his mother pleads
with Mary, Joseph and Jesus,
who have gathered
on a small bedroom altar.

In back of his hut, Fidelio the carpenter
crushes sage and wood lice for lacquer.
He makes burial boxes
that will last forever.
He bores small holes in the sides
so that warm breath may go out and come in.

The Doctor and the Priest Give Counsel

Fidelio's wife is sick,
she cannot sell
firewood in the marketplace.

For three pesos the doctor comes.
She has a disease
of the blood, he says,
and he boils a skunk with mushrooms.
Your wife will drink the broth
and chew the meat
to cleanse her veins.

The priest comes.
Do not wrap her
in mats if she dies,
he says; you must put her
in a box, even one as cheap
as those used for bee hives.
Her dead body
will be sacred,
so bury her properly
in a box.

They leave. Fidelio's wife
must turn herself
into a grasshopper,
go far from here
before her body
is too heavy to leave the ground.

Painted with red amaranth dye,
Inocencio the doctor

230

sorts herbs and seeds:
some for an errant husband's soup
others to put into a lover's ear.
To unite Mario and Matilde
he will offer
the soul of a chicken;
then, with cactus strips
and leafy amaranth stalks,
eat the chicken's flesh.

Beyond the village outskirts,
where houses and huts
half hidden by maguey fences
go disappearing into cornfields,
Mario with his oxen turns the soil.

Heat and dust rise from underfoot:
Mario steps on a volcano,
releases the souls of his ancestors,
sets free the spirits of earth.
They tell him that comets
will cross the sky,
that earthquakes will devour the corn.
They tell him to wear
shining feathers,
to sing and pray
before the peak of the mountain crumbles
and rain drops turn to dust.

Now chasing birds
whose feathers shine like light,
now plucking flowers that dance in the breeze,
Matilde hears the murmur
of her grandfather's voice
in the water of an arroyo.
The voice leaves and approaches her,
tells her it forgets and remembers her.
Matilde places an offering of petals
on her grandfather's face.

Mario Invites Matilde To Go up the Mountain

Our bodies are flowers,
they open a few corollas
then they shrivel up.

Tochihuitzin
Ye Tocuic Toxochiuh

Go with me
far up the mountain
before your mother knows.
We will find small eggs and flowers,
watch butterflies and squirrels.
Clouds and pine smells
will surround us.
I will spread my sarape,
we will be warm.
I will kiss your breasts,
you will leave on my lips
a taste of herbs.
In your lap
a joyful bird will nest.

Fidelio Goes on a Pilgrimage to Chalma

Among ocote trees we dance and sing.
Women cut off their braids,
hang them from branches
with umbilical cords in bags.

We men hang our hats,

kick at pebbles
that contain the souls
of believers who turned back.

In the river below the church
we wash our heads and feet;
then we eat, and rest on mats.

Behind our village streamer we enter,
men on the left,
women on the right,
with candles and flowers
and oil for the lamp of the sanctuary.
With holy water from the river
the priest blesses us.
We follow a smoking incense burner
which takes us to the feet
of Our Father the Lord of Chalma.
We knee to pray.

Behind the banner
of Our Dear Father of Chalma,
dancing and singing,
we come back to Tequistalpa.
The mayordomo receives us
with tamales and acorn coffee.
Musicians play drums and conch shells,
guitars and clay flutes.
We dance and sing,
sing and dance
far from the feet of Our Lord.

Yohualcuacuauhqui
(Nocturnal Woodcutter)

The hostages are herded in the plaza.
Around them, the village sleeps,
dreaming of mushrooms in green sauce;

the village hears a sound
of someone chopping wood.

A man stands near the hostages:
his head is broad, his eyes are large.
An owl leaves his shoulder,
the village murmurs in its sleep.

The man's clothes smell of soil,
his toe nails are sickle-shaped.

The charcoal fires are out,
no ocote torches burn.
The man sees in the dark.

In the plaza, the hostages are silent,
their heads
severed from their bodies.

Matilde Cooks

We have to leave this earth,
we are only on loan to one another.

        Nezahualcoyotl
        Cuicatli Quicaqui

We women grind corn
and knead masa for tamales.
Shooting starts again.
Bodies are tossed
from bayonet to bayonet
to bayonet.
This is done, we are told,
to drive out bad government.

Men of the new government
tell us we are free from Spain,
tell us we are an empire,
that our own beloved Iturbide
is emperor; they tell us
we will eat sweet tamales
filled with sugar and pine seeds,

tell us our men will stay at home
to make pulque and tequila,
eat tamales,
come to us at night.

More shooting.
Our straw sleeping mats
are filled with aves,
glorias and paternosters.
Bad government
is being driven out.
We women
chop chiles and onions
to make dry soup.

Valentín Looks for His Family

I am back from where the land is parched
and plants are shriveled.
Men are sleeping their siesta,
women talk in low tones.
The air is full of insects,
sweet smells come from the soil.

My sister gives birth.
With a machete, the doctor cuts the cord.
My sister crawls with her baby
into a steam bath.
Night birds scream like monkeys.

With picks and shovels and a hired boy
I go through the cemetery.
Wood markers are rotted,
stones have been removed
to pave the village streets.

Women on their knees
grind coffee in stone grinders.
Cracked bells call people to Mass.
Take off your hats, the sacristan says,
God is looking.

Full of snake venom, my mother
lies in a box.

The croaking of frogs
blends with tunes of drunken men.
Dogs bark among marimbas and guitars
and the castanets of donkeys' hooves.
Women roast monkey meat.

Your father? says an old woman
who smells of soil.
He ate field mice
that lay among owl droppings.
His feet are walking
forever away from the village.

From the inner world of the soil,
where all things germinate,
cradle smells come,
and a fragrance of Madonna lilies.
I wrap myself in a sarape,
lie down to rest.
Only the sarape keeps me
from dissolving into the ground.

from *Part III*—When the Owl Cries, Indians Die

Father Hidalgo's Forces Attack the City of Guanajuato and Take the Public Granary

Death to bad government!
Death to the gachupines!
Long live the Virgin of Guadalupe!
Miguel Hidalgo

The Virgin leads us.
Twenty-five thousand strong,
armed with arrows and slings,
farm tools and stones, we come

crashing down the slopes,
boulders that bash in heads,
leaving crushed grapes on the ground.

The soil beneath our feet is holy,
but what is holy for us
to the gachupines does not matter.
They have lawyers with papers
and soldiers with cannon,
they wear shoes and swords
and sit on horses.
They are owls
who take our corn and chickens.

Behind clouds of shrapnel
they fall back to the Granary.
With ocote torches
we burn the door.
The furrows we turn with our plows
are openings of graves.
Death spreads like mushrooms.

We strip three thousand
white and brown bodies.
Priests pray for the fallen.
Most of the dead are us.

Remnants of Hidalgo's Army
Return from Coahuila

Hidalgo's head was fastened to a pole and shown at the Public
Granary.

> Michael C. Meyer and William T. Sherman
> *The Course of Mexican History*

Slowly the men come home.
As if the bottoms of their feet
had been sliced off

and they had been made to run
until they dropped.
Now they are here, where no one
will break their bodies with rifle butts.
The dust, the blood, the hard hooves
of horses will not come through
living cactus fences.
The men are here, far from owls,
in the stillness
and slow time of the soil.

Beyond the charcoal fires,
spirits of God walk in the night.
The doctor has stroked the men with thyme
and coriander and rubbed
their limbs with eggs.
Tomorrow the men go to the canyon
to lay their foreheads on gray stones.
They will eat limes again,
and brown worm salt;
mezcal will run down their throats
like a river cutting its bed.
The men will swallow frogs and snakes,
once more they will dance around God.

Truly do we live on earth?
Not forever on earth;
only a little while here.

Nezahualcoyotl

Where are we going?
We came only to be born.
Our home is beyond:
In the abode of the defleshed ones.

President Polk Addresses Congress

Polk didn't want to be seen as an outright land grabber so he
gave a little speech about the evil ways of the Mexicans.

Thaddeus Colquitt Ivy
Collected Papers

California's no more Spanish
than the land we stand on here
is Indian.
God wills that we settle the west,
where vultures fly low
like Mongol horsemen,
and Mexicans encroach
on our property in Texas,
attack our peace-loving troops,
shed American blood on American soil.
They slink across our border
to rustle jobs, and bathe
only when it rains.
We have no territorial pretensions
beyond a very modest annexation.
Gentlemen: I give you a west
of barbed wire and power lines.
Wild deer will leap into our hands.

Does man possess any truth?
If not, our song is not true.
Is anything stable and lasting?
What reaches its goal?

The butterfly is coming, coming;
It comes flying, opening its wings.

239

On flowers it lives, sucking honey.
Its heart opens to us:
It's a flower.

Seth Thornton Sails for Texas
with Old Zach's Army
New Orleans, July 22, 1845

We muster before midnight
in a street outside a cotton press,
atop of which I see an owl.
Its feathers are swollen; wings,
rotated forward and spread.
Its beak clacks at us—its eyes
have a red glare.

Drums stir my spirit,
fifes pierce my ears.
Our regimental quick-step
inspires my soul.
The owl mummifies
in my mind's roost.

Let us sing,
let us go on
singing
in flowery light
and warmth.
Oh, friends!
Where are
you?

We march to board the ship,
our bayonets glistening
in the bloodlight of the moon.
Faces peer from half-open doors.

We steam for Corpus Christi
at midnight.
Sailors handle lines
with strong, grasping hands.
They glide silently on deck,
see perfectly in the dark.

The captain has thick
tendons in his legs. He stares
straight toward Texas.
The cook hoots and coughs
into a cauldron of rabbit broth.
I glance at my fellow volunteers:
ranks of startled woodchucks.

Mangas Coloradas Is Guarded by
Men of the California Column

The Apache chief fell back off of his elbow.

Daniel Ellis Conner

Colonel West, your men
watch me tuck
an end of my sarape
over one foot with the other.

Night is frozen to the ground
except near the fire.

The men heat bayonets,
rub them against my legs.
I think of ocotillo flowers after rain,
grass running in waves
over my body.

I wish to sleep my own sleep,
have spent many uninterrupted nights
separated from the earth
only by a sarape.

I rise on an elbow
to face your men,
who loom like owls.

Ocotillo flowers
bloom in their guns,

murmurs of stone
go through my ears.

My mouth has
no more words to say.

Letter to George and Mary Gill-hoff, in the Carolina Up Country, from Son Bill

Dear Mother and Daddy,

Like drawings
we erase ourselves,
like flowers
we dry up
on this earth.

Drop what you're doing
and come to Texas.
Everywhere, the topsoil
is bottomland, and cotton
blooms like roses.
The climate's delicioso,
not a case of ague
or sign of yellow fever.
We'll take this land
from the Mexicans
and build plantations
as far as the mountains.
Room here for a million
horses and slaves, and
corn to feed them all.
Kisses for little Kate.

Second Letter from Son Bill
to George and Mary Gillhoff

Dear Mother and Daddy,

Heavy clouds and cool winds
keep the soil soft and moist.
I've made crops of soy beans
and corn; strawberries and
cantaloupes grow by themselves.
I hope you're arranging
matters for your more,
and that's why I've heard
nothing from you in four years.
Got stung by a white scorpion
the other day, and Pawnees
stole the horses. Weary
of buttoning and unbuttoning
his shirt, my neighbor,
a German widower named Kraus,
blew his head off. Kisses
for little sister Kate.

The Navajo to Major Pfanning

My daughter
was just tall enough
to reach a man's heart
when your soldiers came.
Now she dances in cantinas.

My son never wore
hawk feathers in his hair,

only a forage cap
your cook threw at him
as he groveled
among empty fish cans.
My son chips arrowheads
from beer bottles.

My woman took
The Long Walk
to Fort Sumner.

Pfanning: I went
to the prairie
of Illinois.
I bring you
one jacket,
one bonnet,
one petticoat
from your wife.

With Old Zach's Army, Seth Thornton Awaits General Ampudia's Attack at Buena Vista

Ants last night tried to carry off
Bill Gillhoff in his sleep;
I awoke this morning
covered with bat saliva.

We burn green mesquite
in the campfires—the warmth
attracts scorpions and millipedes.

I have a constant taste
for sourwood honey and biscuits,
water in my mouth
from a Carolina mountain stream,
brook trout floating in butter.

The ground burns through our boots.
No friendly breeze
penetrates the chaparral.

244

Today we hear that Santa Anna himself
with twenty thousand reserves
has taken command from Ampudia.
After ants and bats and snakebites
we're ready to show our own fangs:

our infantry strains forward;
Braxton Bragg's artillery boys
load with double shot.
Our cavalry horses form up
to champ the bones of enemy hands.

Chapultepec: Panchito Márquez, Age 13, of the Colegio Militar, Faces Winfield Scott's Victorious Army

Nuestra bandera no caerá en manos enemigas.
Our flag will not fall into enemy hands.

> Juan Escutia, cadet
> Colegio Militar

Moctezuma's halls are dust.
Men with bayonets
advance through shattered crystal.
Our commandant, Nicolás Bravo,
is a prisoner.

My comrades are captured or dead.
Yankees swarm like wild boars
over terraces below;
they uproot gardens
of emperors, viceroys, presidents.

Juan Escutia is wrapping
the flag around his wounds.
He climbs to the parapet.

An avalanche of beards and bayonets
rolls toward me.

I aim at the nearest man,
shoot him between the legs.

Our flag hurtles from the parapet.

I am covered with furious red ants.

> *Even precious stones crumble,*
> *gold cracks and breaks,*
> *bright feathers are torn.*
> *Are we to live on earth forever?*
> *Only a fleeting moment here!*

From Kate Gillhoff's Diary

Mother and Daddy have been dead
these seven years, and today
a letter came from General Taylor.
At a place called Buena Vista
on February 23, my brother Bill,
answering the call of something
always just beyond the next ridge,
was killed. Here, on this muddy
shore of the Santee, birds
are gorging on fiddler crabs.
Clouds skim the tree tops
like swan-maidens, and I would like
to leave the ground to join them.

Rodolfo Fierro

A sociopathic ex-school teacher, Fierro worked his way up to
the rank of colonel. He became Villa's right hand man, and the
scourge of all prisoners.

Thaddeus Colquitt Ivy
Collected Papers

Men are herded into the corral
ten at a time.
I stand my ground.
They flee, I fire,
change pistols,
fire again.

Thirty times
new prisoners enter,
thirty times
I kill myself with work.

My arms tire
like the arms of Moses
before the Red Sea.

The task done,
I retire for the night.
Tomorrow Villa may desire
that I entertain two hundred more.

From the sea of bodies
someone disturbs my dreams
of the secret lives of bullets
to beg for water.

I send my aide
to shoot him.

Elisa Griensen Speaks to the
School Children of Parral

She was an immigrant. Also a school teacher, she became an
avid supporter of the Revolution. One day, near the dusty town
of Parral, Villa was shot in the leg during a skirmish with some of
Pershing's troops.

Ivy, *Ibid*

Our Pancho Villa
hides nearby.
His leg
is dead,
but the rest
of him lives.
One bullet
can't finish him.

Gringo troops
are here
to kill
the rest of him:
the other leg,
both of his arms,
the brain.

Children,
let's bring gifts
for the visitors:
darts,
knives,
stones.

This Mauser
in my hand
has a bullet
for their major.

The Widow

The men are hungry,
lean as snakes,

their machetes
glint in the sun.

From the cabin,
a smell of coffee.

Mountain pines
are off guard,

they talk
to the wind.

The cabin comes closer.
A baby cries.

One sickly dog
drowses in the sun.

The widow pounds corn
in a stone grinder,

a rust-covered rifle
lies on the ground.

The men walk
in single file.

Meadow flowers
tremble in the wind.

Epilog

Witches and trucks
Pass in the dark.
We sleep on mats
Under the wings of God.
Tempered by wind,
Moulded by earth,
Bound to the land,
We thrive like flowers
In rich soil.

Before sunlight strikes
Lonely wayside shrines
And patios filled
With bougainvillea,

We arise and go to market.
Riding and pulling burros
Loaded with avocados
And figs, plums and limes,
Chickpeas and chocolate,
We see forests
And mountains
Emerge like corn
In early dawn.
Like corn
We come into the world,
Like dawn we endure.

We follow
The restless feet
Of an arroyo
Toward the market,
Where birds chirp
In bamboo cages
And hot tortillas
In straw baskets
Listen for the braying
Of our burros.
The crown of thorns
We bear on our brow
Is weightless as we
Hear the arroyo sing
To the living mountains.
On a reed-bottom chair
Fastened to a mule,
Christ rides among us,
Light as a feather.

EVE SHELNUTT

The Musician

I was learning from Juanita what death, or music, meant.

She came, in dreams, not initially to participate but to stand, a coalescense, at the edge of rooms barn-sized, open on two sides, weeds growing to the floor boards. Her shoes made wickets in the grass; between them, mounds, child-length.

Outside it was bright—afternoon sun, the last of definite energy; it hurt the eyes. Once, she stepped forward and displayed her teeth. She flung her head back as I said that I liked them—artificial, even, star-colored. "Oh," she said, "I don't at all," her head seeming to toss involuntarily so that I could observe too its whiteness at the scalp, the blending of hair and scalp by whiteness.

Or, asserting herself, she touched one arm, pulling me gently to her, to whisper, "You can't serve that cake. If you'll travel to Faulkner's hometown, to the museum there, you'll see his mother served a cake like that once."

Luigi, in this dream, was at the sink, saying as he washed his hands that he would buy champagne. He smiled, the water splashed, arcs of light scattering as the droplets fell.

The cake was two-tiered, of rectangles, stacked one upon another, jutting this way and that as if to resemble a hot-climate palace. It was covered with white frosting which gleamed as eggshells sometimes do, or pearls. It sat on a long table, on cardboard, ready for cutting; and, beside it, Juanita sneered.

Moreover, one early morning when the birds still slept, Juanita took my grandmother's place, crouched inside a cupboard, at the farm, on a Saturday night. She waited immobile until my father tried to tiptoe in, the moon head-sized behind his head as the door opened. And, springing out, Juanita beat him with a broom—my father, who had not yet married her, ruined her, tossed her sideways, who wanted in the time of this dream

251

merely not to become a Holy Roller, which keeping of his body off church floors and his writhing at least upright took him, as it turned out, a long, long way.

But, in this version of his youth, Juanita, grown big with age and sipping wine and eating food quickly, swatted his little limping body as it wended its way out, the screen door. I remember, slamming.

Of course Juanita telephoned—my waking life. We had ordinary conversations which were too real, air bubbling from the hooked fishes' mouths. In sleep, not hours before, I would have felt my teeth loosen, as if a tongue could pour! fall on the pillow—pearls beneath a goose's belly. Luigi would find them, scoop them up for safe-keeping.

What makes the world painful? Objects, including the sight of bodies. Cake. When Luigi married me, we served the most beautiful petits fours, roses set on their tops, sweet and lemony, tiny leaves beside them, touching. The minister's robe was the lavender that brides' mothers wear, or girls barely old enough to walk at Eastertime, who lock their baskets in their fists.

He sweated, this minister. His hands shook, his eyes looked shy. And all the while Luigi smiled at me so wide a smile I knew not to turn to stone.

Mornings, straddling me after I curve one arm around his black curls, Luigi says, "You called?" In half-sleep, I smile. He, then, with a toss of his head, sends Juanita packing, her skirts aswish in the long grass, soft light shining on her head, and, seen leaving, her face turned to the other side, she is lovely and, imagine, graceful.

Once, just as Luigi entered me, I noticed Juanita had walked to my father's door. One ravaged hand raised to knock; she knew *he* would have to answer.

"You like?" Luigi always asks me once inside me.

I didn't run to the back of my father's house to warn him. His window was open and near the ground. I could have leaned in, called. But he had turned down the page of his book, one earpiece of his bifocals dangled from his teeth. So I let him get up from the chair, *see* who was at the door.

Luigi, did you know what you were doing? Did our minister wear such a robe to dazzle you? Each anniversary I will send him a note, violets sprayed across it.

But, also, Luigi has a child he's never seen, nor I, though I had shown him *my* child, Paul, the boy almost grown. Often, then, I asked Luigi, "How old did you say she is?"

252

"Him," Luigi would answer. "A boy, age two."

Her, I had met, the mother—sweet, as a method, and thin, and incapable, the baby invisible under her skirt. In time we heard it had arrived, and we did not travel to see it.

"Yes," I said to Luigi, "a boy. I simply forget."

Me and Luigi? Lightning split a blue spruce pine and from its rings our grandmothers, having met by accident, emerged together, holding us. Before we slept at night or when we traveled to the store for groceries, I sang to Luigi songs such as grandmothers know.

And my father had had a child by his last wife, copies of whose pictures he sent by mail. Luigi and I said as we looked at them together that she was beautiful, all, I think, my father got from this girl, our words, over his pictures, which words we remembered to restate in our letters to him. He lived alone, he had pictures stuck everywhere. Sometimes he sent Luigi pictures, yellowed, Juanita's face and body cut from them. "Is that you?" Luigi asked. "That's very sweet."

Thus, we too had pictures everywhere, none, of course, of Luigi's boy. And none, either, of the boy whose twin I had been. On some days I reasoned that Juanita had gone knocking on my father's door to ask for pictures of him—perfect child, Juanita had said, simply without breath, or, as I saw it, a fish contented.

When autumn came, Luigi polished the car, washed its windows, moving then to the house and its windows, the porch, the porch swing, all clean for my exit, our going and returning, should I feel like it. "You may want to take a trip," said Luigi. "So the car's all set, if we want," how, you see, Luigi talked—*you, we.* Language wedded to his body, for Luigi worked with his hands—cars, loose copper drain pipes, broken steps, anything our neighbors wanted. And if it was odd to them that Luigi loved music, simply they didn't know from whence he came. In death, stretched out, his mother wore a look of such repose it put a shame in all the mourners, as if they could not move smoothly. Her look was for having made Luigi. Of course she rested satisfied, I say.

Often and at times without pattern, I thought how Paul's father and I never saw Paul together, never, say, Paul on one side of a room, us on another. I was sure this absence changed the manner in which Paul stood, how he held his head, changed even the air in which he stood.

The days were still hot. "If we take a trip," I said to Luigi, "let's wait until this Indian summer passes," when, I thought, I might be done with the over-sleeping, "the bride's rest," Luigi's cousins called it, not knowing Juanita flitted behind the fence-posts, the old well. Nor looking, really, at my face, neither young nor old, rather, poised, *my* ornamental cousin being Garcia Lorca, who said, "We will nail up the windows and the rain and the long nights will crawl in over the bitter grasses."
Present in mind at Luigi's mother's mourning scene were only, I think, Luigi and his mother. They seemed lonely. Then Luigi turned to me.

Not minding the heat, Luigi's friends or a cousin or two came by in the evenings to visit. They loosened their boots and propped their feet on the porch railing and, leaning back, Luigi's beer in hand, they talked, their voices drifting in to me where I lay on the bed, "the weather," Luigi would explain. Or from where I sat reading, I would watch them repair one of their cars. Before settling down, I would fix sandwiches and, always, Luigi found a way to kiss me privately. He would choose as the place an ear or the inside of one arm.
One afternoon, they oiled the porch swing so that, afterward, when I knew Juanita took her place on it as Luigi and I sat together in the kitchen, I would remember, later as I dreamed, only the sound of her feet on the gray-painted wood. Swish, swish, as if she were a child. Her feet, in reality, were long and bony. Were she to have lived six years more, the doctors might have operated to remove the jutting bone. Luigi's mother's feet were, of course, hidden by flowers and a short yellow coverlet on top of which her arms rested.

In the south, distances seem farther between towns than in other places, except perhaps in Russian novels, in snow. In truth, Luigi and I could have visited Juanita every week. "Just say when, Sweets," Luigi had said.
However, it was as if I had counted every tree between Juanita's house and ours, had seen her red cape flare behind each one as she came inching forward.
Luigi was, I think now, waiting on me, the minister's eyes shy, I suppose, with knowledge beyond us on our Day of Days, the

254

pronouncing of a state, he must have guessed, not rendering it so.

Luigi said he would learn to cook. He said it must be similar to learning how an engine works. I sat by the kitchen window, cooling, watching, Luigi so beautiful. Once I thought I heard Juanita laughing in delight, an apothegm of sorts.

The food was lovely too—baked fish sprinkled with paprika, a billow of sauce around it. And asparagus. Pots and pans everywhere, Luigi sweating. . . .

We were getting Luigi's mother accustomed to me when she died. I had come to sleep pristine on the single bed downstairs. Hearing Luigi as he stooped down to tell me, I had tried to scramble inside a wall, a corner, pale yellow. Time does not flow.

"Luigi," I said, "let's ask Paul to come visit us."

"Well sure," said Luigi. "Here, taste this." And I did, smiling.

Instead, Juanita called. "I'm sick," she said. "I'm not kidding this time."

"All this?" Luigi asked, looking at what I had placed by the door to take. Luigi's records, the old violin he had said he wanted to learn to play, my books, Luigi's huge yellow rain-slicker, his favorite roasting pan. The car was full, the house closed up tight. As we drove, I rested my head on Luigi's shoulder, and it seemed sometimes, at the curves, that Juanita sat beside the door. "Maybe Paul can come there," I said.

We found her as I had imagined we would, when the clomp, clomping of her red shoes would stop, the door left cracked open for us, behind us the late sun and inside the green coolness of her walls and the drawn curtains, her body looking longer yet on the brocade sofa, her shoes off, one arm across her stomach, the other on a cushion, palm up, the head thrown back and, as we pushed open the door, the color white, of hair and face and, for that instant in which her eyes focused on us, the variegated white of her eyes. We dropped our bundles and went forward, both of us crouching by her, me closest to her face. "What's wrong, Momma?" I whispered.

"You think they *know?*" she asked, sitting up, fluffy hair sprayed across her forehead. "Luigi," she asked, brushing one hand across his knee, "would *you* think they know?" She slapped his knee. "No! They don't."

"Should we bring in the rest of our things, Momma?" I asked her, softly still, which was how I talked to her, always, as if the modulated voice would make my body patient.

"Well sure!" said Juanita. "Now let me look at you, Luigi," and she stood up, pulling Luigi with her, to turn him around before her. She was his height; he smiled, smiling still and turning as I went to get our things.

Luigi cooked in the tiny kitchen, doorless, by which Juanita was able to watch as she lay on the couch—the refrigerator door opening, shutting, Luigi pulling out a stool to place a pan on, the windows being flung open, one of Juanita's sponge rollers falling from a sill onto the floor, Luigi calling out, "Hungry, you two?"

That first night, Juanita ate a tremendous amount. As I bent to kiss her, I noticed the smell of spaghetti, that the couch had a stain where she had put her plate. "I like Luigi," she said. And I pulled the quilt close around her, I settled her in.

Outside our window, a wind stirred the oak trees. It was as if we were hemmed in. I raised myself on an elbow and I looked down at Luigi, almost sleeping. "Think," I said, "of how much she *ate*. I really have my doubts. . . ."

"No, no," said Luigi, pulling me to him, "go to sleep. She knows something we don't know."

That night, of course, Juanita did not come sneaking through the grass. She was where she was—sleeping on the couch in her own house, her trees brushing at the window and, under our bed, her shoes in neat little rows.

I think of those days as pewter-colored, though for a long time there was the brightest sun—we watered the willow in the yard and we sprayed down the dirt of the drive. Luigi replaced the screening on all the windows, cut the vines from the carport. I would not leave his side, and so we both browned, by which Juanita, in contrast, seemed whiter.

One day I drove alone to my father's house, and I cleaned it. I took his arm and we walked his property, past the old house Juanita had crouched in, running him off with her broom. The back door hung open and you could see from the road the little cupboard, too small for any human body. He asked, looking at my bare arm, if I needed a watch, and, days later, in the mail, to Juanita's house, came a silver watch, which I hid from Juanita.

The nights, now, were chilly; we closed all the windows, clear before Luigi's new screening. The sky turned gray and the color, I thought, went with Luigi's music. Juanita hummed along, lifting her eyes now and then to flirt with Luigi, a smile, barely apparent, at her lips, which she still painted red. One night she gave him her violin bow. But Luigi couldn't play and Juanita said

she was too tired to teach him now. "You should have," she said
to me, "kept up with the violin."

For reasons I did not understand, Luigi and I did not put away
anything we used, nor the violin case from which Juanita had
taken the bow. So it sat on the green carpet, by the sofa, open,
the three-legged tray sitting over it, and, on the tray, Juanita's
glass of bicarbonate soda and water.

"We can't possibly have Paul come here," I said to Luigi,
looking around.

"Well sure we can," said Luigi. But, instead, I thought of Paul
bringing to our door a girl, saying, "This is my girl." And, after
we had met her, he would send pictures of the two of them, in a
park, taken by a stranger, a relation on *her* side.

Juanita didn't know of my father's other wives—why should
she? I had thought. But, then, too, she never spoke of him. We
brought her magazines and, looking them over, she had Luigi
move the furniture around. The couch, then, faced the windows,
and when Luigi and I came down the rise after going to the store,
we would see, if the curtains were parted, Juanita waiting.

"Don't worry," said Luigi when I tossed at night. "One of the
neighbors is watering the plants. It'll all keep."

I think Luigi was happy. And there was so much for him to do.
Take Juanita for little walks, for instance, the doctors shaking
their heads and saying a little walk might help. I watched them
from Juanita's place on the couch. His black head, hers white,
bobbing over the rise and down, until there was nothing but
quiet in her tiny house. What does she say to him?

"You know," said Luigi, "nothing, just chatter." And he
laughed. I thought he was forgetting his own mother, his stoop-
ing on the floor beside her, one hand at her collarbone, only the
pulse missing.

One morning, Luigi pulling me atop of him, I stopped over him
as a sea gull sometimes will over water. "Do you think," I whispered, "she *hears* us?" which thinking of had made me sick.

"Oh no," said Luigi, "she doesn't hear that well now, I've
noticed," which, I think, was why I came to notice Juanita
watching me. I thought, as I passed her by or brought her a glass
or an ashtray, of the sound in seashells, of the person holding
one to an ear. He squints his eyes, he places himself imagina-
tively on a beach, he tilts his head.

No, Juanita did not die then; in fact, she lasted five years more, and, the last year, we brought her to our house, mine and Luigi's, so that she could have space around her, light and our trees and the sound under the trees of Luigi and his friends, pounding on something or laughing. And Paul, in and out with each new girl, until he settled. Once, in that time, I met Luigi's boy, a formal loving-at-first-sight. And Luigi stayed the same. Anyone would love Luigi, and I have clung. Learning does not take memory away, which is what shells whisper.

I would be reading in the Queen Anne's chair, my legs out before me on the hassock. Luigi might be out with the trash, trying to get it to burn even as a light rain fell. I would turn a page and be thinking of how he looked—yellow and shiny in the coat, the charcoal of its inside surface turned up at the sleeves, Luigi whistling. Then I would notice: Juanita watching me.

Or Luigi would hand me a platter across the table. I would be lifting one hand from my lap to receive it when, suddenly, it would seem so quiet that we both would look at Juanita, is she all right? She would have been watching me.

I thought, some nights, Luigi's hand resting on my back as he slept, that she was jealous, Luigi, at peace, just so. Alone, I decided, I will gather up her shoes from under the bed, when the time comes. I won't, I thought, let Luigi see them.

Then, one night when the rain shook the windows, driven hard against them by a wind, the lights flashing off twice and the tiny house seeming to shake away from the cement slab holding it down, I rested my book in my lap, I turned it over, and I looked up, to Luigi stretched out on the floor by Juanita's couch. *Luigi,* I thought, smiling, though he did not see me, his head resting on an outstretched arm, turned toward the windows, toward the skirt of Juanita's couch. It could have been the only time Luigi was not facing me.

So—which I can say almost smiling now—there was nowhere to look but at Juanita. She looked at me for a long time. The wind died down, it grew still outside and, inside, stiller yet.

Juanita's eyes narrowed, she tilted her head, as if listening. And I think it was this stillness she had waited so long for. And, on this night, her lips were dry, her hair uncurled, flat on her head.

I thought how far away Luigi was, as though there were miles of water between us. I saw it sparkling, without my looking down.

She raised one hand, with which she pointed at me. "You," she said, "have done me an injustice."

It was then, I think, after the air had fallen, as Luigi rose, came walking toward me, that I married him, in sickness and in health.

And Juanita, as we know, went on living.

W. D. SNODGRASS

Diplomacy: The Father

Your mission, in any disputed area, is to find
    (as in yourself)
which group, which element among the contending forces
    seems, by nature, most fit to take control.
Stronger perhaps, more driven, gifted with resources—
    no matter: able to bind in a firm goal
the enervating local passions native to our kind.
      That force, of course, is

your enemy—whom you cannot choose but love.
      As in yourself,
it's this, it's those so loved, that can grow oppressive
    and steal your hard-bought freedom to choose
that you won't love. Act loving, then. Make no aggressive
    move; make friends. Make, though, for future use,
notes on their debts, beliefs, whom they're most fond of—
      their weaknesses.   If

anything, appear more loyal—pretend to feel
      as in yourself
you'd truly want to feel: affectionate and admiring.
    Then hate grows, discovering the way such foes enslave
you worst: if you loved them, you'd *feel* free. Conspiring
    to outwit such subtlety, devise and save
good reasons for your hatred; count wounds. Conceal,
      though, this entire ring

of proofs, excuses, wrongs which you maintain
      as in yourself
might harbor some benign, enfeebling growth.
    As for followers, seek those who'll take your aid:

the weak. In doubt who's weaker, finance both.
    Collect the dawdlers, the brilliant but afraid,
the purchasable losers—those who, merely to gain
        some power they can loathe

would quite as willingly be out of power
        as in. Yourself?—
friend, this is lonely work. Deep cravings will persist
    for true allies, for those you love; you will long
to speak your mind out sometimes, or to assist
    someone who, given that help, might grow strong
and admirable. You've reached your bleakest hour,
        the pitiless test.

But think: why let your own aid diminish you?
        As in yourself,
so in those who take your help, your values or your name,
    you've sought out their best thoughts, their hidden talents
only to buy out, to buy off. Your fixed aim,
    whatever it costs, must still be for a balance
of power in the family, the firm, the whole world through.
        Exactly the same

as a balance of impotence—in any group or nation
        as in yourself.
Suppose some one of them rose up and could succeed
    your foe—he'd *be* your foe. To underlings, dispense
all they can ask, but don't need; give till they need
    your giving. One gift could free them: confidence.
They'd never dare ask. Betray no dedication
        to any creed

or person—talk high ideals; then you'll be known
        as, in yourself,
harmless. Exact no faith from them, no affection;
    suppose they've learned no loyalty to you—
that's one step taken in the right direction.
    Never forbid them. Let no one pay back what's due;
the mere air they breathe should come as a loan
        beyond collection.

Like air, you must be everywhere at once, where-
        as, in your self-
defence, make yourself scarce. Your best disguise

is to turn gray, spreading yourself so thin
you're one with all unknowns—essential. Vaporize
    into the fog all things that happen, happen in
or fail to happen. In the end, you have to appear
        as unworldly in the eyes

of this whole sanctioned world that your care drained
        as in yours. Self-
sacrifice has borne you, then, through that destruction
    programmed into life; you live on in that loving tension
you leave to those who'll still take your instruction.
    You've built their world; an air of soft suspension
which you survive in, as cradled and sustained
        as in yourself.

SUE STANDING

Swimming Lessons for the Dead

> Else what shall they do which are
> baptized for the dead, if the dead
> rise not at all?
>
> 1 Corinthians 15:29

I was baptized by immersion when I was eight.
At fast-and-testimony meeting, the elders
laid their hands on my head to give me
the gift of the Holy Ghost. I could feel
their hands, like ballast, for days after.

At twelve, I was baptized for the dead
in an underground font supported by twelve gold oxen.
After each female ancestor's name was called out,
I was pressed underwater in my white dress.
I saw a clothesline full of white garments, hands.

Now, I dream of a swimming pool full of the dead—
my particular dead. Their bodies float
on the surface like small white life rafts;
their waterwings whisper and rustle
as they drift and spin against each other.

Flutter and fin, I tell them.
If one starts to sink, I dive in
and come up under the shoulders:
breathe out, breathe in.
I am the lifeguard and the deathguard.

Letter to Saint Jerome

Did you think if you did not love
you would not grow old?
I know you will not read this
because you no longer read letters,
though you long for them.
You know too well the long "o" of longing.
Before you entered the desert,
I knew you. I knew you
before your mind started playing
patience with itself,
before your elegant fingers
traced only the spines of books
in your industrious cell,
before you reduced life to the view
from your honeycomb windows.
Now your life is pale and flowers only
with rue and the bitter herbs
you saved from your old garden.
You tried to cut the lover's knot
but not before I was caught in it.
You told me the eyes of angels
are rarely sad. Your homilies
have become more cryptic and twisted.
The traveller's joy in the garden
has all gone to old man's beard.

GIDEON TELPAZ

The Tranquil Heart

Up until the fifth act everything went fine. The turbulent con-
flicts came to an end. Like molten lava poured the bitter words
of wit Shakespeare had put in my mouth. The son of a murdered
father and a sinful mother, I struggled with the palace intrigues; a
marvelous lunatic, a sworn avenger. Then, shortly before the
fencing scene, disaster struck. I was standing in the palace with
Horatio, that loyal friend, by my side, letting out my heartfelt
agony:

> But I am very sorry, good Horatio,
> That to Laertes I forgot myself;
> For, by the image of my cause, I see
> The portraiture of his—

My mouth remained open, alas, I couldn't make a sound. A
curious hush fell upon the auditorium. Hundreds of ears strained
to hear me as I stood on the dusty floor boards, pierced by a
sudden deadly silence. Whispers ruffled the front rows. Heads
turned aside, huddling together. I staggered, the auditorium
swayed before me. With my legs collapsing I escaped backstage.

I lay on a couch in the dressing room, a wet cloth on my
forehead. The theater doctor who had rushed in was bending
over me with a worried face. The stage director leaned against
the wall, biting his nails. My vertigo wouldn't go. I couldn't trust
my voice or my legs. I was unable to die that night, to expire in
that parched voice,

> O, I die, Horatio!
> The potent poison quite o'ercrows my spirit—

My understudy stepped into my shoes eagerly enough, even

though I didn't leave him many good lines; he was an athlete, a fencing buff. Leaning on the doctor's arm, heading for the rear exit, I caught the sound of the mournful trumpets and Fortinbras's instructions what should be done with my body:

> Let four captains
> Bear Hamlet, like a soldier, to the stage;
> For he was likely, had he been put on,
> To have proved most royal—

I took the doctor's advice and left for a convalescent home in one of the Galilee kibbutzim. The place was surrounded by greenery, held in ascetic serenity. On my second day there I ran into a middle-aged bachelor, a short man with a withered, pockmarked face, a tattered mustache and lugubrious eyes hidden behind a pair of thick lenses. He had been a member of a southern kibbutz years ago, until he'd gotten mixed up with some sort of a crime. Though he'd served his time, the kubbutz wouldn't have him back. He drifted around, ending up here as a gardener. In the course of our conversation he revealed that a certain Indian book had fallen into his hands while he was in prison. Out of sheer boredom he'd begun to leaf through it.

"I wouldn't have survived without this book," he said, pulling it out of his overalls pocket and caressing it with his eyes. "The strangest poetry. Sanskrit songs. Dialogues between Krishna and Arjuna."

"Who?"

"God and man."

"Can I see it?"

The gardener edged away hiding the book behind his back.

"Just a peek."

He shook his head with an odd obstinacy. I grabbed the book out of his hand.

"Give it back!" he muttered as a pallor came over him. "No kidding!"

"Don't worry, I won't eat it."

"I'm not worried about the book."

"What are you worried about?"

"You."

I laughed and scooted off down an asphalt path between lawns. He chased me, holding onto his glasses which kept slipping down.

"Give it back!"

"I shall," I promised, "after I take a look at it."

266

A look!

I swallowed the *Bhagavad Gita* in double doses during the two weeks I spent at the convalescent home. What was it in the sadness of Arjuna who refused to go out to battle when the time came, and what was it in the words of the god who tried to encourage him on the battlefield that so beguiled me?

Saturday morning Nina and Natti came for a visit. Natti listened intently to the lines I read aloud. He couldn't comprehend them but was captivated by the melody of my voice and the spell of the foreign names. I saw as much in his wide open eyes. But Nina's face voiced her displeasure. When I lifted my head from the book I ran up against this look of hers.

"Too esoteric for my taste," she said. "Why the Hindu mysticism?"

I failed to suppress a smile.

"Would you prefer that of Rabbi Nachman of Bretslav?"

"More!" Natti pinched my nose between two fingers to turn my head back to the book. "Read more, Daddy."

"You forget you came here to calm your nerves," Nina said.

I had nothing to say to that.

"More, Daddy! More!" the kid urged me on.

"Why not leave mysticism to the mystics? You're only an actor."

She bit her tongue. But the thing was said and in the air now lingered a caustic, bitter echo of an old, unforgotten argument. For Natti's sake I checked myself. I read another song. Natti sat on my knees and to Nina's annoyance swallowed every word. What could I've told her? My ex-wife Nina, the priestess of practicality, felt gauche outside the precinct of her senses or her logic. When I suggested I believed in omens and took them to be attempts at communication from other worlds she would listen with a tense silence. But her sulky face spoke, and I could read her fear: Could it be that I've transmitted my dottiness to Natti?

People unhinged are more inclined to depend on a set routine; three meals a day, lawn chair, eight hours' sleep—not so in my case. I never put the book down. I found myself studying the lines, memorizing them, testing them aloud for how they might carry from the stage.

Shortly after my return to Tel Aviv, as I climbed the theater stairs I tried to imagine the Director's reaction to my request for a year's leave of absence. I wasn't too far off. The man leaned back from his big executive's desk; the thick hairy fingers on his left hand fiddled with his tie; in his right hand he was holding a flyswatter. He was impeccably attired, a crafty dynamo from the

267

business world on loan to the theater from a large chemical corporation where he had scored his first successes. He peered at me, examining with care the odd bird of his exotic aviary which he was now obliged to deal with with patience and respect. Portraits of the theater's founders looked down on me from the wall behind him as he waved his flyswatter across the table and spoke. "You're certainly aware that if we let you go for this length of time, it would be difficult to maintain our repertory."

"You can always find a replacement."

He looked at me askance. "You underestimate yourself that much?"

I stared him out. As an actor he wasn't so hot. It wouldn't take much to yank the rug from beneath him. When I informed him that if the theater could not go along with my request, I would go it alone, he began to show signs of caving in.

"What sort of buried truths do you intend to uncover during this year?"

I realized he'd already had words with Nina. He was wearing the most solemn expression he could find in his prop-room when he said, "Why not go back to the Bible, if all you're looking for is religious stimulation? Leave the Hindu philosophy for the Hindus."

"I'm not looking for religious stimulation."

"What then are you looking for?"

I didn't feel I owed him an answer and stood up to leave.

"We'll see you back soon," he grunted. He remained seated. "The role you're acting has not yet been written."

The fragrance of the wind, the fragrance of the rain, the fragrance of waterbeads on the fresh leaves. The silky air when the clouds are gone, the silence of dawn on the blue ridges. The gilded sun rising, the cascades of light on the gray green olives, the lengthening of shadows on the rocky slopes.

My Himalaya.

"All people struggle on the paths leading to me," says Brahama, and I seemed to have found the beginning of a path in a secluded, white-domed stone house on the hills of Jerusalem.

Fall came with its gusts, cold and sharp. All night long it rained on the hills. The tolling of morning bells from the monastery in the valley woke me at daybreak. The rain closing in on me dispersed the deadly fumes of the world I left behind. Seek the truth within yourself, it was said in the *Upanishads,* but when I looked into myself I was startled.

I drank limpid water on an empty stomach to purify my system and ate nothing until I was sure I was hungry. What I ate was meager. I wouldn't touch meat, just fruit, vegetables and berries. I was fasting a great deal. I practiced for hours out of a Hatha Yoga book. Besides the concentration exercises, meditation and headstands, I was working on the breathing exercises, *prāṇāyāma*. One thing depends on another: without controlling your breathing how could you expect to control your willpower, let alone your concentration? I got up to the monastery bells, took my morning bath, went out on the porch to become one with the view. The olives. The dewdrops glistening on the grass. The distant mountaintops tenderly massaged by the sun's vibrant fingers.

As I hiked through the mountains, wild animals, startled by my footfall, scurried away into the thicket. Summer's thorns and thistles withered up. Rain revived the scorched slopes. Green replaced yellow and brown. Squills rose up, erect and lustrous, autumn crocuses and saffrons embellished the terraces, cyclamen peeped, drooping, from cleft stones. The wild flora encircled deserted orchards, pools carved in the rocks, the ruins of houses, hidden caves. As I approached the ravine flocks of birds would fly up and circle above, flapping their wings to escort me as I walked the firelanes through the forests. I synchronized my breathing exercises with my paces, and learned to climb mountaintops without puffing.

I would watch the sunsets from the porch. The weary fireball dove slowly into a saddle in the mountains. The sky caught fire: now red, now yellow, now rose. Twilight drizzled on the cypresses, streamed in the valleys. The mountains glowed as nature filled with wild softness. The walls of the Italian monastery melted away, twilight fading on the belltowers. I spaced out in the stillness of hills nestling in darkness, beneath the traveling sky, the rising moon, the dangling stars. I read very little in my years on the stage and now a strong hunger awoke in me. *Mahābhārata, Pañcatantra, Rāmāyaṇa,* I kept reading into the dawn.

Nina couldn't take seeing me any more. In her last visit, as she was about to leave, she wondered if I shouldn't seek help. Freddie's name came to her lips.

"You've changed. I hardly recognize you since you took up the role of the holy monk."

"I'm not playing any role." I had to set the record straight. "There's no audience here and I'm not interested in applause."

She seemed little convinced and even on the stairs, holding the boy by the hand, and heading for her car, she was tempted to drag me into another argument. I paid no attention. I was beyond anger, insult, regret.

I had stopped going down to Tel Aviv and from then on she sent Natti in a cab. At a designated time I would wait for him at the cab station in downtown Jerusalem and a few hours later I would put him back in a cab to Tel Aviv. He was thrilled to see my beard, my long, shaggy hair. In his eyes I detected no sign of the pity or distaste which I had grown accustomed to expect in his mother's eyes. These were happy hours—at the zoo, on the park lawns. He was taken with my tales, never tired of hearing about the prince who met many women sent him by heaven, listening eagerly, scratching his head.

"So what is life, Daddy?" he blurted out one day after I had told him about a certain king who wanted to remove the body of a dead man from the gallows to the cemetery but every time the corpse would slip away and return to its place. "Just a fable?"

On Saturday, January 15, a fierce sandstorm blew in from the desert, swirling into the mountains, covering everything with an unpleasant yellow layer. The whirling winds howled three days. The sky was fouled with dust; the sun dimmed and hung miserably, shrouded with hazy scarves. Suddenly it got colder. All through the third night the wind continued to blow. As morning came it died down. In the strange silence I missed the usual noise of the birds. Instead, I could hear sounds of creaks and cracklings from outside. When I got up to look out the window I was taken aback. Snow six inches deep had accumulated on the sill and buried the rose bush. The porch was white. The same white cloth draped the mountains. Heavy flakes drifted up and spiraled away. The crackling was the casuarina branches giving way under the weight of the snow. A snapped electricity wire dangled between the broken branches. I put on a coat and went down to the cellar and brought up wood for the fire. It continued to snow into the night. Just before morning the floodgates opened and a torrential rain came beating down. A thick fog engulfed the valleys. Water gushed down the ditches from the thawing mountains, eroding the roads. When it had passed and the ditches lay silent, a guest arrived.

He wore a black dufflecoat; a plaid cap was pulled down over his droll face. Thin, lanky, cold-eyed Freddie settled near the fireplace, took off his soaked shoes and stood them up to dry. Looking this way and that, he uttered in his crisp voice, "Nirvana? Not yet. A long beard and a cultivated peace of mind are not necessarily a ticket to eternal bliss."

I served him a hot drink. He went on, "I've myself to blame.

270

You've cooked up a dish of curry from leftover psychoanalysis."

I had no intention of correcting him. Still I said, "Your treatment cured me of allergies and nailbiting but did nothing for my soul."

"So it seems, so it seems," Freddie nodded. "You've left my couch to indulge in dilettantish twattle."

I looked at him.

"Freddie," I said, "you may be the greatest shrink but you could never help me touch the abiding roots. No one can understand things human unless he first understands things divine."

Freddie aimed a cold stare at me. "And that's from what? *King Lear?*"

I stretched out on the floor on my back, propping myself on two points of support along my spine, and breathed slowly. The long months of seclusion suddenly came together for me, the energy gushed, overflowed. Freddie stood at my head watching silently. I made contact; the nerve center stood at my command. I loosened up my limbs, one by one, from the tips of my toes to my head. Freddie bent over me, lifted my leg by the ankle and let go. My leg fell like a dead weight. He grabbed my biceps and dropped my arm. The hand fell lifeless. I was floating far above him on the blue, a particle of air, a patch of sky.

"Self-hypnosis," Freddie said, wiping his brow, "I'm a doctor; I can see what you've done."

I stood up. He narrowed his eyes, those droll, piercing eyes, his most prominent feature, and focused them on mine.

The fire was dying; I put more wood on and it rose again.

"Freddie," I said, "how about a card game?"

Freddie smiled. "Don't tell me you have cards here."

"What if I do?"

He was lucky. Yawning, he swept the kitty. At the close of each hand he pulled a silk handkerchief from his jacket and dabbed it to his forehead. After losing the fourth time I had no more than one agora left. Freddie shuffled the cards nonchalantly. I slipped the coin under my elbow and pressed it to the table. Now you're going to lose, Freddie, and that's it, I said inaudibly, I'll beat the socks off you.

Freddie took his first loss without blinking an eye. After his second, the sweat sprouting on his brow increased. His yawning trailed off. As his next loss become clear, the mole on his left cheek began to twitch. I kept pressing my elbow to the table. The coin sunk into my flesh. Freddie blew smoke and sent a puzzled, sullen look out of the corner of his eye, trying to get a glimpse of my cards. It exasperated him to see that everything was on the up and up. His luck went from bad to worse. My elbow was glued to the table. My head began to swim. I hated the coin, loathed it. Freddie pulled out a winning card, confident that his luck would change. I threw my cards on the table. He sat back bewildered. I swept his last penny.

I lifted my elbow, and as the coin loosened and fell out, electricity fled my body. Freddie observed me.

"Beginning to feel like a little god?" he said.

My chest tightened. Outside, the pine trees were rustling in the wind. The pealing of bells swelled from the gloomy monastery, wet, heart-rending. I turned and looked at Freddie. Would he understand now? Would he believe now?

"Don't you see, Freddie?" I heard myself saying; all the while my ears tuned to the bells. "I'm trying to get rid of the crap. I'm trying to find the one true path. To make this superior to this."

I pointed to my head, then my heart.

The mole quivered on Freddie's cheek. His shoes had dried out, but the soles were still steaming when he bent down to tie them.

"Is this an announcement of your retirement from the stage?"

I threw out my arms.

"How do I know? How can I tell? I've acted all my life. After reading these *Vedas,* when I return to the theater, if I do, and resume acting, I won't be the same actor. What else can I say?"

"Aren't you acting right now?" Freddie shot back. "Aren't you acting out the silliest, most pretentious and most dangerous role of your career?"

I turned my back on him. Below, the monastery bells were still wailing.

Sometime after Freddie's visit I received a small package by mail. A thin book with a folded note neatly attached to its dust jacket.

"Let's see what you say after reading this one. Freddie."

Even before I opened it I could feel the bad vibes coming from it. A poisonous dagger lay concealed between the words of the first lines.

"In the world we live in today," or something like that, Huxley wrote in the opening pages of the book Freddie sent me, "a world of Darwin, Newton and Freud, it would be difficult for us to believe in the unbelievable."

I could picture Freddie's troll-like smile. His eyes cut through to me like X-rays from across mountains and valleys.

I pitied him.

Lowering myself to the floor, I set myself for exercise. The breathing sequence, the concentration, crosslegged, inhaling. Even though I had mastered them now, I never did these exercises mechanically. Each time was the first time, the only time.

This time too.

But there was something in the room this time, disturbing, hostile. Could it be Freddie's book? For the first time in a long while my exercises miscarried.

I stood up and went out. Down below the village slept. Streetlights flickered. Mist veiled the stars. The mountains, like a herd of kneeling elephants, huddled together. Could these be atmospheric disturbances? Some fluctuation of the barometer in the vicinity? The moon's play?

Hours passed. When I went in daybreak splattered across the window. I switched on the lamp on the night table and reached for Huxley. I couldn't get past the first page. I hated it bitterly and hurled it away. It was quite a while before I cooled off. I got up out of bed, picked it up and plowed through it until the sun rose, forcing myself to read to the last page and hating Huxley as I've hated nothing before. I took the first bus back into town. The rush-hour bus. By noon I was in Galilee at the convalescent home.

I found the gardener bent over a rosebush, holding pruning shears.

"Read it," I said.

The man glanced at the book, then at me quizzically.

"I want to know what you think of it."

I stayed overnight there. Surely, if something did happen he would contact me right away. I was working alone all this time, without a swami; was I on the wrong track? Follow thy Self and understand it, for it is the root of the Eternal Cosmic Self—it is said in the *Upanishads*. But was I mistaken to set out on this route without a guide? Like an arrow that hits the target and becomes one with it, you must become one with the Brahma. This too was said in the *Upanishads*. But what if I flew wide of the mark? I waited but the gardener didn't show up.

In the morning I went out to the lawn. The gardener was raking dead leaves under the big walnut trees.

"Have you read it?"

The gardener nodded.

"The whole thing?"

"Just the first chapter. Best sleeping pill. Put me to sleep right away."

All the way back to Jerusalem I kept asking myself, How did it happen? Where had I gone wrong? How had I screwed it up?

My lost tranquility, thwarted exercises. At loose ends again, I was roaming the nearby mountains when gradually the strands began to come together. I was still debating with myself but the choice seemed clear. I went to the bank, withdrew all my savings and bought the airplane ticket.

"Didn't I warn you? You start fooling around with the Buddha, you end up off the wall," said Nina when I stopped by on the way to the airport. "First it was off to the mountains. Now it's overseas. What next?"

Her venom I could stomach; saying goodbye to Natti was the hard part.

Tel Aviv disappeared beneath me as the plane soared and flew over the shoreline, heading for the sea. Low, feathery clouds sailed beneath the wings, the sea revealing itself momentarily under their spread. Down below were islands sunk in the water, some set in the sea like swollen toads warming in the sun. One giant island lay on its side, stretched like a crocodile shedding a skin, with mountainous humps on its back. I could see the outline of a huge bay; boats glittered in its water like pin heads. An immense fleet of white clouds floated ahead of us. One cloud had spouted to a great height, like a geyser. We headed toward it but it felt as if the plane was not moving, as if it had frozen in flight, pierced in midair. The geyser drew closer, now a fleecy mountain, and soon it swallowed us.

Like a tired bird, the big silver Boeing glided toward dry land. As I unbuckled my seatbelt, I watched the bustling airport from the porthole on my right, the planes stationed near the gates, flaunting their diverse insignia and blazons in the afternoon sun.

I took a room in Earl's Court, a cheap, small room, listed at the tourist bureau in Victoria station. From a red telephone booth at the nearest street corner I called Henry. His voice came cheery over the phone and he hurried to pick me up and take me to dinner at his club in Chelsea. Henry was an eccentric libertine, bespectacled, moustached. His converstion was spicy, if caustic. We'd hit it off when he'd come to Tel Aviv to direct a Pinter thing, one of the box-office successes from the West End which we used to import. Since then he'd had it with directing, as I found out, and become a critic. I could tell he'd read me clearly the moment he gave me a first look as he opened the car door for me.

"I've come to find a yogi. I need help," I told him as we sat down in the dining room of his club.

Henry tucked his napkin blithely into his collar and peeped at

274

the menu, "Jolly good, and how are you going to go about finding him?"

He looked at me over the lenses of his spectacles.

"He'll turn up sooner or later. What is destined happens in due course," I explained.

"I've heard that line before," Henry grimaced. He spoke with the voice of an old-timer, who has heard all the other lines as well. "This no man's land is swarming with swamis, maharishis, and all sorts of gurus. How will you be able to tell which one is the real McCoy?" He took a sip of his wine and dabbed his lips with the napkin. "Let me go fishing. I may come up with just the right fish for you."

He had to dash off to London's other end. I drove with him a part of the way, to Soho, where he dropped me off.

Henry drove away and I remained standing on the curb. The streetlights poured their dim yellow light on the furious Jaguars that chased showy Rolls Royces up the road. The doors of a nearby cinema opened and a crowd poured out, sweeping me down the street. A hairy black man stepped close to me, "Looking for a good time?"

I felt his warm, sleazy breath before he was carried off in the stream of people. Another movie theater. Well-lit posters advertised the merchandise: nude women, lewdly posed, with big hungry knockers; naked boys, lustfully embracing. I loitered near an Indian restaurant, but none of those I watched going in and out caught my eye. On both sides of the street were sex shops. Rapacious pimps beckoned me from the doorways of striptease joints, the sound of records loudly pouring out into the street from behind them. A long-haired Asian dwarf blocked my path, mumbling, importuning me in an unintelligible garble. He pranced around me and clasped my elbow, which forced him to stand on his tiptoes. I sized him up. Could he hold the key? The thread that would lead me through the labyrinth? The shrimp went on garbling words. His eyes darted about. His clammy fingers touched once at my mouth, then at my heart. He didn't let go until he pulled me inside. It was a shoddy winding staircase. The dwarf skipped quickly down the steps, a smirk twisting his face. One golden tooth shone.

I stood at the bar while my eyes adjusted to the dark. On a small stage a stripper exposed her rolls of fat to a silent audience held closely by a licentious hush. Darkness had swallowed the dwarf. I saw him no more. The music changed, so did the stripper. The one on stage with a big, blond wig, who didn't bother to

275

remove her wedding ring, now was no longer young. With a frozen expression of hate and loathing she gazed off over the heads of her audience. The curtain came down without applause, only to come up again on the next stripper who took off her pink blouse and draped it on a chair. Turning her sagging buttocks to the onlookers she shimmied them dutifully, ran a blue silky scarf over her breasts and hips and between her thighs up over the triangular patch pasted over with silver stars. Suddenly she was overcome by a terrible urge to sneeze. She sneezed and her whole body shook. Without interrupting her shimmy, she turned around to blow her nose.

I picked up my feet and left.

The last underground carried me on a winding midnight ride. The boozers' express: flushed cheeks, disheveled hair, ties askew, eyes bloodshot, the choral droning of drinking songs. The passenger in front of me fished out from under his jacket a big glass lifted from some pub. His neighbor brought out a bottle, chugged it, and threw it under the seat. Then, as if by magic, he produced a new bottle from the pocket of his wrinkled suit. The bottle man drank and sang hoarsely. And from the other cars his chums followed suit. A pug-nosed cockney who had long crossed the fine line between earnestness and insobriety stood sermonizing in the back of the car, confusing it with his Hyde Park corner. I looked at him closely, but he wasn't the man I was looking for, either.

I came across numerous Hindus but none I could stop and exchange code words with. I dropped into several bookstores, lingered near the yoga shelves. I waited and waited.

The weather was capricious: a fair day, the next a continual drizzle. Henry sent me theatre tickets; as a critic he received free passes. I pitched them into the wastecan. Occasionally we would go out and spend an evening together. Henry's favorite haunt was an old pub on the bank of the Thames, Dirty Dick, which had a rather menacing ambiance, stuffed black cats and bats hanging on its walls.

"Well, what sort of fish have you been able to come up with?" I asked him one evening about two weeks after my arrival in London, as we sat at Dirty Dick.

"If you'd settle for just a fish, fine," Henry sighed, wiping the froth from his mustache, "But you, you are looking for the golden fish." He refilled my glass and added, upbeat, "Patience. We'll get your golden fish into the frying pan yet."

One day while I was waiting between trains in Paddington station, my eyes running over the advertising posters on the lit

walls of the tunnel, I noticed a bright patch on one of the rein-
forced concrete pillars. I approached the pillar. It was a piece of
paper the size of a cigarette package taped up with scotch tape.
Under the heading *Hatha Yoga* were three typewritten lines
announcing the date of the course and its place. The course was
scheduled to begin in a few weeks but I copied the address,
somewhere in Finchley Road, and went there right away.

A grey-haired woman opened the door which was held from
inside by a brass safety-chain, and, before I managed to say a
word, she uttered through the narrow crack:

"It's not today. You're three weeks early."

She was about to shut the door on me. I tried to wedge myself
in.

"Sir!"

"Forgive me, I don't mean to disturb you. I need help."

Something in my voice moved her more than my stuttering.
She stood hesitating.

"I'm in trouble. I came from far away. You could help me."

Her fingers fiddled with the chain. She scrutinized me closely
as I told her what I was looking for.

"I'm afraid I can't help you. Perhaps Miss Waterhouse could."

"Miss Waterhouse? Where do I find her?"

"Go straight to the corner and turn right at the Princess Margaret, carry on to The Queen and turn left, then right again until
you reach the Duke of Windsor. On the far side of the street
you'll find a florist's, The Lady With the Camellias. Go in and
ask for Miss Waterhouse. If there aren't too many funerals she
might find time for you."

Miss Waterhouse, a shapely thirty-year-old brunette, listened
to me calmly, while arranging a bouquet of yellow roses that
looked as if they had just been picked from the Regent Park
flowerbeds.

"I know a yogi, but I doubt you could see him without an
appointment," she said.

"Can I call him?"

She didn't recommend it.

"Write to him; he answers letters."

I wrote a note and sent it to the address I received from Miss
Waterhouse. His answer arrived two days later. He had set an
appointment for me for the next day.

It was a two-story house. Red bricks. Flower garden. A posh
Kensington neighborhood. A young crimson-faced maid let me
in.

"Master Rai will see you in the study."

A spiralling wooden staircase with no railing took me to the second floor. The pungent odors of spicy Indian cooking wafted in from the kitchen. The yogi's furnishings consisted of a low, carved desk with two upholstered chairs on opposite sides of it and a leather couch which stood near one wall hung with Gobelin tapestries. As I came into the room he lifted his face to me from behind the desk. A lean, closed face, the color of burnt wheat, with eyes—there was something velvety about them—that had given up coveting things long ago. He was ageless, in a turban and a Saville Row suit. Whom did I expect? A shriveled-up fakir holding a snake charmer's flute?

"How come you were shattered by Huxley?" he said softly, in an Indian singsong, before I quite managed to make myself comfortable in the chair on the other side of the desk.

Tilting his head somewhat he listened to me, the shadow of a smile flickering on his lips. He shaded his eyes with one hand and eyed me intently.

"It's quite perilous to attempt to do what you did without a teacher. Why don't you take up the Kabbala?"

"The Kabbala," I said, surprised.

"In your country you may find plenty of teachers."

"I'm not interested in the Kabbala."

"The paths are different, the goal is one. It may agree with you better."

Without emerging from his supreme self-containment, he sent out his fine antennae toward me; a benevolent radiance from one to whom the secret of eternal bliss was revealed, one who had broken off from the lowland and made it to the heights.

I answered him tersely concerning exactly what I had done and the books I had read.

"You attempted Hatha Yoga as well?"

I told him.

His face clouded. "By yourself?"

"I followed the instructions in the book."

"Studying from a book can do more harm than good. You imagined you'd made certain achievements, but one little nudge from Huxley and you tumble down. Please remove your clothes and lie on the couch."

I looked at him. His eyes were opaque. I undressed and sat on the edge of the couch.

"Lie down on your stomach."

I was embarrassed by my tense body. His fingers were gentle, fluttering up and down my spine. He held his breath, listened deeply. I swallowed and loosened up.

"Breathe. Let's see how you do the *prāṇāyāma*."

I turned over on my back.

His fingers played nimbly over my stomach.

He shook his head, "You could take in more air." His voice was coming as though from beyond high, snowy mountains. "You have done yourself much harm." Then he said, "How long will you be in London?"

I had no answer. I said nothing.

"Drop in again and we'll talk."

I looked at him.

"About your errors."

"My errors?"

I had come from far away. If my efforts were all a delusion and a fallacy, he had better tell me now. The yogi knew what was going through my mind but his face remained imperturbable.

"Your first—renouncing the stage. Had you not withdrawn, had you stayed and finished your act, you would have found peace. One should not participate in the Acts of God before one purifies oneself. Acting is your claim; be not concerned with its fruits. Do not become attached to any action. Renounce neither action, nor inaction. Both redeem, yet action is greater."

"And the second error?"

"All action springs from the Supreme Self. One who is excessive in anything cannot succeed in yoga. Why did you turn your back on reality? Why did you choose seclusion? One should always relate oneself to the other and consider the other's benefit as one's own. How pure was your heart? Haven't you sought self-aggrandizement? Why did Huxley crush you? Because you tried to erase from yourself what earlier incarnation had carved on it—"

He didn't finish. Something had diverted his attention. He grew quiet, listening to voices inside him. He looked back to me: "The road to your Creator is long and its end beyond vision."

I stood up. Near the door I gave him a last look.

"He who chooses the Infinite is chosen by the Infinite." I heard him murmuring, one finger stretched upward like a pointed arrow.

The stuffed black cat stared down at me from the wall as if I were the big fat mouse—put out a paw, seize it. But its eyes were glazed and the voice was Henry's bouyant voice. We had a scotch at the bar. Dirty Dick was rowdy. The crowd grew as the closing hour drew near.

"Chin up, old man. It's not the end of the world."

We were a few glasses older. Henry was trying to wise me up and restore my spirits simultaneously.

"What did you expect anyway?" he belched. "So you were looking for the secret of eternal bliss. Gave those wild geese a good chase. Hic, Hic! Who could win? And who cares? Moses is dead. Jesus is dead. Mohammed is dead. Buddha is dead. Hic, Hic! They all died. Gathered into the bosom of their fathers. We remain orphans, my boy. They took all the secrets to the grave."

I rolled my glass between my hands.

I could still see the image of the blissful man, the man with the enlightened heart, who reached the Supreme Being. Sibylline Rai who dwells in the highest spaces up above me. Above Henry. Above all the mortals creeping here in Dirty Dick. What did I expect? Haven't I brought as much on myself intentionally, pushed myself off the high slope, out of the *Upanishads?*

"Where are you off to?" Henry raised his brows.

"Outside."

"Should I come with you?"

I laughed. Where could he come with me?

My legs carried me along the river. Big Ben chimed above me. The night deepened. A train passed over the bridge. The air trembled. Silent pigeons flew in the dark, taking off and alighting on the damp railing. A tugboat chugged under the bridge. Lights from the far bank flickered in the water. In the breeze coming off the river I suddenly caught the voice,

> But I am very sorry, good Horatio,
> That to Laertes I forgot myself—

The river was dark. And after the shiver passed, I knew I could walk a long hour beside it.

AILEEN WARD

The Spirits of '76: William Blake's *America**

One of the greatest imaginative achievements in all of English poetry was William Blake's creation of a new mythology to replace what he felt were the worn-out inventions of the Greeks and Romans. It is fascinating to watch the gradual development of this myth from its first foreshadowing in the idea of the Poetic Genius or "the True Man," which he put forth in 1788 in *All Religions Are One,* and then in the warring contraries of Energy and Reason in *The Marriage of Heaven and Hell,* a work begun in 1790. These abstract ideas start to take on visible human form in Blake's illustrations to these works and assume individual identity in the action of his poem *A Song of Liberty* (1792), then finally emerge as fully defined characters with their archetypal histories in the two prophetic poems of 1793 and 1794, *America* and *Europe.* Orc and Urizen, the first of his "giant forms" to appear, were what may be called the spirits of '76, mythical embodiments of revolution and reaction, or creative energy and repressive reason. These characters represent new ideas, contained in no previous mythology, for which Blake had to invent new names. In a kind of mythological punning he concocted the name of his revolutionary hero Orc from the Latin name *Orcus,* the King of Hell, combined with the words *orc* or *orca,* meaning a killer whale, and *orcheis,* the Greek term for the genitals, along with an anagram on *cor,* the Latin word for "heart." The name of Urizen, the spirit of reaction and repressive rationality, obviously connotes reason (we are told that Blake's friend, the scientist and radical minister Joseph Priestly, had a habit of quizzing people in conversation with the words "Your reason? your reason?"); but it also suggests the Greek verb *ourizein,* to limit or circumscribe, from which the word "horizon" is derived. These two mythical figures make their debut in *America: A Prophecy,* which Blake wrote in 1792–93 at the height of the French Revolution, some eighteen years after the outbreak of the American Revolution in 1775. It is worth asking why they should appear in his work at just this point, or—to put it another way—why Blake should have created the new poetic form that he called "prophecy" as the vehicle of his new myth, or—to put it more specifically—what is the special or revolutionary significance of *America* in Blake's work as a whole?

To begin with this last question, *America* is a revolutionary achievement because it is the first poem to which Blake applied the term "prophecy." The word itself looks two ways, to the past and to the future, and implies two kinds of prophetic impulse— the Old Testament tradition of moral prophecy, or denunciation of historic evil, and the New Testament tradition of visionary prophecy, the apocalyptic mode of the Book of Revelation with its promise of the ultimate triumph of good. As subtitle, "A Prophecy" denotes a new form of poetic history or symbolic representation of contemporary events, embodying both prophetic impulses, which Blake developed for specific reasons at this time. *America* is also a revolutionary moment in Blake's career in that it is his first fully integrated work of composite art. An artist by profession, Blake invented a unique form that he called "illuminated printing" for his poems. This was based on an ingenious method of relief engraving on copper plates, in which he surrounded the text of his poem with illustrations, then printed it on his own press, and finally colored the illustrations with water color or tempera. The term "composite art" denotes the aesthetic unity thus created of the total text with its illustrations taken together. *America* is also significant as the first of a series of poems on the four continents—America, Europe, Africa, and Asia—that he grouped together in a new and impressive format using plates over twice as large as those of most of his other works. Thus *America* inaugurates Blake's attempt to write a kind of universal history that would not merely embrace the whole globe but reach backward in time to the creation of man and forward to the culmination of history in the apocalyptic present—for many people in 1793 believed that the end of the world described in the Book of Revelation was approaching. Finally, by an accident of bibliographical history, *America* is the only one of Blake's illuminated poems whose early state can be glimpsed, as it survives in proof pages of three plates that he later discarded. This provides not only an interesting insight into his working methods but an important perspective on the motives that impelled him into the revolutionary utterances of the prophetic poems *America, Europe,* and "Africa" and "Asia" in *The Song of Los.*

To understand these motives we must recall a few facts of Blake's earlier life. Born in 1757, Blake was turning nineteen in 1776—just the age of William Wordsworth in 1789, when the storming of the Bastille touched off the French Revolution. As Wordsworth wrote of that time, "Bliss was it in that dawn to be alive, / But to be young was very heaven!" The events of the next five years in Blake's life, from nineteen to twenty-four, were to be as crucial in shaping his later political attitudes as they were for Wordsworth—and indeed are for most men at that age—for reasons that might interest a psychoanalyst. In contrast to Wordsworth, however, Blake remained a revolutionary or a radical opponent of the English monarchy all his life long. It must be remembered that the war with America was widely unpopular in England, with fully as many supporters of the rebel cause on the English side of the Atlantic as there were supporters of George III in the colonies. These sympathizers with the Revolution included not only radicals like Tom Paine but bishops and peers of the realm, historians and members of Parliament, and most of the newspaper editors of England. But even within this liberal environment Blake seems to have been a decidedly rebellious young man. He openly disputed with his teachers at the Royal Academy of Art, he got himself arrested as a suspected spy, and he was present at the storming of the Newgate Prison in London during the Gordon Riots of 1780. That event, which has been called a dress rehearsal for the sack of the Bastille nine years later, inspired Blake's first important design, known as "Albion Rose" from the first line of the inscription he later gave it—"Albion rose from where he labour'd at the Mill with Slaves." The design shows a naked youth with his arms outstretched in a triumphant gesture of release. It is Blake's first version of that great revolutionary symbol of "the dungeons burst & the prisoners set free" (Jer. 77:35) that was to recur in his work all the way through the last chapter of his last poem, *Jerusalem,* and to resound so movingly in the last act of Beethoven's opera *Fidelio.* Blake's antiwar and antimonarchical sympathies in 1780 are also plainly apparent in a number of political poems written during the American Revolution and included in his first volume, *Poetical Sketches,* printed in 1783. Yet it is a striking fact that for the second half of his twenties, from 1783 to 1789, Blake seems to have written no poetry except for a few scraps of nonsense verse and some of the early *Songs of Inno-*

cence. Nothing prepares us for his creative outpouring in the six years beginning with the publication of the *Songs of Innocence* in 1789: fifteen volumes of poetry and imaginative prose, almost all of them illustrated, engraved, and printed by Blake himself. The extraordinary stimulus to this extraordinary production was clearly the French Revolution as it unfolded from the storming of the Bastille in 1789 to its arrest and reversal in 1794–95 with the establishment of the Directory.

Blake's first response to the events of 1789 was his unfinished narrative poem *The French Revolution,* which deals with the two months preceding the storming of the Bastille in the form of an epic debate between the opposing parties at Versailles. This is, however, not prophecy but imaginative history: it presents human and mostly historical characters and events in a background of natural symbolism devoid of supernatural or superhuman reference. The poem was set in type in 1791 and survives in one set of proofs: it is, in fact, Blake's only work after his early volume of *Poetical Sketches* that was intended for publication in the usual form of a type-printed book. But Blake, or more probably his publisher, decided not to risk publishing it in the face of a campaign to suppress radical opinion which the government launched that year. Thereupon Blake resolved to become his own publisher and began to develop his newly invented method of illuminated printing into a medium for political narrative. This decision to bypass the usual publishing process had a crucial effect on the style of his longer poems, for the switch from the printed page to the illuminated or illustrated plate involved an entire reorientation of his poetic method. The style of *America* is much more condensed, elliptical, and allusive than *The French Revolution,* and a great part of the meaning is carried by the illustrations themselves. Thus was born the new poetic form designated by the subtitle of "Prophecy"—the first major aspect of the revolutionary achievement of *America.*

The early form of this poem, which Blake probably began early in 1792 but did not finish engraving until 1793, can be surmised from the proofs of the three discarded plates. The first two pages set the story going in a fashion quite different from the final version, slower in pace, more diffuse in plot. They present a poetic version of George Washington addressing the First Continental Congress in 1775 and of George III convening the British Parliament for a declaration of war. The third page, which came later in the poem, describes the cities and villages of England being mobilized for battle. As yet there is no sign of Orc, the spirit of Revolution, and only an incidental mention of his antagonist Urizen; except for a character called Albion's Angel, a dragon-like personification of George III in his warlike mood, the first two plates give little sense of a mythological dimension to the conflict, despite the epic elevation of the style. The leisurely pace of the narrative and the focus on the historical struggle between earthly powers recalls the method of *The French Revolution.* The close connection to contemporary events is especially interesting on the third page, which contains pencilled alterations that show Blake changing his mind about the meaning of the action as he worked. In the original version, England and Albion's Angel are described as "flaming," "glowing," "ardent," and "eternal"; in the pencilled corrections they appear as "damp," "cold," "cloudy," "heavy," and "aged." These changes apparently reflect Blake's determination to identify the war against the American colonies not with the English people but with their "aged King"—a determination that must have intensified in February 1793 when this king led his people willy-nilly into war against France. In the final version of *America,* however, Blake not only removed the name of George III from the text but virtually eliminated him from the action by cancelling the second and third original plates—a prudent move in view of the Royal Proclamation against Wicked and Seditious Writings of May 1792. Most significantly, he transposed the central action of the poem from the earthly to the cosmic plane by introducing Orc and Urizen as his two leading characters. In a Praeludium later added to the poem, Orc's birth is set in the year 1762, the date of Rousseau's *Social Contract* with its revolutionary assertion that "Man, born free, everywhere is in chains." In 1776 the youthful Orc bursts his chains and emerges as the fiery champion of the revolutionary cause; he defies Albion's Angel, stamps Urizen's "stony Law" to dust, rouses the colonists with the flames of rebellion, and proclaims the triumph of life, liberty, and the pursuit of happiness in terms that suggest the resurrection of the dead at the Day of Judgment:

"The morning comes, the night decays, the watchmen leave
their stations;
The grave is burst, the spices shed, the linen wrapped up;
The bones of death, the cov'ring clay, the sinews shrunk &
dry'd,
Reviving shake, inspiring move, breathing! awakening!
Spring like redeemed captives when their bonds & bars are
burst.
Let the slave grinding at the mill run out into the field:

Let him look up into the heavens & laugh in the bright air;
Let the inchained soul shut up in darkness and in sighing,
Whose face has never seen a smile in thirty weary years,
Rise and look out; his chains are loose, his dungeon doors
   are open.
And let his wife and children return from the oppressor's
   scourge.
They look behind at every step & believe it it is a dream,
Singing, 'The Sun has left his blackness, & has found a
   fresher morning,
'And the fair Moon rejoices in the clear & cloudless night;
'For Empire is no more, and now the Lion & Wolf shall
   cease.' "

                                                    (6:1–15)

Urizen, the sky-god of entrenched and repressive authority, en-
ters the action toward the end of the poem in an ineffectual effort
to rescue Albion's Angel, who is collapsing into madness like
George III; but he succeeds only temporarily in preventing Orc's
flames of revolt from spreading throughout Europe after the
American victory at Yorktown in 1781:

   Over the hills, the vales, the cities, rage the red flames fierce;
   The Heavens melted from north to south; and Urizen who
      sat
   Above all heavens in thunders wrap'd, emerg'd his leprous
      head
   From out his holy shrine, his tears in deluge piteous
   Falling into the deep sublime! Flag'd with grey-brow'd snows
   And thunderous visages, his jealous wings wav'd over the
      deep;
   Weeping in dismal howling woe, he dark descended, howling
   Around the smitten bands, clothed in tears & trembling,
      shudd'ring cold.
   His stored snows he poured forth, and his icy magazines
   He open'd on the deep, and on the Atlantic sea white
      shiv'ring.
   Leprous his limbs, all over white, and hoary was his visage,
   Weeping in dismal howlings before the stern Americans,
   Hiding the Demon red with clouds & cold mists from the
      earth;
   Till Angels & weak men twelve years should govern o'er the
      strong;

286

And then their end should come, when France receiv'd the
  Demon's light.

(16:1–15)

In the action of *America,* still more than in *The French Revolution,* Blake dramatically recreates the events of history—rearranging, condensing, heightening, and translating them into symbolic terms. Throughout we see a gradual escalation of the conflict from the human to the mythological level. The poem starts on the quasi-historical plane with Washington addressing the "Friends of America," "Franklin, Paine & Warren, Gates, Hancock & Green"—three political leaders and the three future heroes of Bunker Hill, Saratoga, and Yorktown (3:1–12). George III replies, threatening the colonists with punishment (3:14–4:1), then the poem moves on to the proclamation of the Declaration of Independence (6:1–17), the defiance of royal authority in Boston (11:1–12:2), the outbreak of war (12:7–12), and a battle that ends with a rout of the British soldiers (13:1–10)—events reflecting faithfully enough the early stages of the Revolution. The account turns symbolic, however, when Albion's Angel sends "enormous plagues," forty million strong, raining down on America in what appears to be the great three-pronged British campaign of 1777:

And as a plague wind fill'd with insects cuts off man & beast,
And as a sea o'erwhelms a land in the day of an earthquake,
Fury! rage! madness! in a wind swept through America; . . .
The citizens of New York close their books & lock their
  chests;
The mariners of Boston drop their anchors and unlade;
The scribe of Pennsylvania casts his pen upon the earth;
The builder of Virginia throws his hammer down in fear.

(14:8–10; 13–16)

But Orc's flames succeed in uniting the colonists, who "rush together in the night"; the plagues then recoil at the Battle of Saratoga and are turned back on England, starting an epidemic of opposition to the war that spreads through all of Britain, rousing the troops to desert and the citizens of Bristol and London to riot and reducing the government to political chaos (14:20–15:10)—all historical events under their symbolic guise.

Another significant aspect of the prophetic form is the vast extension of the symbolic dimension of the poem in comparison with that of *The French Revolution*. Not only is the human and historical action of *America* overshadowed by the superhuman conflict enacted in the heavens and over the sea; the natural imagery that forms the background of the earlier poem—the mountains, valleys, vineyards, and forests of France—gives way in the prophecy to a new type of imagery consisting of biblical and classical allusion and cosmological metaphor, which extends the action outward in space as well as backward and forward in time. For example, when Washington speaks of the Americans as slaves laboring with work-bruised hands and bleeding feet "on sultry sands," and Orc bids the slave grinding at the mill to run out into the fields, the perspective widens to include the Israelites in Egypt and Samson chained in the mill at Gaza. Blake also begins in *America* to manipulate the Miltonic parallels that underlie his later long prophetic poems: Albion's Angel smiting the Americans with plagues, for instance, recalls in a diabolically inverted analogy the Messiah routing Satan's forces with plagues in the sixth book of *Paradise Lost*. A similar type of epic allusion anchors the action to primeval or cosmic history. One example is found in several references to the birth of the sun and the moon as described by contemporary cosmologists (5:1–5; b:1–4, 20–22). Another is provided by the classical myth of Atlantis, the lost continent described by Plato and Herodotus that once joined Europe and America but was submerged in a deluge as punishment for its corruption. Taking a few hints from Isaiah and the Book of Revelation, Blake suggests that this seat of a lost Golden Age will be restored in the Millennium when not only will the desert blossom, but the deeps will "shrink back to their fountains" (8:8). He implies that this return of the Golden Age is already beginning in America when he describes the Thirteen Angels of the American Colonies gathering in council in an ancient palace left unsubmerged on a mountain peak of Atlantis, one of the "vast shady hills" between America and England from whose "bright summits you may pass to the Golden world" (10:5–7). The myth of Atlantis also suggests the meaning of his cryptic illustration on plate 13, which shows a naked woman on a rock at the ocean's edge attacked by a vengeful eagle, and a drowned man on the ocean floor preyed upon by fish. This scene is usually interpreted as depicting simply the horrors of war, or (more obscurely) showing man drowned in what Blake later called the Sea of Time and Space. But it is far more likely that it represents the fate of Ariston "the king of beauty [and] his stolen bride" (10:10)—Ariston the legendary ruler of Atlantis, who by

288

stealing the wife of a friend brought his kingdom to its watery ruin.

This reinforcement of poetic by pictorial symbolism is the second major aspect of the revolutionary achievement of *America*—Blake's first great triumph in composite art. In the *Songs of Innocence,* even though the individual plates show text and design related to one another in increasingly subtle and significant ways, the focus is still on the aesthetic unit of the single page, and the pages could be and actually were arranged in different sequences without any impairment of their aesthetic effect; while in *The Marriage of Heaven and Hell* the text almost totally crowds out the designs in over half the pages. In *America,* by contrast, the larger format permitted a striking new aesthetic unity both within the single page and, more important, in the work as a whole. Almost every visual element in the illustrations of *America* can be referred to some aspect of the poetic text, underlining, extending, or ironically commenting on the action. Plate 13, which represents the punishment of Ariston for his act of treacherous sensuality, is only one of several veiled warnings to George III that monarchs are being brought to judgment for their misdeeds. A clearer example is seen in plate 5, where a ruler is tried by a revolutionary tribunal in the heavens, then hurled downward to what appears to be his fate of beheading—a daring allusion to the death of Louis XVI on the guillotine in January 1793. In the work as a whole, sequential and recurrent images—flames, clouds, trees, plants, birds, beasts, and human beings crouching, soaring, reading, running, mourning, exulting and so forth—link the eighteen plates in a single narrative-pictorial sweep. This flow of visual imagery, along with the dazzling use of color and the suggestion in the text of all varieties and intensities of sound, has been aptly described as the cinerama of William Blake.

We have seen, then, the revolutionary achievement of *America* in its relation to the two central contexts of Blake's work—the poetic form of prophecy and the medium of composite art. Still to be explored, however, is the question posed at the beginning—why his work took this unexpected leap forward in this particular poem—or why the mythical figures of Orc and Urizen first appeared in his work between 1792 and 1793 and not a few years earlier or later. One reason has already been suggested: that the decision in 1791 not to publish *The French Revolution* in the usual fashion impelled Blake to translate his political narratives into the medium of illuminated printing,

The terror answerd: I am Orc, wreath'd round the accursed tree:
The times are ended; shadows pass the morning gins to break;
The fiery joy, that Urizen perverted to ten commands,
What night he led the starry hosts thro' the wide wilderness:
That stony law I stamp to dust: and scatter religion abroad
To the four winds as a torn book, & none shall gather the leaves;
But they shall rot on desart sands, & consume in bottomless deeps;
To make the desarts blossom, & the deeps shrink to their fountains,
And to renew the fiery joy, and burst the stony roof.
That pale religious letchery, seeking Virginity,
May find it in a harlot, and in coarse-clad honesty
The undefild tho' ravishd in her cradle night and morn:
For every thing that lives is holy, life delights in life;
Because the soul of sweet delight can never be defild.
Fires inwrap the earthly globe, yet man is not consumd;
Amidst the lustful fires he walks: his feet become like brass,
His knees and thighs like silver, & his breast and head like gold.

William Blake, *America: A Prophecy*, Plate 8. All four plates appear here by permission of the Lessing J. Rosenwald Collection, Library of Congress.

Thus wept the Angel voice & as he wept the terrible blasts
Of trumpets, blew a loud alarm across the Atlantic deep.
No trumpets answer; no reply of clarions or of fifes,
Silent the Colonies remain and refuse the loud alarm.

On those vast shady hills between America & Albions shore;
Now barrd out by the Atlantic sea: calld Atlantean hills;
Because from their bright summits you may pass to the Golden world
An ancient palace, archetype of mighty Emperies,
Rears its immortal pinnacles, built in the forest of God
By Ariston the king of beauty for his stolen bride.

Here on their magic seats the thirteen Angels sat perturbd
For clouds from the Atlantic hover oer the solemn roof.

Plate 10

What time the thirteen Governors that England sent can-   -vene
In Bernards house; the flames coverd the land, they rouze they
    cry
Shaking their mental chains they rush in fury to the sea
To quench their anguish: at the feet of Washington down falln
They grovel on the sand and writhing lie: while all
The British soldiers thro' the thirteen states sent up a howl
Of anguish: threw their swords & muskets to the earth & ran
From their encampments and dark castles seeking where to hide
From the grim flames; and from the visions of Orc; in sight
Of Albions Angel; who enrag'd his secret clouds open'd
From north to south, and burnt outstretchd on wings of wrath covering
The eastern sky, spreading his awful wings across the heavens;
Beneath him rolld his numerous hosts, all Albions Angels camp'd
Darkend the Atlantic mountains & their trumpets shook the valleys
Arm'd with diseases of the earth to cast upon the Abyss,
Their numbers forty millions, mustring in the eastern sky.

Plate 13

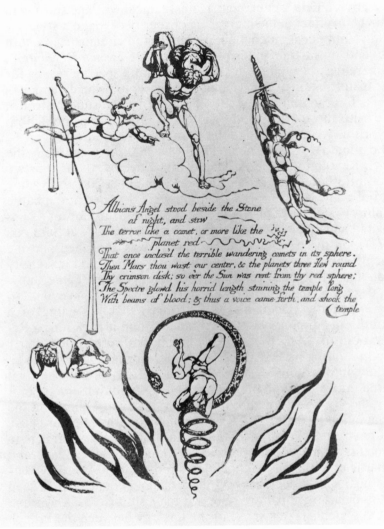

Albions Angel stood beside the Stone
of night, and saw
The terror like a comet, or more like the
planet red
That once inclos'd the terrible wandering comets in its sphere.
Then Mars thou wast our center, & the planets three flew round
Thy crimson disk; so eer the Sun was rent from thy red sphere;
The Spectre glowd his horrid length staining the temple long
With beams of blood; & thus a voice came forth, and shook the
temple

Plate 5

wherein he discovered in the demands of the medium itself the new form of the prophetic poem. Certainly the political influence of the government's campaign against radical writings starting in 1791 had its effect in the increasing obscurity of Blake's style, by forcing him to deal much more obliquely and circumspectly with the events of the time in his poems after *The French Revolution.* But there may be a more significant and more specific reason for the transformation of *America* from its early to its final version— that is, for the shift from the historical to the superhistorical plane with the introduction of Orc and Urizen into the action: and for this we must look to the events of 1792 and 1793.

The month of September 1792 was a turning point in the French Revolution which affected Blake deeply, though in two rather different ways. First of all, on September 20 the invading imperial armies of the First Coalition were defeated at the battle of Valmy—a victory for the French Revolutionary forces as un-expected and consequential as the American victory at Saratoga in 1777. On the next day the monarchy was abolished and the French Republic was proclaimed in Paris—a new political entity threatening all the crowned heads of Europe. Tom Paine, how-ever, described the establishment of the Republic as an event "so transcendentally unequalled" in history "that the name of a Revolution is diminutive of its character, and it rises into a Re-generation of Man." The Revolution had proceeded fairly smoothly during its first three years in changing France from an absolute into a limited and constitutional monarchy before it erupted into warfare in the summer of 1792; but in September it was radically transformed both by the victory at Valmy and the proclamation in Paris. These two triumphs of the popular cause must have set echoing in Blake's mind their heroic parallels in the events of his youth—the Declaration of Independence and the Battle of Saratoga. At the point where history is perceived as repeating itself, it becomes mythical: the individual event is seen as part of a larger pattern. So, we may surmise, this was the point at which Blake's sense of the analogy between the French and American Revolutions began to crystallize—an analogy not at all apparent at the time, when the events of 1775–81 were referred to not as a revolution, but as the American War by English and Americans alike. From his perception of the under-lying unity of the two revolutions was to grow Blake's idea of history as the conflict of vast superpersonal forces, spiritual or ideological in nature, transcending individual human initiative and isolated historical events—the forces epitomized in the giant forms of Orc and Urizen and the later characters of his myth.

294

Finally, the break with the monarchical past marked by the deposition of Louis XVI appears to have called up in his mind the unfinished business of the English Revolution of the mid-seventeenth century—the Civil War and the brief experiment with republican government under Oliver Cromwell. The hope that the English Revolution might also now be brought to a triumphant completion seems to underlie the prophetic glimpse into the future at the end of *America,* where the twelve years of reaction in England following the American victory at Yorktown in 1781 are envisioned as Urizen's last futile attempt to quench the flames of Orc. In 1793 Blake looks confidently forward to the final triumph of popular rule that began when "France receiv'd the Demon's light" of revolution in 1789.

But September 1792 also brought a profoundly disturbing event—the September Massacres in which hundreds of royalist prisoners lost their lives; and four months later Louis XVI was beheaded for treason. The Revolution was turning violent in its moment of victory, and this unforeseen development was forcing Blake, along with the other English supporters of the Revolution, to shift the grounds of his defense. The liberal apologists of the early 1790s, poets and political writers alike, had found an analogue for the first hopeful years of the Revolution in the prophecy of Isaiah, with its promise of the peaceful transformation of all nature with the coming of the Messiah. But as the Terror began, they turned to the Book of Revelation to justify the bloodshed as Armageddon, the great battle between the forces of good and evil that ends with the defeat of Antichrist and the start of the Millennium. Blake drew on both these strains of imagery, apocalyptic and millennial, in *America:* but he was unique among the poets of his time in that his confidence in some glorious outcome to the revolutionary struggle in France was reenforced by an analogue much closer to the present than Armageddon—the victories of Saratoga and Yorktown. So, long after most of his fellow liberals such as Wordsworth and Coleridge became disillusioned by events in France and deserted the revolutionary cause, Blake remained faithful to the original ideals of the Revolution—liberty, equality, and the brotherhood of man.

The final significance of Blake's *America*—its sense of the enduring revolutionary impulse linking the French and American Revolutions—becomes clear when it is compared with other poems of the time dealing with the events of 1776. What is striking about the impact of the American Revolution on English poetry of the 1770s and 1780s is that it had almost no impact: and yet this should not be surprising. Poetry in those decades was at a low ebb; but the failure of the poets of that time to rise above the level of, say, the Poet Laureate William Whitehead's clay-footed "Ode for the Year 1777," with its feeble reproof of the Americans as "wayward children of a distant clime," should not be laid simply to their inability to respond to a great occasion. Rather their failure suggests the need for at least a decade to elapse before an event of the magnitude of the American Revolution could be absorbed and recreated by the imagination: at least the length of time, for example, between the end of the First World War and the publication of *All Quiet on the Western Front.* But in the 1790s English poets were overwhelmed by the impact of a second revolution, much closer to home and more threatening in its possible consequences. Only Blake had experienced the American Revolution in the full flush of youthful ardor and the French Revolution in his intellectual maturity; only Blake, then, could perceive and communicate the essential continuity of the two events and build on this analogy a new prophetic view of history linking past, present, and future. *America: A Prophecy* is thus the only work of English poetry to do justice to the imaginative challenge of the American Revolution. For Blake quite literally, the shot fired at Lexington was heard around the world.

JOHN WHEATCROFT

Oysters

i

Barnacle-covered, the color and weight
of zinc, dredged from the sand
and shingles of some Carolina inlet,
life locked in a rock.

The oyster knife won't split them.
I, determined housebreaker,
jimmy and pry with a chisel.

We've arrived at this point
between ocean and sound
during storm, hungry and late,
with a bottle of gin and the oysters.

ii

Scraping their flesh from its mother-of-pearl,
we swallow them raw.
Mucousy, they slither down our throats,
martyrs making smooth their own rough ends.

Cannibal as sharks we pinch and gulp
the tiny crabs that scurry in the shells.
Our teeth grind grit, we spit
potential pearls, then flush
ourselves with gin.

After the booze and the oysters
it's the bed. Both of our marriages
cracked, our children caught
between undertow and the tide,
we writhe to make a match,
half shells that don't quite fit.

At the zero hour we trust
the little killer loop
is doing its inside job.

Afterward, each clutches other,
barnacle on a barnacle.

Dozing, I move through water,
struggle against a current,
thrash to stay afloat,

while through the jalousie of sleep
I hear nor'easter's howl
scourge southward from Nantucket
and the upraised arm of Cape Cod.

CARL WOODS

Letters from the Colonies

Introduced and edited by Peter Klappert

Carl Woods arrived at VCCA from Santa Barbara in March, 1978. He'd come for a month's residency, fees abated, and hoped to go on to other colonies; when those plans were delayed, Bill Smart invited him to stay on as a fellow in exchange for a few hours of work each day. This was VCCA's first year at Mount San Angelo, and there was a great deal to be done. Carl's double status, part fellow-in-poetry and part staff, made it easy to get to know him; at the same time, I don't think any of us really knew him well.

I arrived on May 16 for a two-month stay. Here are some notes on my first encounter with Carl:

Annoyed myself at dinner.

                  Carl Woods (Francis Becker,
Grove Becker, Fred Decker—Bill Craig calls him all of these,
also "Beaver") has been reading my books
and worse, talking them up.
                        Funny old coot—60s—thinning
longish white hair, goatee and glasses,
poverty wardrobe. Slight,
sinewy, and very tan.
                  Hash-slinger,
pot-scrubber, night clerk, local grocery boy
who does ashes, windows, hedges, leaves,
gets ahead three months on a furnished room

and quits, on a fine warm day,
                              out to the park
down to the beach off to read at the library
and type his poems up, 25¢/hr,
on the machine kept locked in a milkgreen room.

In short, I like him, he means well, but *Damnit*.
This was conversation before the poetry reading.
Must one be interviewed across a plate of peas?

*Carl was 57, but most of us took him for mid-sixties. He seemed
to be an autodidact, a noble primitive of poetry who'd dropped
out somewhere along the line to get by as best he could and
devote himself to writing. I immediately typed him, both rightly
and wrongly, as part of that immense cottage industry of poetry
that meets in local groups, publishes in the littlest of little magazines, and rigorously maintains, in the French sense of the word,
its* amateur *status. He was capable of great generosity and spontaneous, childlike enthusiasm, and he was capable of an equally
unexpected abruptness. He was forthright enough about his
values, but as a man who lived on the fringes, he was also a little
guarded and crafty, a bit of a cadger. He did not reveal much of
his history, but the glimpses he permitted were interesting, and
sometimes heart-breaking.*

*In 1978 I was preoccupied with my own work and personal
problems, and I was frankly put-off by the number of poems Carl
was writing and sending out. He was proud (but not boastful) of
the nearly three hundred poems he'd published in about ninety
different magazines, he kept over two hundred manuscripts in
circulation at all times, and he was writing two to three poems a
day: we were about as far apart as two temperaments could be. I
left VCCA before him and lost touch. I didn't know he'd gone on
to the Millay Colony in Austerlitz, New York, and from there to
the Ossabaw Island Project off the coast of Georgia, and I didn't
know he'd been invited back to VCCA on a more-or-less permanent basis, until March 1979, when Bill Smart sent me a copy of
the memorial service for Carl.*

*Walking along the shoulder of Route 29 on a raining, February
evening, on his way back from town to Mount San Angelo, Carl
was struck from behind by a hit-and-run driver and killed outright. He left no family, and most of his papers are now at VCCA
in a file cabinet known as "The Carl Woods Archive." Carl's*

300

body was cremated, and in the summer of 1979, when a number of us who had known him were in residence, we held an impromptu ceremony in his memory. We rowed across the lake he had come to think of as his studio, bringing Carl's ashes and a young birch tree with us in the battered rowboat; on a point of land not far from the beaver island, we planted the birch, scattered the ashes, and read some of Carl's poems.

Since that day, I've become interested in Carl's work and life in a way, I regret to say, I was not interested while he was alive. The mysteries of his life mainly deepen. What is clear, as I read through the "archive," is that in his last year Carl grew tremendously as a poet. The poems become more vivid, more specific, and they are confident enough of their images and metaphors that the poet can refrain from intruding with glosses and interpretations. And there has been a further, unsuspected reward. Among the hundreds and hundreds of pages of poems in that file cabinet are copies of a few long letters Carl wrote to his friends in Santa Barbara. They give a rich sense of colony life—of experiences comparable to those of many fellows, but particularly of Carl's experiences.

I'm indebted to Carl's friends for sharing their copies of his letters and poems with me. I've gone over the letters included here with the directors of The Millay Colony, The Ossabaw Island Project, and The Virginia Center for the Creative Arts. We've determined that the cameos of other fellows are all composite portraits or pure invention. In the very few cases where references might (correctly or incorrectly) suggest actual people, the references have been removed to preserve that privacy so crucial to any artists' colony. I've also compared the numerous versions of the poems that follow, choosing the latest version (or, when that could not be determined, the version that seems most fully realized). I hope the appearance of the work here may be one more step toward the publication of a book by Carl Woods.

April 10 '78
C Woods
The Virginia Center for the
Creative Arts at Sweet Briar
Sweet Briar College
Sweet Briar, VA

Dear Don and Dorothy:

Well, I'm here in Virginia, writing 2 or 3 poems a day and loving the whole southern scene: the weeping cherries, the red buds, the cardinals. There are some real characters here who sound off every night at dinner. They've all had 4 or 5 books published by big New York firms, so I guess I'm lucky to be here.

The trip out was a real gas. Had the front seat all the way, but was on the 2nd section, so had to change busses three times.

In L.A. I didn't see the baggage men load on my typewriter or the box of poems—new unfinished stuff. So I went into the baggage room looking for them. Nothing. Nobody knew anything. (I've lost everything I owned twice on Greyhound busses. Ask at your destination every day for months, and all you get is, "Oh, back North. Tha's a whole nother cumpny. Dun nobody here know nothing bout tha." So I was a bit paranoid.) Back at my gate, minus box and typewriter, some guy says, "Yer bus jus lef." I see this monster lumbering out, sprint after, catch it at the exit turn—Yes, we got a happy ending here, folks!—and climb on section 3 of the Memphis run. About 10 minutes on and this bus pulls up in front of a stalled one, which was my number 2 for Memphis. Something wrong with the heating system, so we went back to the garage. But we caught up in Dallas and I saw some of my stuff on the section 1 bus. Got it all together in Roanoke, Virginia.

The trip was great. Slept well, took a pill only one night, and enjoyed sight-seeing and the people on board. Wrote six poems on the way. Lost them all, but rewrote all but one, which I'm remembering just now, about a bony old alcoholic cook going from San Diego to Florida for a cook's helper job. Well! He was a real beauty. Snored and drooled both. But I lost him in El Paso.

Memphis was great, the Mississippi river, too. The Arizona desert was a bore, except for Superstition Mountain. And a couple of incredibly desolate and polluted mining towns. God! People live their lives in those places? And the Comanche Reservation, the south-eastern 50 miles of Arkansas. I didn't see any-

302

thing living—not a bird, not a lizard, not a rabbit. A real pallette: brown and gray. Braque in a nightmare! A huge gate and fence there. What the hell for? Certainly no one was about to break in! Some redneck started bragging about how big the reservation was that we in our generosity had given those Indians. I argued with him about how generous we really had been, when two rich green little valleys hove into view. So the redneck started telling us about how them pieces belonged to some farming concern back in Arizona. That's a coincidence, isn't it? I asked him. He was too far gone to insult, but there were some blacks and an Indian on board who laughed.

William Smart, the director here, says I may be able to stay here a month longer on my grant. And he's said that when my time is up, I can work part-time for room and board till I have somehwere else to go to. There are a couple of other places I'm looking into but, of course, I could just stay here till my stay at The Millay Colony begins.

I got another letter from Wilbur, and I'm going to read some Wilbur at Sweet Briar College soon. My work is going very well, I think. Quality is always hard to evaluate when one works so fast. Polishing changes things round drastically. And there isn't really time to decide what's good or bad. I'm sending you 3 pieces, but if you have any doubts about them, then please don't show them to anybody. I don't figure I'm going to spend much of this precious creative time on revisions. That'll come later.

The food here is good, the rooms comfortable—in a huge old plantation mansion—and the studios are fine, quiet and re-moved. Nobody bugs nobody. This afternoon I hiked up over a cow pasture—really heifer and yearling steers—into a piece of sloping ground which I think is being readied for new pasture when what they're on now is used up. Lay down in the sun and mused—wrote one piece I'd planned some days before, another about two butterflies that fell, in flagrante delicto, on my paper; and walking back to the big house to shower, another thought struck me about a lake in a small valley beside the place, and I finished that while I set the dining table for dinner.

Well, as you can see, all's well.

Carl

July 16 '78
Carl Woods—*F. G. Becker*
VCCA
Sweet Briar, VA 24595

Dear Elizabeth:

Sorry to be *so* late with this letter. I didn't have your address, just the phone no., in my little book, and nobody I wrote to about it remembered to send it on. Going to get it today from the Phone Co.

Everything's going very well. Nearly 200 poems in the 3½ months—some among my best. My fellowship here at the Virginia Center for the Creative Arts—VCCA—has been extended indefinitely, till Ossabaw & The Millay Colony finalize my dates.

Elizabeth, most of the poems are writ in my "studio," a battered oarless rowboat on a beautiful lake. Let me tell you about it: There are 5 or 6 beaver in 3 lodges along the edge. Raccoon, opossum, woodchuck, rabbit, fox, muskrat, & mink. A pair of 2 small blue herons, that are really *blue,* and a family of 2 red-wing blackbirds, with a very quarrelsome "uncle"—a 3rd gear. Hawks, crows, swallows, and later, after the fireflies come out, a pair of bats.

In the water bream, crappie, perch, bass—turtles, one the size of a trash can cover, really hormongous! And, of course, my favorites, the beavers. Insects: a dozen varieties of dragonflies alone, whizzing and diving at the baby mosquitoes. Water spiders, ticks, ants, "flies"—etc. Did you know that all spiders can walk on water?

Lots of 2-yard-long blacksnakes rippling purple thru the grass, but haven't seen a snake in the water, tho I'm sure they're here. The water's too murky to swim in, anyway. Road crew dumped fill in 5 or 6 years ago, & the lake's never cleared up.

Most of my letters are typed, but this one's written, pad on my paddle, as I sit in the boat rocking gently in the evening breeze, tied to a snag from a pine tree fallen into the lake. The beavers didn't do that—don't eat pine. Poplar, alder, cottonwood, and a few others. They eat leaves, twigs, & bark. Underwater, because they're slow & clumsy on land.

The first binoculars were stolen at the Faulding Hotel, my new pair were bought here—16 power, very fine for birds & such.

I'm sitting here after dinner—it's now 8:07—been here 45 minutes—waiting for the beavers to start cruising, for my huge turtle to show, for whatever's going to happen. There's one of the bat-pair, very early tonight—the sun's just down. Thought it was a swallow, but the flying style's a bat. There's a Sweet Briar College about a mile away that has leased the Italian Villa-Southern mansion & the 400 acre grounds for 50 years to the VCCA for $1.00 yearly. They're helping pay for restoration. And "my" boat is theirs. A black worker for the college, Dewey

Johnson, came down with his fishing gear a few mintues after I arrived, & I believe he's a bit disgusted that I'm in the boat. He brought it over here in a college truck &, naturally, likes to fish from it. Hey, there's a new bird gliding in on a submerged tree. Damn! It's a kingfisher! Still no beavers, tho. A couple of fellows from the dinner table are strolling by the far shore. Hope they don't yell "Hello" & scare everything off.

Well—he knows the boat'll be free after dark, unless there's a good moon. Oh, oh! There it is—almost full, and here's the first beaver! The big one, scouting the surface. Back & forth, quite near the boat. There's a couple of swallows. Very odd to see them *after* a bat appears. He's vanished now.

It's about time for the fireflies to start flashing, or do they stop when the moon's full? Seems to me that happened in June. It's 8:40 & still very light. There's an increase in activity by the surface insects—striders & spiders. The fisherman, Mr. Johnson, left, & the beaver came out. He came back, & they went away. Now Dewey has left again, presumably for good. Maybe 3 or 4 will come out now. They're used to me!

I rock the boat & make a Chinese lantern out of the reflection of the moon. I was gross enough to flash the glasses on the 2 fellows: a very bad painter—no color sense at all—and a loud, lazy, sloppy writer who does quite good short stories.

Well, Elizabeth, it's 9:00, getting dark; but that big moon is rising. Ah, & there was the first firefly. How many more? Another! But, really just a few. I've never been on the lake in moonlight. Eager to see how it is. Hope not too dark to see anything. Well, I can't see to write anymore, sooo—

Thank you very much,
& Goodnight

Carl

October 16 '78
Ossabaw Island
Box 13397
Savannah, Ga 31406

Dear Elizabeth:

Hope all's well with you. Let me fill you in on my adventures: the train ride from the Millay Colony in Austerlitz NY to NYC was beautiful—along the Hudson River just at sunset. Then, the next day, the Frick Collection, my favorite of any gallery I've seen.

Didn't like Washington. Ugly, pretentious public buildings, and the slums falling down against them. But the National Gallery was splendid: Ginevra di Benci, of da Vinci, whom I'd seen so often in books; Erasmus and Cromwell by Holbein; the Rembrandts, Raphaels, Sassettas, Giottos. The Alba Madonna, to which my "Figures in a Field" is written. But the bucolic French were too sweet for my taste, and the English portraits too pretentious.

Was that room of smeary black Whistler portraits at the Frick? But I like the English landscapes, and also, Whistler's. The Flemish, and the Dutch interiors. Such great fun to discover someone new: Benvenuto da Giovanni—new to me, anyway—great stuff, marvellous Tintoretto-like draftmanship. And what an intriguing name. "Welcome to Joy," isn't it?

Went to the East wing. Disaster area! I don't really believe I'm another old fossil. I like about half of the modern work I see. But am I blind, or are these frauds?

What this country would be if the people refused to let the grocers cheat them!

Out of Washington, I slept on the bus through Virginia, which I'd planned: I know it a bit. But I also slept through both Carolinas, which I regretted. Woke up to flat old Georgia. But the woods were pleasant. All young stuff, lots of logging. Then—Savannah. Named for the marshes though the word "savannah"—Hummm—let me go down and check the definition. . . . Yes, the word means a treeless plain or wide grassland. Nothing about marshes, swamp grass. Maybe there were real savannahs on the mainland at Savannah when it was named. Sidney Lanier, flautist and poet who died about 100 years ago, wrote about the "Marshes of Glynn." Have to look it up. A young colony member here said he'd gone to the library and found no Yeats, but 2 shelves of Lanier!

Savannah has the unique rich colors and soft shapes of decay, though there is evidence of a losing battle to renovate. Much water and air pollution. There's a short but pleasant promenade by the Savannah River, and a boat trip through the barrier islands for sale for $5. A wonderful inexpensive cafeteria downtown. The black slums are grisly, but the center of town is rich with "Squares" (like South American Plazas, but to me, more beautiful) full of bad sculpture and magnificent old trees, mostly live oak festooned with Spanish moss. That's very interesting stuff—not a parasite, it just lies on a twig and feeds on the air,

306

dust and water vapor. Savannah was settled, they say, in 1733, so there's lots of history. Some splendid limestone houses in the center of town. Maybe one for every 10,000 shacks.

Nobody at the stores even knew what anagrams were, and nobody had scrabble. Hummm. Went out to the college. Pretty minor affair. The Art Gallery cost $1.75. The Frick: $1; The Met: a quarter, or a penny, if you are short. Well! Stayed out.

Then the boat trip to Ossabaw! A gusty sparkling day—low islands and swamp-grass everywhere. Through canals to the island—live oaks, pines, and palmettoes. Also, juniper trees, poplars, magnolias. And, fringing all but the west, seaward shore, the marshes. Flat! Don't think there's a spot over ten feet high. Tsunami, come and get me!

Arrived Friday afternoon. Saturday went for a five-hour ramble. Saw—where's that list?—made it on the side of a first draft of a poem. Here it is: crab spider, golden orb spider. (These, like others, were identified for me, from my descriptions, by scientists on the island.) 6 wild pigs—mostly black—hermit crabs, fiddler crabs, 5 deer, lizards, 6 wild turkeys, an otter, a great blue heron, redbirds, 6 kinds of butterflies, squirrels, turkey buzzards, a ring-tailed wildcat which turned out to be a skinny raccoon. Wood ibis, cattle egret. You can imagine my euphoria. (I don't know why I delight so in seeing things I know are there, in seeing wild things. Must think about that, and write a poem on it.) In the next few days I added mink, wild turkey—and, (are you ready for this?) a yearling alligator sunning himself on a hummock island off the edge of a marsh near a causeway.

I'm beginning now to classify the big wading birds—so spectacular—the different kinds of heron, ibis, and egret. There are hundreds of small birds, almost none of which I know. The birds weave the Spanish moss into nests. Saw something yesterday that looked much like an oriole's home. The main house and the studios are on the north edge of the island; west, facing the mainland channel, are the marshes, and east, seaward, is the beach. It's too far to walk, so van-loads go out there on Tuesdays, to swim and sun.

Well, an ocean beach is not all that exciting to me, so I take advantage of the trip east to give me a one-way lift to areas of the island I couldn't reach and return from in one day. I leave the beach immediately for a 6 or 7 hour walk back through new country. Here's what I saw on a rise:

Ossabaw Egret

An egret appears in the tawny savannah
in a silent descent of light
Glides a windy curve to a tussock
and stands   blessing the marsh

The soul of the island
shines whiter   in green-gold reeds
than cloud sun-struck   or May lily
No radiance so potent has ever found
a shape so blithe

     They say she swallows frogs whole
     snorts like a pig in a stench of dead fish

I see her kindle-dazzle   lifting
the fire of her wings   planing away
to her home   hidden in blue afternoon

Boar

Under the island's live oak dusk-at-noon
shoulder arches black
darkness prying   leafmold for acorns
shaking palmettoes for beetles
glittering in the mile-wide marsh   to munch
fiddler crabs and water moccasins

He walks lean through the stained light
of a pine barren   crunching cones
runs over the grass of a clearing with his brother
short legs   hoofs a blur

On the beach he unties the green knots
of a dune   unshovels turtle eggs

He will share a meadow with a cow   deer   dog
horse   or ibis   But when he sees me watching
he scurries off   snorting   rattling the woods

Sorry, Elizabeth, about the carbons—no xerox. If you have time for comments, I'd be pleased to hear—

Carl

January 8 '79
Carl Woods
VCCA
Sweet Briar, VA 24595

Dear Bob, Jane and Jenner:

Well, my nine-month adventure in the wilds of Art-Colony-Land is over! I've spent 2 weeks back at the Virginia Center for the Creative Arts recuperating from all those poems. Director William Smart invited me to return as a 2-hour-a-day room-and-board employee, to give me a couple of months, I thought, to find a permanent security-guard post back in Santa Barbara, or some such job which would provide writing time. And also because he knew of my wanting to see Winter, after 20 years.

But I am flattered to learn that Mr. Smart wants me to settle permanently at San Angelo, to work with the handyman, to baby-sit for his little girl, and to house-sit for him on his frequent absences. The tremendous advantage of being close to someone who deeply and genuinely likes both me and my poems, added to the stimulation of rubbing elbows with many gifted people, seems to me a marvelous opportunity that I must take gratefully.

Of course, should a chance to carry on my work appear in SB, a return to my quasi-native haunts and my loyal friends would be likely. In any case, in a few months, I'll be back, to arrange for my mss., books, desk, and some other effects, and I hope to see many familiar faces then and discharge some of my many obligations.

There's an incredible heap of new poems to edit (by the way, excuse, please, my using both sides of the paper. But I'm planning to make this a moderately mammoth letter, and want to save postage) mostly place-oriented: from the woods around the lake here at the VCCA; from the teeming island, Ossabaw; and from the Millay Colony on the New York-Massachusetts state line. The book ms. must be up-dated: strongest new work added, the weaker oldies deleted, 60 or so poems—85 or so pages—finished, and the book *PUBLISHED!!* by Saint or Satan, hook or crook.

Then I shall return to writing, much more slowly, a couple of the best poems possible to me every month. Moving back into forms, some my own, measured rhythms, rhymes. This year will be my best.

Looking back over these fabulous months—to say "Why not 30 years ago?" is futile—I see what was slighted was the people, the other artists: The blimp who made mysterious walrussy noises for hours in the bathtub, who left wine bibbers and bourbon slurpers at the long table every evening to drive off, sometimes 50 miles, to another AA session.

The four-year-old, very beautiful daughter of the chief mechanic, everyone's darling, who, when someone slapped her puppy, hissed, "She eva do dat agin, I gonna slap her up longside da haid!"

The shy, unconfident artist, about 22, from Harlem, who gave me 3 delicate drawings of the baby oppossum her huge white dog so carefully brought her from the deep grass where its mother had dropped it; who worked days on tiny watercolors of finches on vines, and whose terrifying, stupid guardian was killed on the highway her last day at the colony, and who, then, utterly alone, had to move to a part of New York she couldn't afford.

The lanky, way-out-of-the-closet novelist and teacher at some unfortunate college, who worked 18 hours a day, and chattered nonstop through every dinner about getting published to get tenure.

The erudite philosopher, who could not only identify any misplaced quotation, but could also quote it, with the paragraph preceding and following—who apparently never forgot a page ever read; who played Mozart on his cornet and Brahms every afternoon by the beach, proclaiming for us all the true melody of sunset.

And, of course, last but not least—the pauper potwasher and night-watchman from California, who, despairing at his inability to keep a job to support his poetry writing, wondered, a year ago, if he mightn't find time to write by trying for a few residencies at artists' colonies!

So you can see what a marvel of value has come from your

310

help. I want to assure you that, no matter what happens, I will
see to it that your bread returns to you on the waters! I hope you
enjoy the poem included, and that you'll find time to let me know
what you think of it.

Gratefully,
Carl

Willows Road

At the torn edge of miles of marsh
the creek glitters along the causeway I walk   sky blue
By the far palmetto-wall   east
stands a donkey   watching

Ten yards away a great blue heron
is probing the grass for snails and shrimp
with an ibis and her child   Blue crabs slide
under the shallows   a flock of fish breaks water
On his island hummock lolls the apprentice alligator

The grandfather boar of the island
charges black across the middle width
The natives dive away beneath colors to dark
fly off beyond trees   gallop into brush
Heart widens with the sway of the
empty savannah   with the tall sky

Now an egret flies slow over reeds
whitely measuring quiet   I have seen this
holy place   I can go home

Notes on the Contributors

JOEL AGEE was born in New York City in 1940 and grew up in Mexico and East Germany. He has published poetry, essays, stories, and critical reviews in *The New Yorker, Harper's,* and *The New York Times Book Review,* and has translated two works of fiction from German into English: *The Ballad of Typhoid Mary* by J. F. Federspiel and *Poff the Cat or When We Care* by Hartmut von Hentig. He is the author of *Twelve Years: An American Boyhood in East Germany* (Farrar, Straus, & Giroux, 1981). The German edition of his book (in his own translation) won the "Buch des Monats" prize of the Darmstadt critics' circle in February 1983. At present he is at work on a novel and is a Contributing Editor to *Harper's.*

SALLIE BINGHAM was born in Louisville, Kentucky, and published her first novel, *After Such Knowledge,* in 1959. Two collections of short stories, *The Touching Hand* and *The Way It Is Now* followed. Her stories have been published in *Mademoiselle, The Atlantic Monthly, New Letters, Redbook, Shenandoah,* and *The Spirit That Moves Us.* Her stories have been included in The O. Henry Awards (1964) *40 Best Stories from Mademoiselle, Harvard Advocate Centennial Anthology,* and *The Best American Short Stories.* Her first play, *Milk of Paradise,* was produced by The Womens Project at The American Place Theatre in New York. She lives in Louisville and is book editor of *The Courier-Journal.*

MARGUERITE GUZMAN BOUVARD was born in Trieste, Italy, and grew up in Wilmette, Illinois. She has been Poet-in-Residence at the University of Maryland and has taught poetry at the Radcliffe Seminars. At Regis College she conducts poetry workshops and teaches international relations while chairing the political science department. As a poet, she has published in many little magazines. Her first collection, *Journey's Over Water,* was published in 1982 by the *Quarterly Review of Literature.*

DAVID BRADLEY was born in Bedford, Pennsylvania, in 1950, and was raised there. He attended the University of Pennsylvania and the University of London. He is the author of two novels, *South Street* (1975) and *The Chaneysville Incident* (1981), which received the PEN/Faulkner Award in Fiction for 1982. His father, the late Reverend David H. Bradley, was born in 1905, was also raised in Bedford, and was also the author of two books. Rev. Bradley died in 1979. David Bradley is a professor of English at Temple University.

MARTHA CLARK was born and raised in Kingsport, Tennessee. A past winner of the American Poets Honorary Prize from Brandeis University and a Major Hopwood Award for Poetry from the University of Michigan, she has published in magazines including *Green House* and *Iowa Review.* She has an M.A. in social work from the University of Michigan and is now a geriatric social worker. She continues writing from her home in Ypsilanti, Michigan.

MARTHA COLLINS grew up in Des Moines, Iowa, went to Stanford University for her B.A., and earned her M.A. and Ph.D. at the University of Iowa. She has taught at the University of Massachusetts-Boston since 1966, and is currently Director of Creative Writing. In 1982–83 she was a Fellow at the Bunting Institute at Radcliffe. Her poetry has appeared in *Field, Ironwood, Poetry, Southern Review, Commonweal, American Poetry Review,* and many other magazines.

JAMES MADISON DAVIS was born in Charlottesville, Virginia, and educated at the University of Maryland, Johns Hopkins University, and the University of Southern Mississippi. He currently teaches at Pennsylvania State University, Behrend College, in Erie. He has published numerous short stories in such periodicals as *Swallow's Tale, Antithesis, Pulpsmith, Antietam Review,* and *Constellations.* His novella *Blackletter* is scheduled to be published by Perivale Press in early 1984. He is currently working on a novel and a critical book on Polish writer Stanislaw Lem.

CORNELIUS EADY was born and grew up in Rochester, New York. He has worked as a Poet-in-the-schools in New York,

Vermont, and Virginia and was coproducer of "Writers' Block," a monthly poetry show broadcast over WBAI in New York City. In 1981 he was the National Arts Club Scholar in Poetry at the Breadloaf Writers' Conference. His first book, *Kartunes,* was published in 1980 by Warthog Press. "Victims of the Latest Dance Craze" is the title poem of his second book, a cycle of dance poems. From 1982 to 1984 he was Margaret Banister Writer-in-Residence at Sweet Briar College.

LYNN EMANUEL was born in New York City and grew up there and in Denver. She teaches at the University of Pittsburgh. She has received a Pennsylvania Council on the Arts Fellowship, and her work has been published in *Poetry, The American Poetry Review, The Georgia Review, The William Morrow Anthology of Younger American Poets, The Iowa Review's Anthology of Writing by Contemporary American Women, Pushcart Prize VIII,* and *The Anthology of Magazine Verse and Yearbook of American Poetry, 1984.*

SUSAN FAWCETT was born in Cleveland, Ohio, and grew up in Macedonia, Ohio. She currently lives in New York City. Her poems have appeared in *The Nation, Michigan Quarterly Review, Poetry Now, Kayak, Ms Magazine,* and other publications. She is the co-author of two college writing textbooks— *Grassroots: The Writer's Workbook* and *Evergreen: A Guide to Writing.*

ROLAND FLINT was born and grew up in Park River, North Dakota. He now lives in Silver Spring, Maryland. His third book of poems was published in 1983—*Resuming Green: Selected Poems, 1965–1982.* In 1981 he received his second grant from the NEA. He teaches literature and writing at Georgetown University.

ANNE HOBSON FREEMAN was born in Richmond, Virginia, and lived there most of her childhood. After graduating from Bryn Mawr College and spending a year at London University on a Fulbright scholarship, she returned to Richmond in 1958, married a lawyer, and has lived there ever since. She commutes to Charlottesville once a week to teach a prose writing class at the University of Virginia. Her essays, stories, and poems have appeared in *McCall's, Cosmopolitan, The Virginia Quarterly Review, The Denver Quarterly, The New Virginia Review, The Richmond Quarterly,* and various anthologies, including *Prize*

314

Stories from Mademoiselle, A Green Place, edited by William Jay Smith, and *The Best American Short Stories, 1982.*

JAN HAAGENSEN was born in Washington, D.C., and grew up in McLean, Virginia, and the suburbs of Pittsburg, Pennsylvania. After graduating from Sweet Briar College in 1968 she received an M.F.A. from the Writers' Workshop, University of Iowa, and a Ph.D. from the University of Connecticut. At Connecticut she won the Wallace Stevens Prize in poetry. Her first collection, *Like a Diamondback in the Trunk of a Witness's Buick,* was published by Cleveland State University Poetry Center in 1977. She lives on her family's farm in Enon Valley, Pennsylvania.

JACQUES HNIZDOVSKY was born in the Ukraine in 1915 and came to America in 1949. Since his first exhibit in 1954, Hnizdovsky has had more than one hundred one-man shows in America and abroad. A catalogue, *HNIZDOVSKY: Woodcuts, 1944–1975,* was published by Pelican Press in 1976. He has illustrated many books, among them the poems of Coleridge, Keats, Robert Frost, and William Jay Smith, and is also well known for his *ex libris* bookplates. He now lives in New York with his wife and daughter.

EDWIN HONIG was born and grew up in New York City. He graduated from the University of Wisconsin in 1941, and three years later published the first critical study in English of the Spanish poet, Federico García Lorca. He has also published critical studies of Calderon and Cervantes, as well as *Dark Conceit: The Making of Allegory.* Primarily a poet, Honig has published twelve collections, most recently *Gifts of Light.* From 1949 to 1957 he taught at Harvard University, and from 1960 until his retirement in 1983 he was a professor of English and comparative literature at Brown University.

DAVID HUDDLE was born in Ivanhoe, Virginia. He is a graduate of the University of Virginia, Hollins College, and Columbia University. His work has appeared in *Esquire, Harper's, Field, The Hudson Review,* and other journals. He is the author of a collection of stories, *A Dream with No Stump Roots in It,* and a book of poems, *Paper Boy.* Professor of English at the University of Vermont, Huddle has also taught at the Breadloaf School of English, Goddard College, Middlebury College, and the Warren Wilson College M.F.A. Program for Writers.

PETER KLAPPERT's first book, *Lugging Vegetables to Nantucket*, was the Yale Series of Younger Poets volume for 1971. His next book was *Circular Stairs, Distress in the Mirrors* (1975), followed by *Non Sequitor O'Connor* (1977). *The Idiot Princess of The Last Dynasty* and *'52 Pick-up: Scenes from the Conspiracy, A Documentary* will be published in 1984. "Stages of a Journey Inland" is part of a work-in-progress tentatively titled *Scattering Carl.* Klappert has taught at Harvard University, the College of William and Mary, and George Mason University.

MILTON KLONSKY was born on Staten Island and received his education in the New York public schools, Brooklyn College, and Columbia University. Among his books were *The Fabulous Ego: Absolute Power in History, William Blake: The Seer and His Visions,* and *Blake's Dante.* His essays appeared in *Commentary, Partisan Review, Hudson Review, Sewanee Review, New American Review,* and *The New Republic.* At the time of his death in 1981 he was writing an essay on his acquaintance with W. H. Auden and Chester Kallman. "Maxim Gorky in Coney Island" was one of several essays found among his papers by his widow, Gloria Rabinowitz.

EDITH KONECKY's fiction has appeared in *The Virginia Quarterly, The Massachusetts Review, Kenyon Review, Esquire, Mademoiselle,* and other magazines as well as a number of anthologies. Her novel, *Allegra Maud Goldman,* was published by Harper & Row and Dell.

DOUGLAS LAWDER was born in New York City, grew up in Connecticut, and attended Kenyon College. His poems have been published in *Virginia Quarterly Review, The Nation, Poetry, Northwest Review,* and many other magazines. His first collection, *Trolling,* published by Little, Brown & Co. in 1977, received much praise. He has just finished a novel titled *Under Storm Mountain.* Lawder is an Associate Professor of English at Michigan State University.

DAVID MCALEAVEY teaches at George Washington University in Washington, D.C. Ithaca House has published three volumes of his poetry, most recently *Shrine, Shelter, Cave* (1980). He won the 1983 Kreymborg Award from the Poetry Society of America, and his poems have appeared in magazines such as *Poetry, Virginia Quarterly, Epoch, Seneca Review,* and *Greenfield Review.*

316

PETER MEINKE directs the Writing Workshop at Eckerd College in St. Petersburg, Florida. His story, "The Ponoes," is in the 1983 O'Henry collection, and "A Decent Life" won the 1982 Emily Clark Balch Prize for Short Fiction. His latest book of poems is *Trying To Surprise God* (1981).

TAYLOR MORRIS was born in Rayville, Louisiana, and grew up in New Orleans. He is a graduate of Tulane University and received a master's degree from Columbia University. He is an associate professor at Franklin Pierce College in Rindge, New Hampshire. His stories, articles, and poetry have appeared in *The New Yorker, New Age, Windfall, Northern New England Review, The Boston Globe,* and other publications. *The Walk of the Conscious Ants* was published by Alfred A. Knopf in 1972.

HARVEY OXENHORN is director of the Public Policy Communications Program at Harvard University. His poetry and prose have appeared in *The Atlantic Monthly, The Southern Review, Boston Review, New Letters,* and other magazines, and his book, *Elemental Things: The Poetry of Hugh MacDiarmid* will be published by Edinburgh University Press. Born in Westbury, New York, and educated at Swarthmore and Stanford University, he has worked in Ireland, East Africa, and aboard U.S. naval vessels in the Pacific Ocean. His book-in-progress concerns a recent stint as crewman on a tall ship's expedition to the Arctic.

MOLLY PEACOCK was born in Buffalo, New York, and now lives in New York City. She was educated at SUNY-Binghamton and Johns Hopkins University. She is the author of *And Live Apart* published by University of Missouri Press in 1980. Her poems have appeared in such magazines as *Paris Review, Mississippi Review, Shenandoah,* and *New Letters.* She has recently completed a manuscript of sonnets titled *Raw Heaven.*

DAVID RAY was born in Oklahoma and educated at the University of Chicago. Professor of English at the University of Missouri-Kansas City, he edits the quarterly, *New Letters,* and produces a weekly radio program, "New Letters on the Air," for National Public Radio. His books include *The Mulberries of Mingo* (stories) and several poetry volumes, most recently *The Touched Life* (Scarecrow Press). His awards include a PEN/NEA Newspaper Syndication Award in fiction and the William Carlos Williams Award from the Poetry Society of America for his book *The Tramp's Cup.*

MARK RICHARD grew up in Franklin, Virginia, and attended Washington and Lee University. His story "Twenty-one Days Back" was a finalist in the 1980 American Short Story contest sponsored by *The Atlantic Monthly* and was subsequently published in *Shenandoah*. From 1977 to 1979 he worked aboard ocean-going trawlers in the Atlantic, as deckhand, winchman, night helmsman, crew boss, channel pilot, and keeper of ships' logs and finances. He is currently living and writing in Virginia Beach, Virginia.

J. W. RIVERS was born and grew up in Chicago. He has a B.A. and M.A. from the Universidad de las Americas (formerly Mexico City College). He has published poetry and fiction in English and Spanish in many magazines. His first collection of poems, *Proud and on My Feet,* was published by the University of Georgia Press in 1982. The twenty-eight poems from *When the Owl Cries, Indians Die* comprise nearly half of that as-yet-unpublished manuscript. He is currently working on a book-length poem tentatively entitled *The True History of Colonies and Settlements.*

EVE SHELNUTT was born in South Carolina and was educated at the University of Cincinnati and the University of North Carolina at Greensboro. She is an Associate Professor at the University of Pittsburgh, teaching in the M.F.A. Writing Program. Her two short story collections, *The Love Child* and *The Formal Voice,* were published by Black Sparrow Press and, in 1983, her collection of poems, *Air and Salt,* was published by Carnegie-Mellon Press. Her work has appeared in *The American Review, Mother Jones, Agni Review, Virginia Quarterly Review,* and in many other magazines. Her short stories have appeared in numerous anthologies, including *The O. Henry Awards.* Her current projects include the completion of a third collection of stories and a second book of poetry.

WILLIAM SMART grew up in Missouri, attended Kenyon College and the University of Connecticut, and has been teaching creative writing at Sweet Briar College since 1966. Since 1975 he has also been Director of the Virginia Center for the Creative Arts. He has published poems and short stories in *The Kenyon Review, Carleton Miscellany,* and *New Republic,* among others, and has edited four previous anthologies, *Eight Modern Essayists* (1965, 1973, 1980) and *Women & Men/Men & Women* (1975).

W. D. Snodgrass grew up in Beaver Falls, Pennsylvania, and attended Geneva College. Following service in the Navy during World War II, he went to the Writers' Workshop at the University of Iowa where he studied under Robert Lowell. He was awarded the Pulitzer Prize in poetry for his first book, *Heart's Needle*. His second book of poems was *After Experience*, and he has also published a collection of critical essays, *In Radical Pursuit*. In recent years he has been translating, adapting to music, and performing early songs, and adapting his own works for the stage *(The Führer Bunker)*. He currently is in Mexico on sabbatical leave from the University of Delaware. An earlier version of "Diplomacy: The Father" appeared in the cycle *Remains* under the pseudonym S. S. Gardons, published by The Perishable Press in 1970.

Sue Standing teaches poetry and fiction writing at Wheaton College in Norton, Massachusetts. She holds degrees from Oberlin College and Boston University, and was a Fellow at the Bunting Institute of Radcliffe College. Her poems have appeared in *The American Poetry Review, The Nation, Poetry Northwest,* and other magazines. Her book, *Amphibious Weather,* was published by Zephyr Press in 1981.

Gideon Telpaz was born in Israel and now lives in the United States. He was educated at the Hebrew University in Jerusalem and at the University of Oxford from which he received his doctorate degree. He has taught at several American universities, was a fellow at the International Writing Program at Iowa City, and took part in editing the *Oxford English-Hebrew Dictionary*. He currently writes both in Hebrew and in English and is the author of five collections of short stories; several novels; and plays for radio, television, and the stage. He is currently working on a new novel in English.

Aileen Ward was born in Newark, New Jersey, and grew up in Summit, New Jersey. She attended Smith College and received her Ph.D. degree from Radcliffe College. Her biography *John Keats: The Making of a Poet* won the Duff Cooper Prize in England and the National Book Award in Arts and Letters in 1964. Her articles and reviews have appeared in *Tri-Quarterly, The New York Times Book Review,* the *Times Literary Supplement,* and elsewhere. She now lives in New York and is Schweitzer Professor of Humanities at New York University. At present she is writing a biography of William Blake.

JOHN WHEATCROFT has had seven books published—four volumes of poetry, two novels, and a play. Most recently released is his novel *Catherine, Her Book.* His play, *Ofoti,* winner of an Alcoa Playwriting Award, ran on the NET Playhouse television series and received the National Educational Television Award for the best original play of the year. A new novel and a volume of stories will appear in 1984. John Wheatcroft is Presidential Professor of English at Bucknell University.

CARL WOODS was the pseudonym of Francis B. Becker (a.k.a. Grove Becker). He was born in Muskegon, Michigan, in 1920 and was raised in orphanages and by foster parents. During the 1940s and 1950s he earned his living by playing the guitar and singing in clubs in New York City and South America. Sometime in the 1950s he moved to California, where he earned his living by teaching children to play the guitar and doing odd jobs— short-order cook, night watchman, hotel clerk, groundskeeper. In March 1978 he came East to take up residencies at the Virginia Center for the Creative Arts, the Millay Colony for the Arts, and the Ossabaw Project. In February 1979 he was struck and killed by a hit-and-run driver on the highway near the VCCA. In the eight years before his death Carl Woods published an enormous number of poems in small magazines, but never a book.